"Gob is the only band my parents ever told me not to listen to. Obviously, I did anyway. When Dave Brownsound emerged from that swimming pool shredding [in Sum 41's music video for "In Too Deep"], he made it cool as hell to be awesome at guitar in punk rock. I think that was truly one of the most important moments in guitar history."

—Mike Warne, Pkew Pkew Pkew

Advance Praise for *In Too Deep*

"This book is a vivid snapshot of a pre-streaming era in the music industry when major labels were still willing to lavish spiky-haired misfits with $3,000 steak dinners, and a reminder that when a band makes the leap from playing rec centres to arenas, they're not necessarily violating punk principles—they're opening up a crucial gateway that inspires the next generation of disaffected suburban kids to make some noise of their own."

—Stuart Berman, author of
This Book Is Broken: A Broken Social Scene Story

"An essential addition to a growing canon celebrating the sickest music this country has ever produced, *In Too Deep* venerates a group of artists that were rarely afforded the respect they deserved during their commercial peak. Picks up where great books like *Treat Me Like Dirt* and *Tomorrow Is Too Late* left off to document Canadian punks launching themselves out of the primordial ooze of the underground and into stadiums around the world."

—Sam Sutherland, author of
Perfect Youth: The Birth of Canadian Punk

"While the U.S. and the U.K. get most of the glory when it comes to punk, Canada was certainly no slouch. In fact, there's a whole hidden history waiting to be discovered with this book."

—Alan Cross, host of *The Ongoing History of New Music*

"This book was exactly what I wanted: a vivid, expansive unpacking of Canada's raucous aughts."

—Andrea Warner, author of *We Oughta Know: How Céline, Shania, Alanis, and Sarah Ruled the '90s and Changed Music*

"Canadian music history is rarely taken seriously. Neither is pop-punk of the Warped generation. By combining the two in this book, Bobkin and Feibel set themselves an ambitious task and pull it off with all the audacity this music demands. It helps to have characters this colourful. But the narrative writing here displays rich storytelling and an ear for dialogue that puts the reader in the recording studio and backstage. This book just catapulted into the Canadian canon."

—Michael Barclay, author of *The Never-Ending Present: The Story of Gord Downie and the Tragically Hip*

"As a band, we spent our early years touring Canada so disproportionately that people just assumed we were Canadian. What we found was a tight-knit, supportive, and nuanced punk scene. A scene that was watered and nurtured so well in its own garden that it thrived and quietly spread across every border, onto the airwaves of stations far away. This scene adopted Rise Against in many ways and we've never forgotten it. When it comes to Canadian punk, it's not being dramatic to claim that the music world is simply a better place for it."

—Tim McIlrath, Rise Against

"It was beyond exciting that Sum 41 hailed from a small town close to ours. Their success was an inspiration to all of us. When Billy Talent and Alexisonfire broke through, it hammered home the point that geography was not a significant impediment to playing music as a career. It was profound."

—The Dirty Nil

"Artists like Avril Lavigne and Fefe Dobson had such an influential impact on newer bands like us entering the pop-punk space. The paths they paved inspired us to want to pave our own path as well."

—Téa Campbell, Meet Me @ The Altar

IN TOO DEEP

IN TOO DEEP

WHEN CANADIAN PUNKS TOOK OVER THE WORLD

MATT BOBKIN &
ADAM FEIBEL

ANANSI

Published in Canada in 2025 and the USA in 2025 by House of Anansi Press Inc.
houseofanansi.com

House of Anansi Press is committed to protecting our natural environment. This book is made of material from well-managed FSC®-certified forests, recycled materials, and other controlled sources.

House of Anansi Press is a Global Certified Accessible™ (GCA by Benetech) publisher. The ebook version of this book meets stringent accessibility standards and is available to readers with print disabilities.

29 28 27 26 25   1 2 3 4 5

Library and Archives Canada Cataloguing in Publication

Title: In too deep : when Canadian punks took over the world /
Matt Bobkin & Adam Feibel.
Names: Bobkin, Matt, author. | Feibel, Adam, author.
Description: Includes bibliographical references and index.
Identifiers: Canadiana (print) 20250114143 | Canadiana (ebook) 20250114283 |
ISBN 9781487012687 (softcover) | ISBN 9781487012694 (EPUB)
Subjects: LCSH: Punk rock music—Canada—History and criticism. |
LCSH: Punk rock musicians—Canada—Interviews.
Classification: LCC ML3534.6.C2 B663 2025 | DDC 781.660971—dc23

Cover and book design: Alysia Shewchuk
Cover image: BillionPhotos.com/stock.adobe.com

House of Anansi Press is grateful for the privilege to work on and create from the Traditional Territory of many Nations, including the Anishinabeg, the Wendat, and the Haudenosaunee, as well as the Treaty Lands of the Mississaugas of the Credit.

Canada Council for the Arts
Conseil des Arts du Canada

With the participation of the Government of Canada
Avec la participation du gouvernement du Canada | Canadä

We acknowledge for their financial support of our publishing program the Canada Council for the Arts, the Ontario Arts Council, and the Government of Canada.

Printed and bound in Canada

For Harry and Sally Weltman, who let me stay up late to watch the 2004 MMVAs.

—M.B.

For my friends and family, and for every kid who puts their faith in four chords.

—A.F.

CONTENTS

PROLOGUE

Just about every chapter in the long history of punk rock begins with a group of teenagers in a garage or a basement. Canada's began in 1975, when four high school students in Hamilton, Ontario, picked up their instruments and started a band called Teenage Head. The group played their first show that year in the cafeteria at Westdale High School, and over the next few years started gigging around town and then in Toronto, where a countercultural music scene would take shape just as similar movements were cropping up in the United States and the United Kingdom. In New York City, the Ramones, Blondie, and Patti Smith were turning the dive bar CBGB into the birthplace of punk rock. In London, the Clash, the Sex Pistols, and the Damned were rising from the gutters to become chart-climbing British icons. In Toronto, Teenage Head, along with bands like the Viletones and the Diodes, formed their own explosive scene with its own legendary stories—the "Toronto Weekend" showcase at CBGB in 1977, *The Last Pogo* concert at the Horseshoe Tavern in 1978, and the Teenage Head show at Ontario Place in 1980 that came to be known as the "Toronto Punk Rock Riot" in headlines across the country—to make the city a supporting player on the world's stage of first-wave punk rock.

Within the Toronto scene, Teenage Head stood above the rest. Known to some as the "Canadian Ramones," the band earned a reputation as one of the wildest live acts on the local club circuit and gained a rabid fan base across the country, especially after their infamous show at Ontario Place, which drew an estimated fifteen thousand people to the outdoor theatre—about six times its 2,500-seat capacity—and resulted in fifty-eight arrests, numerous injuries, three totalled cop cars, and one near-drowning. Teenage Head's second album, 1980's *Frantic City*, sold so well across Canada that it was certified platinum within three years.

Despite their success at home, Teenage Head struggled to find an audience outside of Canada. The band's efforts to break out south of the border were thwarted when they crashed their van, breaking guitarist Gord Lewis's back, just before the group was due to head out on their first major U.S. tour. The band eventually got fed up with their lack of U.S. distribution and broke things off with their label, Attic Records. And so, by the end of 1982, one of Canada's hottest bands no longer had a record deal.

Just as quickly, Teenage Head's fortunes changed. The U.S. major label MCA Records stepped up to offer the Hamilton punks a recording contract, but it came with several conditions:

the band would have to change their name to the pluralized Teenage Heads, to avoid any potential controversy; they would start by releasing an EP, not a full-length album, to test the waters in the U.S. market; and they would need to significantly polish their sound to appeal to radio programmers. The resulting EP, 1983's six-song *Tornado*, was a complete disappointment. Many fans decried the overly produced, radio-friendly sound. Critics' reviews were mixed, at best. And MCA Records, in the midst of internal upheaval, completely abandoned them. "The entire team that had signed us was gone," bassist Steve Mahon said in a 2023 retrospective for uDiscoverMusic. "We got a one-page letter in the mail that basically said we were off the label. And ... good luck."

Within a year, Teenage Head were back in Canada, destined to spend the rest of their career on independent labels in their own backyard. For many years, it was the closest a Canadian punk band would come to breaking through internationally—and it wasn't really that close at all.

TEENAGE HEAD WERE JUST one of many victims of a common theme among Canadian recording artists: you could be a big deal in your own country, but in all likelihood, people living outside of those borders wouldn't even know your name. Neil Young, Joni Mitchell, and Rush were among the rare exceptions. The Tragically Hip was the rule: national headliners; international footnotes.

"At the time, and still today, Canadian artists look at companies in a very binary fashion: you're either a conduit for me to get out of Canada, or an obstacle," says Michael

McCarty, a veteran of the Canadian music industry who was president of EMI Music Publishing Canada from 1992 to 2008. "Unfortunately, the Canadian label system all too often has been perceived as an obstacle."

It was a tricky situation to navigate, filled with geopolitical pitfalls and easily bruised egos. Signing to a Canadian label meant international labels were unlikely to pay attention, while signing outside of Canada could breed resentment among the nation's music industry bigwigs. You could be popular in Canada or outside of Canada, but rarely both.

THROUGHOUT THE REMAINDER OF the twentieth century, punk rock was constantly evolving, largely without any major involvement of Canadian acts—though not entirely. By the end of the '70s, the punk pioneers in New York and London had moved in different directions, while punk scenes had popped up in practically every county seat in California. This ignited a frenzy on the West Coast, turning into a lively touring circuit that brought punk rock to the suburbs, a type of punk that was harder, faster, and more ferocious.

It wasn't long before this more aggressive sound moved north of the border—this time to Vancouver, on the West Coast. One of the biggest names in the city's early punk scene was D.O.A., led by the inimitable Joey Shithead. When the band called their second album *Hardcore '81*, the name stuck. D.O.A. went on to be one of the pioneers of the subgenre called "hardcore punk," alongside U.S. acts Black Flag, Dead Kennedys, and Bad Brains.[1]

1 D.O.A. released their third album, 1985's *Let's Wreck the Party*, on Dead Kennedys' label Alternative Tentacles.

Canada didn't birth hardcore, but it almost certainly named it.

"Being Canadian meant we had to work twice as hard 'cause we were from the Great White North and we weren't accepted that easily in the States," Keithley wrote in a short essay displayed at the Punk Rock Museum in Las Vegas. "I think the Canadian bands went out on tour with a bit of a chip on their shoulders."

In the early '90s, a new crop of bands from Southern California turned punk rock into a widespread commercial success. One by one, yet seemingly all at once, they signed major-label deals, recorded hit songs, and sold millions of records, transforming a mostly underground scene into a full-blown mainstream movement. The Sex Pistols and the Clash had managed to climb the charts in the U.K. in the late '70s, but this was different; when Nirvana emerged from the Seattle punk scene to become world-conquering superstars as 1991's *Nevermind* sold more than five million records in two years, they blew the door open for other underground bands to step through. Green Day's *Dookie* soon followed in 1994, along with the Offspring's *Smash*, and then Blink-182's *Enema of the State* in 1999. Between them, an abundance of other successful and influential punk-rock records—NOFX's *Punk in Drublic*, Rancid's *... And Out Come the Wolves*, Bad Religion's *Stranger Than Fiction*, and many more—each sold hundreds of thousands of copies and shaped the counterculture of the '90s and beyond.

For the first twenty-five years of punk rock's history, the bands that rose to international fame emerged from the places you'd expect: New York City, London, Los Angeles, and a few other parts of California—highly populated cities that served as major hubs of music, arts, and culture in the global superpowers of the United States and the United Kingdom. Meanwhile, the influential acts that were breaking new ground and stirring up trouble in places like Toronto and Vancouver were relegated to mythical cult status among diehard punk rockers, far from the notoriety that had been achieved by punk rock's big breakthroughs. Only the real-deal punks know Teenage Head or D.O.A., but even your parents know Green Day.

But at the turn of the century, something unexpected happened: a bunch of Canadian teenagers started their own punk bands in the garages and basements of their small-town and suburban homes and managed to break through the barriers of their domestic music industry to become the face of their generation's own counterculture.

These bands were coming from small, sleepy suburbs and unassuming towns in Canada that most Americans couldn't even begin to place on a map—places where the suits and ties at the big record labels hadn't thought to send their talent scouts. Within just a few years, these artists went from playing sparsely attended gigs in basements, community halls, and mom-and-pop restaurants to performing for millions of TV viewers at the MTV Video Music Awards, the Grammy Awards, and *Saturday Night Live*, and to thousands of rabid fans at the main stages of some of the world's biggest music festivals. And twenty years later, they'd be embraced by a new generation of kids who weren't even alive when all of this was happening.

This is the story of the Canadian punks who defied the odds to become the world-conquering icons they never dreamed they could be.

1

GOB

Seventeen seconds into the music video for Gob's "I Hear You Calling," a sickly grey arm breaks forth from a grass-covered pitch to grab the ankle of the band's lead singer, Tom Thacker. He's frantically freed by his bandmates, and they watch in shock as a zombie and several of its comrades emerge from the ground, complete with mottled skin and soccer jerseys. What unfolds isn't just a supernatural soccer match between the foursome and their undead adversaries, but a breakthrough moment for the Vancouver punk band.

It's the fall of 2000, when many millennial kids are stepping off the school bus every day and running home to play *Pokémon* and watch MTV—or, in Canada, MuchMusic. Kids these days are mostly listening to boy bands, girl groups, pop stars, and rappers, but punk rock is becoming increasingly popular, having moved beyond the skaters and snowboarders, pranksters and burnouts, and other misfits that kept the torch burning in the '90s.

Gob are four of those misfits, and they've been having a pretty good time over the past seven years touring around North America, writing and performing fun and irreverent punk tunes, and pushing video after video onto Canadian TV to become their country's first real answer to Green Day and the California punk scene they idolize. But it hasn't been easy. Beneath the Hollywood-size concept of their music video's thrilling soccer match between humans and the undead are four guys from the Vancouver suburbs who have spent their career toughing it out in an era of punk rock that wasn't quite ready for them.

Now, they're being rewarded for it. After living it up in the subcultural trenches, the stage is set and the world is primed for a punk band like theirs to make it big. These days, the music industry is more willing to lend a hand. Their older videos were made with minimal costs, but "I Hear You Calling" was made with a six-figure budget, which included costumes, choreography, and a host of actors playing zombie soccer players and zombie cheerleaders. It all looks pretty professional. And within the next couple of years, "I Hear You Calling" will be among a handful of songs by Canadian punk bands to be heard through the speakers of hi-fi systems, boomboxes, clock radios, and family minivans across the country.

Now, all they have left to do is make the leap from the Canadian underground to the international stage. When Gob started in the early '90s, that felt as likely as raising the dead.

* * *

HIGH SCHOOL BUDDIES Tom Thacker and Theo Goutzinakis grew up together in Langley, British Columbia, a small city on the other side of the Fraser River from Vancouver with a population, at the time, of just under twenty thousand. After they graduated high school, Thacker and Goutzinakis decided to stick around town instead of going to university, where they could work dead-end jobs, ride their BMX bikes, and make music together. Thacker and Goutzinakis looked like punks (especially Thacker, with his six-inch spiked mohawk dyed a deep blue), they listened to punk bands, they went to punk shows, and they admired their local punk legends. Naturally, they wanted to start their own punk band. But they weren't interested in pursuing the hardcore punk sound that dominated Vancouver throughout the '80s thanks to local legends D.O.A. They were more into a new strain of poppier, Ramones-influenced punk rock being released by bands on Lookout! Records, an independent label in Berkeley, California.

Lookout had been born out of a Berkeley venue known as 924 Gilman Street. It was the closest thing the West Coast had to CBGB, and it helped birth a new wave of bands that, coincidentally, were more inspired by the melodic stylings of that original New York scene than the West Coast–led hardcore style that followed. Bands on the label's early roster, namely Green Day, Operation Ivy, Rancid, and Screeching Weasel, had begun influencing a new generation of punks, and even teetered on the cusp of mainstream viability, which Green Day would achieve with their 1994 album, *Dookie*.[2]

---

2 When Green Day signed to major label Reprise Records in 1993, they were banned from 924 Gilman.

But that hadn't hit Vancouver yet. When Thacker and Goutzinakis started their new Lookout-inspired project in late 1993, it was so out of step with the local scene that they struggled to find a drummer, even after putting an ad in the local alt-weekly, the *Georgia Straight*. "People would call up and be like, 'Yeah, I love punk rock.' It's like, 'Great, what do you listen to?' They're like, 'Nazareth.' I mean, Nazareth's great, but it's not going to work," says Thacker. "We had an idea of what we wanted to do. It was going to take a specific personality—someone with a high tolerance for playing as fast and as hard as they could." That person was Patrick Paszana, known as "Wolfman Pat," a slightly older guy with long hair and a dark beard who was already a veteran of the local music scene. Along with bassist Kelly Macauley, who worked with Thacker at the A&B Sound electronics store in nearby Surrey, the quartet set out to introduce Vancouver to the Lookout school of punk rock. Wanting to separate themselves from the bands in their scene who they thought were taking themselves too seriously, they gave themselves a short, unserious name: Gob.

FURTHER LISTENING

PROPAGANDHI

Hometown: Portage la Prairie, Manitoba
Years active: 1986–present

After playing a show with NOFX in 1992, punk trio Propagandhi impressed Fat Mike so much that he signed them to his label, Fat Wreck Chords, on the spot. Their 1993 debut album *How to Clean Everything* sounded like standard '90s pop-punk, but for their 1996 follow-up, *Less Talk, More Rock*, Propagandhi displayed a political vehemence more in line with their '70s and '80s forebears than their '90s scenemates, proudly emblazoning the album cover with a declaration that they were "animal-friendly, anti-fascist, gay-positive, pro-feminist." (After this album, bassist John K. Samson left to form indie rock band the Weakerthans.) Propagandhi was seen as so radical that their song lyrics and vocalist Chris Hannah's onstage speeches put a target on their heads even at their own shows, and they were often subject to verbal and physical threats. The band has continued to move forward on their own terms, running their own record label—G7 Welcoming Committee Records—from 1997 to 2012, and moving musically into a heavier, more metal-influenced sound starting with 2001's *Today's Empires, Tomorrow's Ashes*.

As Vancouver's lone ambassadors for this poppier new punk style, Gob initially struggled to connect with local audiences and developed an irreverent attitude. "The fans didn't really accept bands like us. It was a little *too* different. If we sounded exactly like D.O.A. or Bad Brains or something, yeah, but we set out to sound like something newer," says Thacker. "Not many people had dyed hair or punk clothing. We really stood out everywhere we went, so we'd push people's buttons in a friendly way. We never meant any harm. We weren't fighters or anything like that. We kind of avoided that scene—that was the old punk scene. We just liked to fuck with people."

Shortly after forming, Gob piled into Ridge Recordings studio in Maple Ridge, just north of Langley, and recorded their self-titled debut EP, cramming nine songs into just fourteen minutes. They first released the EP in 1994 on Thacker's one-man label Positive Records, and it was reissued a few months later on Landspeed Records, an imprint started by music scene friend Jay Clark. They brought in Jamie Fawkes as the band's new bassist and followed that EP with two seven-inch records in 1995: the first was a four-track effort called *Dildozer*, with record packaging that included a cartoon of the titular vehicle looking exactly like you'd think it would, along with crass wordplay and ass-related humour. The second, another four-song collection titled *Green Beans and Almonds*, showed off the group's humour with more restraint—the cover art was a parody of the mascot for the frozen food company Green Giant, and two of the songs were called "I Don't Want You Back Baby" and "I Want You Back Baby."

While Gob was a novelty in Vancouver, their first few releases were very clearly cut from the same cloth as the American bands signed to Lookout. That meant their sound was perfectly viable and marketable south of the border, but it also meant that they faced stiff competition. That reality set in on their first tour of California, when they finally got to check out the region's storied punk-rock scene for themselves. "It became clear to us just by reading the population on the *Road Atlas*: there's more people in California than there are in Canada," says Thacker. "So, when we got down there, we saw how many bands there were and how good those bands were. Like, 'I don't know if we could ever make a dent here.'"

Of course, that didn't mean they weren't going to try.

A BAND WITH A strong work ethic to counterbalance their mischievous, goofball personalities, Gob were staunch proponents of the punk DIY philosophy—"do it yourself"—and, well, insisted on doing everything themselves. "We weren't gonna wait around and try to get a record contract," says Thacker. "We're gonna do everything ourselves: the recording, contacting the CD pressing plant, the cassette plant, the record plant. We did every single thing; we were just going to do it."

Like any good DIY band, Gob sent their music to campus radio stations and a few record labels. They were soon contacted by Vancouver music scenester Grant Lawrence who, along with singing in garage rock band the Smugglers and booking concerts around town, was working as a publicist, booking agent, and A&R rep for a fresh local label called Mint Records. Lawrence was a fan of Lookout! Records, particularly bands like the Queers and Screeching Weasel, and a friend had told him about this wild crew from Langley and sent him one of the band's demos. The Mint staff began listening to it on repeat.

"It was very raw, and it was not that well formed, but you could hear both Tom and Theo's ability to write a catchy song," Lawrence says. "Rancid were like the Clash reborn, and Green Day were like the Jam reborn, so I felt that Gob could be a Canadian answer to those American bands. That's what labels were starting to look for at the time."

Mint offered Gob a one-album contract, gave them some money, and hoped for the best.

Presented with the opportunity to record their debut album, Gob took their fast-and-furious punk approach to the next level, tracking twenty songs that clocked in at just over half an hour. The resulting album was an explosion of suburban alienation and sexual frustration that included an interlude composed of a kazoo melody and a bunch of fart noises, and as a tribute to Lawrence, a cover of the Smugglers' song "Hey Stephanie" to close out the album. When Thacker and Goutzinakis went into the Mint office to pitch their vision for the album cover—a photograph of a "total loser-type guy" sprawled out on the ground after wiping out on his bike—they had one person in mind: Lawrence, who dutifully sprawled on the asphalt outside of the Vancouver Film School in blue coveralls while a pair of students stood nonchalantly behind him.[3] Gob called the album *Too Late... No Friends*, a playground saying they'd use to taunt each other.

Gob had no real expectations that their debut album of minute-long punk jams would change their lives in any tangible way. And yet it did.

---

3 In the liner notes, Gob claimed the cover model was *Beverly Hills, 90210* star Luke Perry.

* * *

BY THE TIME MINT was ready to release *Too Late... No Friends* in the summer of 1995, Gob had amassed a small but dedicated base of supporters, with fans, allies in similarly minded local band d.b.s., and steady label support. But Mint felt that there was one promotional tactic that the band still needed to help them break out: a music video.

In the mid-'90s, music videos were a vital way for new artists to find an audience. MTV had revolutionized the way young Americans listened to music in 1981, followed by MuchMusic in Canada three years later, featuring a similarly styled lineup of original, music-centric programming.[4] Just like its American counterpart, MuchMusic filled the all-important need of creating a place where new artists could find their audiences, whether through more general programs like *The NewMusic* and *Videoflow*, genre-specific shows like *RapCity* (hip-hop), *Electric Circus* (dance), *Power 30* (hard rock), and *The Wedge* (indie rock), or regional programs like *Much East* and *Much West* that fought against the Canadian music industry's bias toward Ontario, not coincidentally the station's home province.

Canadian artists were also given a leg up due to laws that mandated broadcasters to air a certain percentage of Canadian content—material created in Canada or by Canadians, also

4 MuchMusic's presence was the reason why MTV never really took off in Canada. There have been a few MTV-branded channels in Canada over the years, but they were all severely limited in how much music-related programming they could air due to Canadian broadcasting protections around genre exclusivity. Not satisfied to be branded as a mere MTV rip-off, MuchMusic expanded into the U.S. via the channel MuchMusic USA in 1994, which was rebranded as Fuse in 2003.

known as Cancon. Plus, Lawrence was privy to a MuchMusic loophole that could give an edge to bands like Gob: the shorter the song, the more likely it was to get played at the end of the hour, between programs. "It's not exactly an endorsement of your art," Lawrence concedes, but it was a strategy that had worked for the Smugglers' single "Vancouver BC" a few years earlier. The only downside: the songs couldn't contain any swearing, and Gob, as Lawrence puts it, "swore so fucking much—irony intended."

Mint asked Gob to make a music video to promote *Too Late... No Friends*, and the band went to the office to meet with the label with every intention of laughing off the suggestion. They thought music videos were stupid. But on the way to the meeting, the band came up with a better idea: "If we build a ramp, we can go lake jumping, and then we can make a video of that. The label will like it because it's cool, and we will get to go lake jumping. It'll be fucking awesome."

Buried halfway through *Too Late... No Friends* was "Soda," ninety-five seconds of thrashing guitars, Thacker's sneering vocals—miraculously free of swearing—and a simple

FURTHER LISTENING

D.B.S.

Hometown: North Vancouver, British Columbia
Years active: 1992–2001

Many pop-punk bands built their brands on acting like children, but d.b.s. didn't have to play such games: they formed the band when they were in Grade 8 and released their debut album *Tales from the Crib* when they were still in high school. *Tales from the Crib* straddles the line between new-school irreverence and old-school aggression—among its twenty-one tracks are speedy takedowns of racism and the education system and a hilarious sendup of the Canadian national identity that features one of the best-timed burps in recorded history. The scene agreed: Gob took the teens on a California tour in 1995, D.O.A. took them on a six-week tour of Europe, and Joey Shithead released d.b.s.'s *I Is for Insignificant* on his label Sudden Death Records in 1998. The band broke up in 2001 and moved on to other artistic pursuits. Vocalist Jesse Gander went on to be a recording engineer for hundreds of artists including Japandroids, the Pack A.D., and Misery Signals, while guitarist, Andy Dixon became an acclaimed painter.

chorus about wanting to jump in a lake on a sunny summer day. It would be the perfect soundtrack to a video of dudes biking off a ramp into Cultus Lake in the Fraser Valley. Mint loved the concept and gave the band roughly $1,400 to make the video.

Gob left the meeting thinking they had totally pulled one over on their label. Mint knew they had a hit on their hands, and it barely cost them anything.

The "Soda" video was filmed by Goutzinakis's cousin, Peter Papas, and mostly features the band and their friends riding their BMX bikes around the streets of Langley, at a skatepark, and, as promised, off a giant ramp into the water. The most "incredibly dangerous" part, according to Thacker, wasn't flying off the ramp, but lip-syncing into the camera while biking. "We're on the street in Langley, someone's driving the van, Peter's filming, we're looking forward once in a while because a car could come out at any time and hit us." While filming the opening scene, one of their friends got a concussion attempting a 360 tabletop.

The video was supposed to end with a top-down shot of the bikers in the water, singing along, but Goutzinakis was the only person who showed up to the last day of shooting; Thacker had to work, and the other guys only showed up for the bike shots. (Plus, Thacker admits, it was an idea "we clearly did not have a budget for.") So, the cousins had to improvise. Goutzinakis caught at least a dozen daddy-long-legs spiders, shoved them into his mouth, and dramatically stuck his tongue out to the camera as the bugs crawled back out and wriggled off his chin. It was a delightfully impish gross-out gag that capped off a spot-on moving portrait of a summer day as a young person with nothing better to do than goof off.

The video was an instant hit on MuchMusic, appealing at first to the channel's video jockeys, or "VJs," who hosted the programs. Though the VJs were the face of the channel, they weren't just wannabe actors hoping to parlay the gig into something more glamorous—they were bona fide music nerds who often hand-selected the music videos they played on their programs, more like community radio than commercial radio. MuchMusic put the "Soda" video on *The Wedge*, their indie-rock specialty show that aired on weekday afternoons—just in time for kids to get home from school—hosted by Sook-Yin Lee, an early friend and fan of Gob. But then it got added to *Videoflow*, the channel's round-the-clock stream of music videos that occupied most of the daily schedule. As its exposure grew, the "Soda" clip became a cult classic among Canadian teenagers who identified with its carefree, fun-loving spirit and low-budget, camcorder-style presentation.

"Skate culture and VHS tapes were circulating widely back then, the same stuff that would end up creating *Jackass* on MTV. There was this vibe that lo-fi and independent was really *you*," says George Stroumboulopoulos, who at the time hosted the *Punkorama* radio show on Toronto station 102.1 The Edge, and a few years later would become one of MuchMusic's most recognizable VJs. "Those Gob videos look like the videos you'd make with your friends, but just a little bit better."

Every week, staff at the Mint Records office would watch the fax machine slowly print out pages marked with the MuchMusic logo. Their eyes would dart straight to the *G* section to see where Gob's video had landed that week: usually "light rotation," sometimes even "medium rotation," though never the most-coveted "high rotation." Still, the label was ecstatic. "That's like printing money in Canada in the '90s," says Lawrence.

Gob was on a cross-Canada tour when the "Soda" video came out, and they noticed the "MuchMusic bump" overnight. There were a hundred or so people at the shows at first, but once the video came out, the audiences exploded in size. "I remember the day after it aired, there were five hundred people at the show," says Thacker. "It was a feverish kind of feeling. Everything changed once MuchMusic started playing it." From that point, music videos became a central part of Gob's promotional strategy. Next came a film shoot for "You're Too Cool," which captured the band curling, playing hockey, snowboarding, and throwing snowballs—a fitting counterpart to the summery "Soda" clip, and perhaps the most stereotypically Canadian music video of all time. They'd become cult classics among a generation of Canadian youth, and Gob would double down on those successes in the years to come.

As Gob's popularity on MuchMusic took hold, they became one of the fastest-growing bands in Canada. But it was their notoriety everywhere else that was about to become a problem.

FURTHER LISTENING

CHIXDIGGIT!

Hometown: Calgary, Alberta
Years active: 1991–present

Four songs into their self-titled 1996 debut album, Chixdiggit! spells out their ethos: "Henry Rollins Is No Fun." In other words, hardcore was too serious—punk rock is about having a blast. And that's exactly what Chixdiggit! were all about, with straightforward songs about hot girls, smoking weed, and growing up. They signed to Sub Pop for their first album before moving to Fat Wreck Chords, where they've been the rest of their career, by way of the latter's Honest Don's subsidiary. And, unlike many of their peers, Chixdiggit! were proudly Canadian, even as they toured the globe—lead singer K.J. Jansen's cartoon avatar wears a maple leaf T-shirt on their self-titled album cover, while their second album is called *Born on the First of July*. After releasing their fifth album, *Chixdiggit! II*, in 2007, they've stuck mostly to touring, with the exception of two EPs. Other than the occasional mid-tempo track, their musical formula is basically the same as when they started, which has kept them as dependable supporting players in the punk-rock nostalgia touring circuit.

* * *

SHORTLY AFTER THE RELEASE of *Too Late... No Friends*, Mint Records struck up a partnership with Lookout! Records, the very label whose roster of artists had inspired Gob. First spearheaded by Grant Lawrence after the Smugglers had played a show in California with Lookout founder Larry Livermore's band, the Potatomen, the deal eventually took shape in September 1995 with the co-release of a new album by the Mr. T Experience, an established punk band from the San Francisco Bay Area. To the owners of each company, Mint and Lookout felt like a natural fit: they had both started out as modest, independently run imprints that cared more about music and community than money and profits, and the teams shared a mutual respect for each other's passion, professionalism, and DIY spirit.

The partnership presented a huge opportunity for Gob, who would now be allied with the most influential punk imprint in America. It also didn't hurt that by 1995, Lookout! Records had reportedly accrued an astonishing $10 million in sales.[5] Gob was a perfect fit.

On Mint, Gob was an outlier. They were the label's first straight-up punk band. They were the first signees who had not already been part of the label's trusted community of friends. And their brand of primal chaos contrasted with Mint's progressive, family-friendly aesthetic. Case in point: Mint's flagship act was Cub, whose warm, earnest tracks led them to be dubbed

5 Lookout's impressive sales figures can be largely attributed to sales of Green Day's back catalogue following the success of their major-label debut *Dookie* in 1994.

"cuddlecore," an admission of softness that was the polar opposite of Gob's raging hedonism.

"Mint Records had a pretty squeaky-clean image," says Lawrence. "And Gob came in like a runaway punk train."

Gob had developed a reputation for pranks, immaturity, and generally unruly misbehaviour. As the band's main point of contact at Mint, Lawrence was often fielding angry calls from club owners, show promoters, and band managers.

"Some people think that goes with the territory of rock and roll," Lawrence says. "Mint was a little bit different in that we tried to build up a network of friends that would help our bands out—like, we would have a promoter in Moncton that would book every Mint band, and Gob got on to that network. But if there was misbehaviour, then that promoter would be like, 'Ahh, the backstage got wrecked! I'm not gonna book any more Mint bands!' So, that was becoming a problem. Now, whether that was their fans, whether that was maybe a hired gun for the tour, I don't really know. We wouldn't get a lot of details. But the common denominator was the band name, Gob."

Worse yet, the band's poor reputation caused problems within the Mint organization: Gob's labelmates began asking Lawrence to stop booking them and Gob on shows together, and they were even causing friction with the new partnership with Lookout. "People that were really important to us on the Lookout side were getting upset," Mint co-founder Bill Baker later recalled in *Fresh at Twenty: The Oral History of Mint Records*. "Gob was touring with the Queers, and we'd get these phone messages when we came in to work from Dave and Joe of the Queers, and it would be, you know, screaming, 'These fucking idiots that you've got touring with us down here!'"

Finally, Mint had had enough. Lawrence and the label were done fielding angry phone calls. So, when Gob returned home from a tour in California, Mint invited them into the office to talk. Blissfully unaware of the situation that was unfolding, the band rolled in and asked the label to buy them a new van. "We tour all the time, we need to get a van," Thacker pitched them. They were Mint's new moneymakers—that was the least the label could do, right?

Lawrence countered, "We've actually decided we're not going to renew your contract."

The band was shocked. *Too Late... No Friends* was selling thousands of copies and Gob was raking in royalty payments—no small feat, especially on an indie label like Mint. But the label valued community over everything, even sales. "Things had gotten kind of tense. We were hard to manage," Thacker concedes now.

Gob left the office in a fit of confusion. Eventually, they bought themselves their own van. They knew they'd be all right—they still had their fans, and they still had their music.

As it turned out, the label drama was just beginning.

WHEN GOB WAS DROPPED from Mint, their chances of ever getting signed to Lookout! Records went from slim to none. But by 1996, Lookout was far from the only trendsetting punk label in America. Labels like Epitaph and Fat Wreck Chords had also released some massive albums, like the Offspring's *Smash* (which eventually set an all-time record for most units sold by a band on an independent label), NOFX's *Punk in Drublic*, and Rancid's *... And Out Come the Wolves*. These successes showed that punk rock was commercially lucrative enough that bands could sell hundreds of thousands of records no matter where they were signed. Major label or indie, punk was popular. All that really seemed to matter was that the label was from California. It wasn't a golden ticket to instant fame and fortune, but being part of that scene certainly gave you a good shot.

Gob got to work tightening up their act in their bid to become Canada's first '90s punk breakouts. Thacker and Goutzinakis recruited bassist Craig Wood and drummer Gabe Mantle to be the band's new rhythm section, and in 1998 they self-funded recording sessions for their second record, *How Far Shallow Takes You*. On the album, the reconfigured band sounded crisper, punchier, and more professional than they had before, notching up both the in-your-face aggression and the innate catchiness of their pop hooks. All they needed was a record label to release it—ideally, an American one.

Later that year, Gob managed to land a deal with Fearless Records to release their new album, priming themselves to hopefully make the jump from a moderately popular Canadian act to a widely known pop-punk force on America's much, much larger stage. Fearless was founded in 1994 by Bob Becker, a punk scenester in Culver City, California, who had promoted local shows for bands like Sublime, Lagwagon, Strung Out, and Pennywise. Fearless's first few signings were mostly bands from the Los Angeles metro area like Glue Gun, Straight Faced, and the White Kaps, and the label had achieved modest successes with albums by Bigwig, 30footFALL, and At the Drive-In. Gob signed with Fearless, mastered their album in Los Angeles, and readied it for release in late November 1998. But Gob's second record deal fell apart even quicker than the first one.

Details of Gob's divorce with Fearless are hard to come by. According to Thacker, Gob's manager wanted Fearless to reimburse them for the costs of shooting the music video for "Beauville," and when the label refused, a conflict ensued that ultimately brought their relationship to an abrupt end. Weeks after *How Far Shallow Takes You* was released, Gob and Fearless had cut ties, and Gob rereleased the album on Landspeed Records, the small imprint that had released their early seven-inches. After flirting with the SoCal punk scene, Gob found themselves back on a Vancouver label, but this time on a one-man operation with little reach outside of the city.

A second chance was rare enough. A third chance would be a miracle.

JUST THREE MONTHS AFTER Gob's split with Fearless, the apparently ungovernable band found a new home. Ric Arboit, one of the founders of Nettwerk Music Group, had been heavily involved in Vancouver's hardcore punk scene since the early '80s and loved what he was hearing from Gob. That said, Nettwerk wasn't known for punk rock. Not even close. When friends Terry McBride and Mark Jowett started the record label in 1984, they released the debut albums by the folksy alt-rock group the Grapes of Wrath and the electro-industrial band Skinny Puppy, and used them to land a distribution deal with Capitol Records. Nettwerk went on to develop an eclectic, genre-agnostic roster throughout the remainder of the '80s, but they soon earned a global reputation as a specialist in industrial dance music. Then in 1988, Nettwerk signed a young singer from Halifax named Sarah McLachlan, whose fourth album *Surfacing* was a huge success upon its release in 1997.[6] By then, Nettwerk had also moved into artist management, adding the Barenaked Ladies and Dido to its growing roster. By the end of the '90s, people who had heard of Nettwerk would have known them either as a record label that had churned out pioneers of industrial dance music, or as a management company that represented several of the top hitmakers on adult contemporary radio.

Gob was the furthest thing from either of those: a band of punks, pranksters, and shit-disturbers who had felt burned by two record labels. But Nettwerk didn't care if an artist fit with the reputation that had been assigned to them. When Arboit came to the team wanting to sign a punk band that he thought was great, that was all they needed.

"Gob wrote some great songs," McBride says. "Barenaked Ladies wrote some great songs. Sarah McLachlan wrote some great songs. To me, they're all singer-songwriters. How they decided to dress it up and express themselves as individuals, that was the difference."

Nettwerk signed Gob to a multi-album deal and re-released *How Far Shallow Takes You* in May 1999, giving the ill-fated record its third release in a span of six months.

With a new deal in hand and Nettwerk's financial backing and industry connections, Gob went back to making music videos that kids would love to see on TV. When they set out to make a video for the song "What to Do," they got a seemingly unlikely offer: Jason Priestley, the Canadian actor who had just wrapped a nine-season run on the teen drama series *Beverly Hills, 90210*, wanted to direct it for them.

---

6 McLachlan and Nettwerk also launched Lilith Fair, the women-only travelling festival that was the top-grossing festival tour between 1997 and 1999.

"We were saying, 'What the hell?' We didn't believe it," Goutzinakis said in an interview with Sun Media at the time. "It was cool to see this clean-cut, ex-*90210* star was actually an old-school punk rocker."

They soon learned that before he moved to Hollywood and became a TV star, Priestley used to go to punk shows in his hometown of Vancouver, seeing bands like D.O.A. and the Dead Kennedys—and he also loved *How Far Shallow Takes You.* With Priestley in the director's chair, the music video for "What to Do" starred former MuchMusic VJ Terry David Mulligan in a spoof of *The Jerry Springer Show.* In his introduction to the *The Mulligan Show*'s latest guests, the namesake tabloid host fittingly described Gob as "the world's most dysfunctional band."

"I would have done anything for Gob," Mulligan says now. "I loved that they didn't take themselves seriously. I was surrounded by bands where this was the be-all and end-all. This was their entire life wrapped up in twelve bars. Gob stood out because they had a sense of humour and they brought it out on stage."

"What to Do" was later included in the soundtrack to the Disney Channel's 2000 made-for-TV horror comedy *Mom's Got a Date with a Vampire.* And the band's cover of the Rolling Stones' "Paint It Black"—a bonus track included on Nettwerk's re-release of *How Far Shallow Takes You*—was featured in the 1999 supernatural thriller *Stir of Echoes* starring Kevin Bacon.

"Nettwerk opened so many more doors for us," Goutzinakis told Sun Media. "It seems like they're doing everything but wiping our—"

When the clock struck midnight to mark the end of the twentieth century, Gob had two studio albums under their belt, a handful of music videos in rotation on MuchMusic, and about forty thousand in total record sales.

Gob were the self-described "shithead kids" of Canadian punk rock, and that had made it challenging to make things work in the professional world of the music industry. But most of the people who got to know them loved their songs and, even better, loved their personalities. Now that they had a strong, stable ally in Nettwerk, Gob was in a position to capitalize on the potential so many people had seen in them. Just as long as they didn't fuck it up. As it turned out, the new millennium was going to be very lucrative for punks, pranksters, and jokesters like them. Shithead kids were taking over.

EVEN WITH ALL THE mainstream exposure punk rock experienced throughout the '90s, it paled in comparison to the phenomenon it would become in the early twenty-first century.

In 1999, *Enema of the State* catapulted a punk trio from San Diego County called Blink-182 into stardom with "What's My Age Again" and "All the Small Things" crossing over to pop radio to become global smashes. All three of the album's singles were mainstays on MTV's *Total Request Live*, and the band's big-budget music videos, glossy production, and incredibly catchy songs made *Enema of the State* such a success that Blink-182 became the new model for punk supremacy.

That same year, the genre became increasingly ubiquitous in pop culture. Hollywood movies like *Varsity Blues* and *American Pie* added Green Day, the Offspring, and Blink-182 to their soundtracks, and the video game *Tony Hawk's Pro Skater* introduced a whole generation of young people to punk and skater culture thanks to its soundtrack that put a spotlight on the best of modern punk and hip-hop.

Then, in the fall of 2000, the debut of the MTV series *Jackass* validated a teen instinct for pranks, antics, and hijinks and developed an appreciation for mischief and immaturity among American adolescents. The program's devil-may-care and "bigger is better" attitudes captivated millions of kids across the country, giving them a crash course in punk music that further attuned them to the influences of the day's biggest bands.

But for Canadian punks like Gob, it was like looking through a one-way mirror. Canada's reputation as America's dorky upstairs neighbour was hard to shake.

With Mint, Gob was on a fairly well-connected Canadian independent label, which likely would have been enough to turn them into something between a regional curiosity and a moderately famous band in their own country. With Fearless, they were on a small-time but quickly rising American independent label, which could have fast-tracked them to a bigger audience in the U.S., even if it meant they might not be known as hometown heroes in Canada. If Gob had stuck with Mint, they probably would have gotten stuck at the border. If they had stuck with Fearless, they could've had some success in the bigger American market, but not so much in Canada. Now that they'd fallen ass-backward onto Nettwerk's roster, they had a shot at cracking both markets. Nettwerk had a worldwide distribution deal with Sony Music and a proven track record of turning Canadian acts into international stars.

"Nettwerk were in a different place in the industry," says Thacker. "I mean, Sarah McLachlan was their bread and butter.

They were a very mainstream place to be, which was good for us for some reasons. Our antics weren't going to throw a monkey wrench into the machinery."

In the year 2000, Nettwerk re-issued *Too Late... No Friends* after reclaiming the masters from Mint, giving Gob's debut album a wide release in the United States. Then Gob made an appearance at the Juno Awards, where they were nominated for Best New Group. They spent part of that summer, for the third consecutive year, on the Warped Tour, the annual travelling music festival that over the previous five years had become the biggest punk-rock event of the summer in cities across North America. And finally, Gob prepared to release their new album with Nettwerk, possibly the closest a punk band could come to making a major-label debut without being called a total sellout.

On Gob's third album, the songs got a bit slower and a bit longer, and they were written with a structure more like traditional midtempo rock songs. They had been listening to bands like Jets to Brazil, Jawbreaker, and the Promise Ring, who played in less of a hurry and with more restraint and sensitivity. It was still punk rock, but it was more "radio friendly." That wasn't really their intention; Thacker and Goutzinakis had always written catchy, pop-oriented songs that were disguised by their speed and aggression, so when they slowed them down and cleaned them up a bit, they naturally sounded like something more accessible. All Gob wanted to do was continue to write good songs that didn't make them sound like uninspired, fame-chasing copycats of the big-league bands from California.

"We were trying to carve out our place," Thacker says. "By that time, Green Day was a mainstay, so we didn't want to sound like that. And then Blink-182 came along, and we didn't want to sound like that. We were finding our place."

As the demos trickled into Nettwerk's offices, their bosses were "freaking out," as Thacker tells it. Songs like "For the Moment" and "No Regrets" emerged as clear picks to be singles thanks to their catchy verses and catchier choruses. Then there was a song that Thacker had been working on but wasn't really sure about—it seemed like it might be too different from anything they had ever done. He showed the rest of the band a mostly instrumental demo, and they were sold within the first twelve seconds; the song opened with a guitar riff that was arguably more melodic and catchier than anything they had ever done.

"We need to do this song," Goutzinakis told him.

The band started working on the song that same day, playing it as a full band and Thacker repurposing the guitar riff as the vocal melody for the verses. They sealed the deal by punching up the chorus with gang vocals sung by Thacker, Gouzinakis, and Wood. Even just hearing the demo version, the band and their label felt confident they had a hit.

"When we gave it to Nettwerk, they were like, 'All right, let's do it! We're making a record,'" Thacker recalls.

"I Hear You Calling" became the signature song from Gob's third album *The World According to Gob*,[7] released in the fall of 2000. Not only did the music video become another MuchMusic favourite, but the song finally gave the band a hit on Canadian radio.

"When you start getting radio adds in the Kelownas and the Red Deers, you know that something's starting to bubble," says

---

7 The album title is a play on *The World According to Garp*, the 1978 novel by John Irving.

Arboit. "They never jump on anything until the major markets have jumped on it. When the little markets start adding, it's always a good sign."

"I Hear You Calling" wasn't a global smash like "Basket Case" or "All the Small Things," but it was nonetheless a hit. It took a while, but in January 2002 it even got added to KROQ, the Los Angeles station that was a driving force in alternative rock radio across America. "In Los Angeles, we went from selling something like two copies of the album to eighty to 180 within three weeks of KROQ's airplay," Tom Gates, Nettwerk's head of promotion, told *Radio & Records* magazine.

But while American radio helped, Gob got their biggest boost from the video game industry. All three of the singles from *The World According to Gob*—"I Hear You Calling," "No Regrets," and "For the Moment"—were included on the soundtrack to EA Sports' *NHL 2002*, a result of Gob having a fan at the video game developer's Vancouver studio. The game sold more than 1.5 million copies (mostly in Canada, the U.S., and Europe), unexpectedly exposing Gob to a wider audience than they had ever seen.

"Your record label does whatever they can do to promote the band. Obviously, indies can't do it as much as majors, but they do what they can. Their campaigns didn't touch what those EA Sports games did for us," says Thacker. "We would be on Warped Tour and fans would come up to us and be like, 'I know this song, but I had no idea who played it. Now I know it's you guys.' Those games had a massive reach, and that was awesome."

By 2002, *The World According to Gob* had sold fifty thousand copies in Canada—enough to become the band's first gold-certified record.

For their next record, Gob set their sights even higher. Unfortunately, so did their bosses.

GOB HAD CONQUERED CANADA and was finally starting to break into the United States and other international markets. The next step was obvious: sign to a major label.

Nettwerk had formed a fruitful working relationship with the New York–based major Arista Records, as the company's management arm had been working with several of Arista's signees. Arista's flagship acts at the turn of the century were mostly R&B artists like Toni Braxton, Babyface, and Usher, and they had just landed a major breakthrough with P!nk's smash pop-rock album *Missundaztood.* Once again, Gob would be the odd ones out at company-wide functions—a group of punk troublemakers in a room full of pop hitmakers. Nevertheless, Gob took Nettwerk's help, signed with Arista in the summer of 2002,[8] and set out to make their major-label debut.

Before they even got there, it became clear that the band and Arista had differing expectations. Thacker recalls a conversation with one of the operations managers that immediately raised a red flag.

"How many records do you expect to sell?" Thacker asked.

"Ah, like two million," he recalls the Arista rep replying.

Thacker's eyes widened. Gob's last record hadn't even sold a hundred thousand copies. Arista was apparently forecasting they'd outsell that by a factor of more than twenty.

---

8 While Arista signed Gob internationally, Nettwerk retained the band in Canada.

"I know it happens, but it sounded unreal to me," he says. "And it was."

When Gob released *Foot in Mouth Disease* in the spring of 2003, they scored another hit on MuchMusic with the lead single "Give Up the Grudge." But before they could start touring and properly promoting the record, they hit another wall. At the time, Arista was hemorrhaging money; the company reportedly lost an estimated $110 million in 2003, which followed significant losses from the previous year. The label had to tighten its purse strings and only prioritize their most successful acts—and Gob wasn't one of them. Gob's well of major-label funding quickly dried up.

In June, two months after *Foot in Mouth Disease* shipped to record stores, Gob had flights booked for their first European tour with Motion City Soundtrack and Sugarcult. But they couldn't get the funding to pay for the rest of the costs of the tour, so they cancelled. Thacker decided to go anyway, since he already had the plane ticket—might as well take a vacation. He even went to the first show of the tour at Melkweg in Amsterdam, just to watch.

"It was so heartbreaking," he says now. "I saw the audience. It was perfect for us. In this industry, funding can get pulled like *that*."

Gob got some mileage out of *Foot in Mouth Disease*—three of the tracks appeared on EA's *NHL 2003* and *NHL 2004*, and "Give Up the Grudge" made it to both EA's *Madden NFL 2004* and the 2003 film *American Wedding*—but the album was ultimately a story of disappointment. Gob asked to be let go from Arista, and the label agreed.

* * *

GOB WASN'T THE FIRST punk band to have a bad experience on a major label, and they wouldn't be the last. After parting with Arista, the group dusted themselves off and put out two more albums on Canadian independent labels in 2007 and 2014 as they transitioned from a hot new band on the rise to the "elder statesmen for Canadian pop-punk," as Thacker once put it. By the time Gob had hit their peak, they had sold tens of thousands of records, way more than they would have ever imagined when they were a bunch of teenagers riding their BMX bikes around the streets of Langley and pissing off everyone they met. But there's also a sense of perpetual frustration: every time they caught a break that could help them make a big splash, there was something—a financial disagreement, an industry obstacle, or even their own misbehaviour—that came along to ensure they came up just short of their aspirations.

But while Gob's story is full of almosts, it's also full of unprecedented accomplishments. Within a highly concentrated punk rock scene that thrived almost entirely in Southern California, and within a music industry that made it exceedingly difficult for a Canadian artist to achieve widespread international acclaim, this band of goofballs from the suburbs of Vancouver became role models for a younger cohort of teenage punks across Canada—several of whom were already on their way to chasing the widespread success that had eluded Gob.

"Thinking back, there was no one in that space, and we started that off," says Thacker. "It's funny, over the years, people talk about Gob like, 'You guys are greatly respected.' I'm like . . . we are? I guess when you pave that way, you can't unpave it."

What Gob had started wouldn't take long to become a full-blown movement. While they spent their twenties trying to navigate the pitfalls of the Canadian music industry, kids across the country were growing up watching MuchMusic, playing pranks on their neighbours, picking up instruments, and dreaming of one day playing the Warped Tour. As it happened, a bunch of teenagers in a small town in Ontario were about to become world-famous for doing just that.

2

SUM 41

In the first week of September 2001, just a few nights before the MTV Video Music Awards, Sum 41 is sitting at a table in a New York bar. The four bandmates are already so wasted on booze and mushrooms that they can barely see straight. Bassist Jason "Cone" McCaslin is celebrating his twenty-first birthday—making him legal in the U.S., not that it changed much—and he's been throwing back B-52 shots all night, egged on by singer Deryck Whibley, guitarist Dave Baksh, and drummer Steve Jocz.

One of them passes over another shot. McCaslin throws back the liquor and pauses for a beat. As the room starts spinning, he pukes all over the table and onto the floor—and, incidentally, onto the shoes of singer Nikka Costa, one of their fellow nominees for Best New Artist, who's unlucky enough to be sitting at the table next to him. Whibley and Baksh erupt in laughter. McCaslin laughs, too, even as he continues to vomit. Jocz is busy making out with a girl at the bar, so he misses it.

The party doesn't end there. Back at the band's hotel, they empty the minibar, then head across the hall to their tour manager's room to look for more booze. But they don't have the minibar key, so they're trying to jostle it open somehow. It's tucked into a big armoire that's almost as tall as the ceiling, and in their drunken fumbling, the whole cabinet comes crashing down, smashing the TV and breaking a bunch of other stuff. If they hadn't already kept everyone on their floor awake with their drunken partying, the loud crash of their failed attempt to get more booze at 5:00 a.m. surely rouses their neighbours from sleep.

It's a special night for the members of Sum 41, but this is what a lot of nights have looked like over the past couple of months. They've been partying nonstop ever since their debut album *All Killer No Filler* became a smash hit thanks to the lead single "Fat Lip." Since releasing just three months prior, *All Killer No Filler* has already been certified platinum in the U.S., selling more than a million copies. During that time, Sum 41 have been touring constantly, and their time on the road has been filled with nightly escapades of drunken mayhem and physical destruction. They're barely into their twenties and they're already on top of the world, shamelessly riding the high of their quick ascent to fame and fortune. They're young and indestructible.

Two days after their big night in New York, they receive a bill for the damages at the hotel: they owe roughly $4,000. Fortunately for them, none of the members of Sum 41 will have to pay a cent. They've already been given a licence for destruction by Lyor Cohen, the president of the Island Def Jam

Music Group, the big-league record company bent on turning Sum 41 into international superstars.

"Go out and destroy the world," Cohen said. "Just make sure you get it on tape."

BY THE AGE OF SIX, Deryck Whibley had developed a fondness for the sound of breaking glass—which, of course, motivated him to break things that were made of glass. By his teens, he was leading a crew of pranksters on cartoonish crusades to egg neighbourhood houses and spray strangers with water guns. In another time and place, this behaviour might have meant nothing—or at least, nothing good. But for a kid living in an era that was quickly developing an appetite for juvenile hijinks—within a few years *Jackass* would debut on MTV to great acclaim—it might just pay to be a walking demolition derby.

Born in the Toronto suburb of Scarborough on the second day of spring in 1980, Whibley was a short blond kid who was quiet, kept to himself, and didn't have many friends. Whibley's mother, Michelle, was only seventeen when he was born, so the two lived with her parents during the earliest years of his life. "We didn't have any money; we didn't really do much," Whibley recalled in a 2016 interview with *VICE*. When Whibley was in his early teens, he and his mom moved to nearby Ajax, Ontario, a suburban town in Durham Region, the catch-all municipality that represents the cluster of cities and towns located just east of Toronto.

Whibley became infatuated with music from a young age, taking an early liking to rock bands like Nirvana, Guns N' Roses, the Sex Pistols, and Aerosmith, and hip-hop acts like

LL Cool J, Run-DMC, and the Beastie Boys. When he was eleven, he started a rap group with his cousin called Powerful Young Hustlers. His mom would give him a dollar whenever he rapped for her. That was the first time Whibley made money from music.

As a student at Exeter High School in Ajax, Whibley skipped class as much as he could. "I hated it," he told *VICE.* "I hardly went, I couldn't stand it. I hated it so much. I think I knew so young that I was never going to do anything with it. You just have that feeling. Everything seemed pointless to me. None of it seemed relevant to anything I wanted to do." As he entered his teenage years, Whibley's fashion choices reflected his rebellious attitude: he dyed his hair and slicked it into bright-orange spikes, and he wore the type of baggy streetwear that was popular at the local skate park.

By age fourteen, Whibley had learned to play the guitar and started a band called Kaspir with his friend Grant McVittie. That year, 1994, was also when he became friends with Steve Jocz, a hyperactive kid a grade behind him at Exeter. Like Whibley, Jocz loved music and hated school. "None of us liked school. None of us were into sports," Jocz says now. "We were always into music. That was the culture we had gotten into." Kaspir added Jocz as their drummer and their friend Jon Marshall as lead singer and played songs that sounded like an amalgam of Nirvana and Weezer. But pretty soon, their tastes would change.

By the mid-'90s, punk rock had broken into the mainstream in a big way. Young people across North America got hooked on Green Day and the Offspring, and they started hanging out at skate parks, wearing baggy clothes, spiking their hair with copious amounts of gel, and running to their local music stores to buy more of the fast-paced, hard-nosed music that encouraged them to embrace their angst and lash out at "society," even if they weren't entirely sure what they were supposed to be angry about. Bands like NOFX, Rancid, Bad Religion, Pennywise, Lagwagon, and MxPx weren't just making a style of music that was in high demand, they were projecting an image of social dissent and youthful rebellion. This was the realm of middle fingers, anti-corporate fashion, and anarchy symbols spray-painted on half-pipes. They wanted to be loud and impolite. They wanted to be reckless and free. They wanted to rebel. When they heard punk rock, they knew almost instantly that this was how they would do it.

Whibley and Jocz were among those kids. On July 27, 1996, the members of Kaspir travelled to nearby Bowmanville to attend the Warped Tour, the best place for any punk-rock kid to be that summer and many that followed. It was the second year of the travelling outdoor music festival, and founder Kevin Lyman had refocused the lineup to turn it from an eclectic mix of alt-rock into a punk-rock circus, aided in part by a cash infusion from its new title sponsor, shoe manufacturer Vans. A couple dozen bands descended upon twenty-eight cities and towns across the United States and Canada, including some of the boys' favourites like NOFX, Lagwagon, and Pennywise. On their way home from the show, buzzing with adrenalin and excitement, the group made two big decisions. First, they were going to start over as a new band that would sound just like their punk-rock heroes so that in a few years they'd be playing the Warped Tour themselves. And second, since it was the forty-first day of their summer vacation, they'd call themselves Sum 41.

* * *

AS TEENAGERS, WHIBLEY AND Jocz had become fans of the band Treble Charger, who hailed from the Northern Ontario border town of Sault Ste. Marie. Treble Charger had released their debut album *NC17* in 1994, and their single "Red" was getting regular airplay on campus radio stations and MuchMusic. By the time they released their *Self=Title* EP in early 1995, they were fielding offers from major labels and signed with RCA. Whibley and Jocz went to see Treble Charger when they played in Oshawa, Ajax's larger neighbour to the east. They managed to sneak backstage to give singer Greig Nori their demo tape and ask him to come see their band, which then comprised Whibley, Jocz, Marshall, and new bassist Richard "Twitch" Roy. A few weeks later, in September 1996, the group played their first show as Sum 41 at a Battle of the Bands showcase at Toronto's Opera House, where they rented a school bus to bring all of their friends from Ajax. Nori was there, and he brought his friend Marc Costanzo of the band Len.

Impressed by what they saw, Nori and Costanzo both took an interest in Whibley and the band, using their connections as professional musicians with their own recording contracts to help the young group break into the music industry. By 1997, Treble Charger's major-label debut, *Maybe It's Me*, had notched a radio hit with "Friend of Mine," and Len was selling tens of thousands of copies of their first two albums. These guys weren't exactly rock stars—not yet, anyway—but they had enough experience and credentials to shape the kids' trajectory in music.

Sum 41 took every bit of help that Whibley's new friends were willing to offer; Costanzo helped them record their first set of demos, and Nori would soon become their manager.[9]

One night, Whibley was hanging out at Costanzo's place while the older musician recorded the lyrics to a mid-tempo dance-pop beat he had built around a sample of a disco song that a friend had played in a DJ set.[10] A few weeks later, Costanzo brought that song to his publisher, Michael McCarty of EMI Music Publishing Canada. Word quickly spread through the music industry, and before long, Len had landed a major-label record deal. In the summer of 1999, "Steal My Sunshine" would dominate Top 40 radio stations around the world, cracking the top 10 in Canada, the U.S., the U.K., Ireland, and Australia.

McCarty had signed Len to a publishing deal a few years earlier, after

FURTHER LISTENING

NOT BY CHOICE

Hometown: Ajax, Ontario
Years active: 1997-2008

They say a rising tide lifts all boats, and that was certainly the case in Ajax. When talent agents descended upon the Ontario city to poach its talent, Sum 41's scenemates Not By Choice got a taste of the big time. They received quite a bit of love from MuchMusic on the strength of their pop-punk debut album, *Maybe One Day*, in 2002: the music videos for "Standing All Alone" and "Now That You Are Leaving" aired frequently, and both tracks ended up on the channel's storied *Big Shiny Tunes* compilation CD series. ("Standing All Alone" may be the catchier song, but the "Now That You Are Leaving" video is particularly memorable—it's a pitch-perfect parody of MTV show *Becoming*, where fans re-create iconic music videos from their favourite bands—and earned them the MuchMusic Video Award for Best Independent Video.) The band opened for Avril Lavigne and Simple Plan, but their second album *Secondhand Opinions* wasn't as successful. Both of their albums were released in partnership with major labels, but only in Canada, which perhaps explains why they quietly disappeared a few years later.

---

9 In his 2024 memoir, *Walking Disaster: My Life Through Heaven and Hell*, Whibley would allege that Nori groomed and sexually abused him for years, beginning not long after they met, when Whibley was sixteen and Nori was in his mid-thirties. As of the time of writing, Nori has denied the allegations, and both Whibley and Nori have filed competing defamation lawsuits.

10 That friend was Brendan Canning, an Ajax-born musician who, at the time, was playing in alt-rock band hHead, and a few years later would co-found indie rock collective Broken Social Scene.

Costanzo and his sister Sharon—the band's core duo—had gotten themselves kicked out of every label office in Toronto. "They were real punky, and they had a real sort of small-g gangster mentality, like, 'We don't trust you or like you until you prove otherwise,'" McCarty recalls.

EMI Music Publishing Canada wasn't a label, but they threw around cash like one.[11] McCarty would sign promising young songwriters to publishing deals that would help bankroll early recordings to court attention from record labels. Once an artist got signed, the label would start footing the bill, but McCarty and his team would pocket some cash from songwriting royalties and move on to building up their other acts. This arrangement gave wild-card artists like Len the money and freedom to do whatever they wanted, like wrapping copies of their debut album *Superstar* in yellow fur without hearing some bigwig prattle on about their "bottom line." And through his work with Len, McCarty was developing a reputation for helping free spirits navigate a music industry often reluctant to take risks.

Costanzo was urging McCarty to sign Whibley, so he took him up on his invitation to see Sum 41 play in Ajax. Costanzo, McCarty, and Barbara Sedun (EMI's vice-president of A&R) drove from Toronto to watch the band wreak havoc on a bunch of tunes in Roy's basement. As McCarty recalls now, "It was really raw, but we were blown away by the personality, the presence, the musicality—it all seemed to work."

With EMI on board as the band's publisher, Sum 41 hopped into Metalworks Studios west of Toronto in 1998 to

---

11 EMI Music Publishing was a separate company from EMI Records. The label would get right of first refusal for any act signed to the publisher, but if the label said no, the publisher had free rein to shop the artist around.

make their first official demo—a quick, efficient, four-track blast of pop-punk that clocked in at under ten minutes and included the song "Summer," an early Sum 41 live staple. Among Sum 41's growing fan base of local punks, that demo tape was informally titled *Rock Out with Your Cock Out*. They sent it to major labels across North America, and they heard back from ... nobody.

A little while later, along came Aquarius Records. The Montreal-based indie label had recently had success with a rap-rock band from Newmarket, Ontario, called Serial Joe, who sold fifty thousand copies of their debut album in three months. When co-founder Terry Flood happened to check out a performance by Sum 41 one day, he was impressed; they were doing the rock thing, the rap thing, and the metal thing—all the stuff the kids loved. And so Aquarius promptly started up negotiations on a worldwide deal for Sum 41.

It should've been an easy sell. Aquarius had been around since 1969, with flagship artists that included April Wine, Corey Hart, and Bif Naked. They even had a young Ontario transplant, Mike Renaud, who had worked his way up from the mailroom to become the A&R rep for the label's younger artists, like Serial Joe. Renaud was the perfect guy to convince the young Sum 41 that Aquarius was a cool label worth signing with.

"There was no doubt we wanted to sign them right away," Renaud says.

But Sum 41 had set their sights higher than an independent Canadian label. McCarty had advised them that a label of Aquarius' size wouldn't have the inroads to break the band internationally. Had they signed to Aquarius worldwide, their best-case scenario might've been ending up as, well, April Wine,

Corey Hart, or Bif Naked. If Sum 41 really wanted to go for it, McCarty explained, they needed to aim for an American major label. So, the band balked at the one record label that had shown them any interest and kept looking.

Everyone was stumped. How was it that Sum 41, with all of their talent and showmanship, weren't connecting with major-label scouts, many of whom were actively looking for pop-punk bands just like them?

The answer came from Sum 41 themselves: "All people hear is the music. They say we just sound like Green Day or whatever, that we're just derivative," McCarty recalls the band telling him. "They don't understand what characters we are."

So, the band and their team put their heads together to figure out how to show the music industry who they were. The answer was closer than they thought.

BY 1999, SUM 41 had settled into a stable lineup of four keen, fun-loving kids who not only had a mutual love of punk rock, but also a shared interest in hip hop, heavy metal, rock 'n' roll theatrics, and good old-fashioned mischief. When Marshall left the band in 1997 and Whibley took over as lead singer, Sum 41 was left with an open spot on guitar that was filled by another high school friend, Dave Baksh, who had previously played in heavy metal bands 747 and Embodiment. He, Whibley, and Jocz had become friends at Exeter when they were kicked out of class together. A metalhead who could already shred on the guitar, Baksh went by the nickname "Brownsound," a reference to both his Indo-Guyanese background and his love of the signature guitar tone of Eddie Van Halen. A year later, Roy left the band and was replaced as bassist by Jason McCaslin. Another Exeter classmate, he had played in a grunge band called Second Opinion. They'd all hang out together at school, where Whibley gave McCaslin the nickname "Cone" because he would never pack a lunch and would buy a Chapman's ice cream cone from the cafeteria instead.[12]

As Sum 41 was bringing their memorable live show to cities across Canada throughout 1998 and early 1999, Jocz's trusty camcorder, practically welded to his forehead, had been accumulating footage of the quartet goofing off and being rambunctious teens. With some money from EMI, the band compiled that footage into a promotional video that showed them pulling a bunch of pranks, including driving around town and blasting unsuspecting passersby with Super Soakers.[13] While so much of the music at the time was being sold to suburban teens looking to let loose from their cul-de-sac monotony, the appeal of the Sum 41 VHS tape was that it showed viewers that they actually *were* those kids.

As soon as he saw the completed video, McCarty knew it was going to work. "I was probably the most excited I've ever been in my entire career. It just blew my mind how good it was. We immediately knew this was a game changer, and it did exactly what they said it would do—it communicated what characters they were. And, just as importantly, it showed that they could communicate using the medium of video."

Immediately, Sum 41's team got busy showing the video to

12 In a rude bit of irony, McCaslin would later discover he was actually lactose intolerant, a diagnosis he received after eating "a lot of fucking pizza on tour" with Sum 41 in 2004 and ending up in the hospital.

13 This is known in the industry as an "electronic press kit" or "EPK," a punchy introduction to an artist designed to get people in the music industry up to speed.

the labels who had previously turned them down. McCarty connected the band with a lawyer named Chris Taylor, who had played in the reggae-rock band One in the early '90s before beginning his law practice. He had just made an early splash by discovering Nelly Furtado and securing the young pop singer a big-time contract with DreamWorks in 1999, and he wanted Sum 41 to be his next big success story. Taylor, McCarty, and Nori sent the VHS tape to A&R reps at several labels, and this time, they heard back from practically all of them. The tape itself quickly became legendary, as it was repeatedly copied and passed around—the '90s equivalent of going viral.[14] Within weeks, nearly a dozen U.S. record labels were preparing to send their scouts to Toronto to see what was up with this group of ill-behaved Canadian kids.

While the band's team fielded calls from American labels, Sum 41 was busy working on bringing that authentic sense of self-expression to their live shows. Over the years, McCarty had seen plenty of bands blow deals at high-pressure showcases, playing in empty rooms except for the suits sitting there assessing them. The band needed to be comfortable. McCarty reached out to Toronto booking agent Yvonne Matsell, who secured the band a midweek residency in late 1999 at Ted's Wrecking Yard, a punky dive bar with a sizable stage in Toronto's Little Italy neighbourhood, so the corporate stooges could properly see what Sum 41 was all about.

Right away, Sum 41 made the space their own. They littered

---

14 Among the people who got a copy of Sum 41's infamous VHS tape were Green Day's Billie Joe Armstrong, who thought it "hysterical," and NOFX's Fat Mike, who considered signing them to his label Fat Wreck Chords, but decided they should probably be on a major instead.

the stage with exercise trampolines and a life-size cutout of comedian Martin Lawrence that McCaslin had poached from his job at a Cineplex movie theatre in Scarborough, and they attached sparklers to the ends of their guitars. "We were a young band trying to stand out," says McCaslin. "We did stuff so people would be able to walk away saying, 'Ah, I remember that Sum 41 band, they had trampolines.' That shit works! Just single trampolines, and people still remember it to this day." Even though the only people in the audience for that first show were their team and the venue staff, Sum 41 gave it their all. Whibley, Baksh, and McCaslin piled onto the drum riser, surrounding Jocz and his kit. On the count of four, the three guitarists leapt onto the trampolines, bounced ten feet into the air, and started playing their hearts out the moment they landed. By the end of the night, there had been pinwheels, frenetic medleys, and even some fireworks. "I'm going, 'This is the greatest thing I've ever seen in my life!'" recalls McCarty, his voice still teeming with enthusiasm more than twenty years later. "We were just absolutely gobsmacked by how good it was."

By the time the residency was wrapping up six weeks later, Sum 41 was selling out Ted's every week, packing the two-hundred-capacity venue with a healthy mix of industry insiders who had flown in for the event, local scenesters, and the band's friends with fake IDs. Afterward, Sum 41 fielded interest from a handful of record companies including DreamWorks, Hollywood, Interscope, Island Def Jam, Arista, and Maverick. "We went from having zero labels interested in us to having every single label," Jocz recalls. Now, Sum 41 could afford to be picky. And they wanted to sign with a company whose people really believed in the band and would commit to them long-term. "With a lot of these label guys, it's a pissing contest," says Jocz. "They just want to fuck the hot chick at the bar. They don't want to marry her; they just want another notch on the belt." Out of all of them, it was Island Def Jam and Interscope—two major American labels—that emerged as the frontrunners in the Sum 41 sweepstakes.

One of the industry guys who had travelled to Toronto was Lewis Largent, a former MTV VJ who had moved offscreen in the mid-'90s to focus on his role as the channel's vice-president of music programming. In 1999, he was in the process of leaving MTV to run A&R at Island Def Jam when another former MTV-er—Rick Krim, then a VP at EMI Music Publishing in New York—showed him Sum 41's promo vid. From his time at MTV, Largent had a strong instinct for what made a band telegenic. And Sum 41 had it. "I'm thirty-five years old. I've seen the Clash, I've seen the Sex Pistols, I've seen the Jam, I've seen them all," Largent said in an interview on MuchMusic. "And I'm just tellin' ya, *this* is the band. They're bigger than life."

After Interscope had treated Sum 41 to a $3,000 steakhouse dinner, Largent and his colleague Rob Stevenson, the director of A&R at Island Def Jam, took the band out for their own meeting—at a Subway sandwich shop. Their lunch couldn't have cost more than $50. "We were like, 'We just ate at the best steakhouse in town. These assholes have taken us to Subway,'" says Jocz. "We were like, 'Fuck these guys,' you know? But then after talking to them a little bit, we realized that actually these guys are kind of cool."

Toward the end of Sum 41's residency at Ted's, it had become clear to just about everyone that the band would go with Interscope or Island Def Jam. But behind the scenes, the band still hadn't made a decision. During one of their last shows, Whibley got on the mic and made a half-joking declaration: "Whoever comes up on the stage and jumps on the trampoline, we're signing with them." Sum 41 had impressed Largent with their high-energy and daredevilish displays, and Largent wanted to show the band that he could keep up. He rushed the stage, leapt onto the trampoline, and gave the whole room the finger as he gleefully bounced up and down.

It wasn't the only factor in Sum 41's decision, but it certainly helped. Largent's willingness to cut loose showed the band that he was the type of guy they wanted to work with. And more than any of the others, Largent's team at Island Def Jam had shown that they really understood the band. The result of a merger of fourteen record labels, most notably the pop- and rock-focused Island Records and the hip-hop specialists Def Jam Recordings, the barely year-old conglomerate was ready to capitalize on the rising popularity of hip-hop while also bolstering its roster of rock bands. "We can get good contracts out of anybody, but it really starts with the team," says Taylor, Sum 41's lawyer. "Island Def Jam was really well resourced, stacking up on the rock side. Hungry as hell. Perfect timing."

Sum 41's music would land on the Island side of the company, but they'd also be on the same roster as their hip-hop idols LL Cool J and DMX. The company's president, Lyor Cohen, even had a history of booking shows in Los Angeles featuring iconic hip-hop and punk acts, and he had spent time as the tour manager for Run-DMC and the Beastie Boys. When he stepped in, they finally sealed a deal. "Lyor just had a way of talking to you where he was on your level," McCaslin recalls. At the end of 1999, Sum 41 officially signed to Island Def Jam.

But while a worldwide record deal with a major label would be good for the band's long-term viability, McCarty felt that it could actually sink them in their own country. Canada wasn't a priority for major labels like Island, with deep pockets and offices all over the world. Why spend time and resources in Canada when they could focus on places with more people and more money? "I think that the hardest job in the music business in the entire world is doing A&R in Canada for a major label," says McCarty. "If you sign with an American label or a British label, then the Canadians could resent it, and they don't work your record very strongly in Canada. And yet, the chances of you being successful with your records [on a Canadian label] outside of Canada are very small."

Plus, Aquarius had been good to them before anybody else was interested; the label had made Sum 41 their first offer, had helped them when their van broke down while on tour—an inevitability for the old 1982 Ford Econoline with no air conditioning, no heat, and holes in the floor that allowed rain and snow to come through—and had even gotten them onto the side stages at the Toronto and Montreal stops of that summer's Warped Tour, a dream come true for a band that had formed three years earlier precisely because of how much they loved the Warped Tour. Sum 41 wanted to repay them with their loyalty, so they carved out a spot for the independent imprint within their worldwide major-label deal. Looking to keep ties with their home country, Sum 41 went back to Aquarius asking for a Canada-exclusive deal, and Aquarius agreed. Finally, with Island Def Jam on their side, and Aquarius holding down the fort at home, Sum 41 was ready to take on the world.

* * *

BY THE END OF the '90s, punk rock's time in the mainstream was proving to be more than just a passing fad. Punk bands were reaching bigger audiences and developing a sound that was more melodic and commercially palatable: "pop-punk." And this new wave already had a forerunner in Blink-182, who were successfully challenging Green Day as rock radio and MTV's punk band of choice. Blink-182's knack for catchy melodies, unbridled fondness for sex jokes and toilet humour, and undisguised ambition for stardom was far removed from punk's traditional anti-establishment ideals. They wrote gag songs about incontinence and incest, and they released a music video of the three bandmates running naked through the streets of Los Angeles. Such behaviour made them a prized commodity of mass entertainment, particularly with their third album, *Enema of the State*, in 1999. While the album garnered Blink-182 a good share of critics—many of them punk rockers who heatedly contended that the group was nothing more than the Backstreet Boys of punk rock—it went quadruple-platinum in less than a year and turned them into icons.

So when Island signed Sum 41 to a major recording contract the same year that *Enema of the State* blew up, they had a clear blueprint of what success would look like for the Canadian teens. And if Sum 41 wanted to feed the appetite for pop-punk before listeners got their fill somewhere else, they had to act quickly. The band headed back into Metalworks in early 2000 to record their first proper release, an eleven-song EP called *Half Hour of Power* that reproduced the exact thirty-minute setlist they had been playing at their shows.[15]

Kicking off with a minute of thrash metal riffage, *Half Hour of Power* wastes no time showing off the band's eclectic interests. There are power chords, guitar solos, tight doo-wop harmonies, fake vomiting, and screaming—and that's only the second track, "Machine Gun." Near the end of the EP, the chugging guitars of "Dave's Possessed Hair" abruptly give way to "It's What We're All About," featuring Beastie Boys–style rap trade-offs between Whibley, Jocz, and Baksh, which in turn transitions seamlessly into heavy metal flareup "Ride the Chariot to the Devil." Though still a pop-punk recording at heart, *Half Hour of Power* showed off a surprising amount of versatility and was in keeping with the band's penchant for relentless thrill-seeking and sky-high ambitions.

If there had been any lingering doubts that Aquarius wasn't as perfect a fit for Sum 41 as Island, it was put to rest when the Canadian label arranged for the band to launch *Half Hour of Power* at Zanzibar, one of Toronto's most iconic strip clubs. The quartet hit the stage and stripped down to thongs and little else—a bowtie for Jocz, a cowboy hat for Whibley, and a shaggy black wig for McCaslin. Baksh was the most conservatively dressed, being the only one to cover his chest, which he did with a breastplate printed to make him look like a busty, bikini-clad lady. When they turned around, the crowd could see they had written "Aquarius" on their butt cheeks.

When *Half Hour of Power* was released to music stores in late June 2000, the EP performed modestly, sneaking onto the

---

15 This is, however, a technicality. The EP contains only 26 minutes and 30 seconds of music; they added three-and-a-half minutes of silence to the end of the final song to bring the total length to half an hour.

charts in the U.S., the U.K., and Japan. The single "Makes No Difference" had the biggest impact, landing in comedy movies like *Bring It On* and *National Lampoon's Van Wilder* and the MTV animated series *Daria*. For the music video, the label even managed to get rapper DMX to make a cameo.

Half Hour of Power didn't turn Sum 41 into a household name, but it wasn't really meant to. "There wasn't a massive push on that album—it was just an introduction," McCaslin says. "Island really wanted us to tour for about a year and a half to build an underground following." In that regard, *Half Hour of Power* more than succeeded in introducing an unknown Canadian group to a receptive audience and getting them sucked into the machinery of American mass media. Now, it was time to go all in.

•

TO HELP SUM 41 record an album that could stand next to Green Day's *Dookie* and Blink-182's *Enema of the State*, there was only one guy for the job: Jerry Finn, who had worked on both those albums. Before *Dookie*, Finn was, in his own words, "an assistant [engineer] making eight bucks an hour." But after mixing the album alongside producer Rob Cavallo, Finn's career prospects exploded. By the time Blink-182 went to record what would become *Enema of the State* in 1999, Finn was an in-demand producer who had helmed records by punk superstars Rancid and Pennywise. If there was anyone who could polish Sum 41's sound enough to dominate the charts while retaining their punk and metal edge, it was Finn.

Only a few months after *Half Hour of Power* was released, Sum 41 headed back into Metalworks to start working with

Finn on their debut full-length album. The group had rented the backroom of the Chameleon Café, a small Ajax venue that Whibley and Jocz had persuaded to host local punk shows, and where they had spent their time between tours working on new songs for the record. Progress was slow, and they only had a handful of songs finished by the time they entered the studio with Finn. The producer assured them that once they started recording, inspiration would strike, and the songs would start flowing out of them. But after nearly three months at Metalworks, they barely had any new material for the record. "The problem was we were partying way too much," Whibley said in a 2019 interview with *Alternative Press*. "We were nineteen and we'd been given a bunch of money by the record company. And it was our first big record. All we were doing was eating really expensive dinners, going out to strip clubs, and doing whatever we felt like—everything except working, really. There was no writing being done."

At the end of 2000, the band took a three-month break from the studio and Whibley tried to focus on writing new material. But his living situation and the band's touring schedule weren't exactly conducive to productive writing sessions, either. He would write in short spurts whenever and wherever he could while the band was on tour—in green rooms, hotels, the back of the van—and when he'd get home to his parents' house in Ajax, he'd sit in their car in the freezing cold Canadian winter and write songs with an acoustic guitar and a tape recorder. By March, Whibley had managed to finish four more songs, and the band also added the intro and outro tracks "Introduction to Destruction" and "Pain for Pleasure," two half-jokey heavy-metal tributes to Iron Maiden's *The Number of the Beast.* (Jocz spent a total of ten minutes writing the lyrics to the latter while he was sitting on the toilet.)

When the band was ready to head back into the studio, Island sent them to Cello Studios in Los Angeles. That way, none of their friends would be around to distract them, and they wouldn't be old enough to go drinking in the bars anyway.[16] At Cello, they finally got some work done. The band was happy, and Finn's team was impressed. At one point, while listening back to the raw mixes, engineer Joe McGrath remarked, "Jesus, this album is all killer, no filler." And so the album found its name: *All Killer No Filler*. It was all coming together nicely. But it was still missing something.

Over a period of several months, Whibley had been slowly cobbling together a song out of several spare parts: a hard-rock riff, a hip-hop verse, a big pop-punk chorus. "The very, very first thing I wrote was the guitar riff," Whibley said in a 2021 interview with Stereogum. "I didn't necessarily write it for this idea that I had for this sort of punk-rock-rap kind of thing. I knew I had this old-school rap idea mixed with punk-rock sort of stuff, but I wrote this riff just as a riff. And then I ended up writing a chorus, like, months later. And then I had this verse. And none of them were supposed to be together. They were just separate things that I was writing over time. And then one day it kind of clicked, and I thought, 'Well, these all kind of work. They're all around the same tempo, they're all the same key.' I changed a few things and made it work, and now all of a sudden, I was like, 'Okay, I've got the rap part, I've got a riff, and I've got a chorus. But I don't have the rest of the song.'

---

16 For American readers: the legal drinking age in Ontario is nineteen.

And then it took a long time before pieces just kind of came together." A vision slowly materialized, but Whibley still wasn't sold on it. "I played it for a few people, friends, and I don't even think half the band really liked it," Whibley told Stereogum. "And it wasn't really like it was this great song that everyone loved. It was kind of like, 'Meh, it's kind of stupid-sounding. And are you really gonna rap over it?'"

The one person he convinced was Finn. "That's your first single," he told the band. "That's gonna be a hit."

That song, "Fat Lip," is Sum 41's origin story told in three minutes, distilling *Half Hour of Power*'s sugar-high sense of exploration into a tenth of the space; there are spunky guitar riffs, three-man rap bars, fast-paced, palm-muted power chords, and a big, shiny pop chorus. The lyrics are both self-deprecating and snot-nosed, with no shortage of quotable zingers perfect for a generation whose brains had been primed by the likes of *American Pie*.

"It's this weird Frankenstein song, and I'm amazed it worked," Jocz says. "It's a perfect example of what Sum 41 was. It's a metal song, it's a rap song, it's a punk song. It's all over the place, because we could never focus on one thing. But somehow we made it work."

Taking Finn's advice, the band decided that "Fat Lip" would be the album's lead single. For the music video, they hired director Marc Klasfeld, who was known at the time for rap videos like Nelly's "Country Grammar"—which was exactly the type of video Sum 41 wanted. They filmed it over two hot, sunny days in Pomona, California, where the band had already built a decent fan base, even in those early days. Klasfeld got hundreds of punks, freaks, and weirdos to hang out, bounce around, and be funny in front of the camera. The band spent part of the video playing for the mass of people and the other taking part in the chaos and hijinks themselves. After two days, they left the shoot with smiles, sunburns, and no idea if they had made a good music video or not.

Their record labels, though, knew right away. "When we got the video, it was like, 'This is unbelievable,'" says Renaud, their Aquarius rep. "This video is basically a montage of every subset of kids who feel disenfranchised or not part of the mainstream."

The first inkling the band got that they had created something special came just after Klasfeld sent them the first cut of the music video. They were in L.A. again and bumped into Joel and Benji Madden of Good Charlotte at their hotel, so they showed it to them. "They were just freaking out. 'Oh my god! This is such a great music video. You guys are gonna be such huge stars,'" Whibley told Stereogum. "They're like, 'This is it. This is the last day we're gonna know you before you're famous. You guys are famous now because of this.'"

"FAT LIP" WAS RELEASED on April 22, 2001, and *All Killer No Filler* followed two weeks later. But while the album sold well, the single didn't make a major impact right away—and the band wasn't sure it ever would. "It's a challenging song, if you think about it. Nothing like that had ever come out," McCaslin says. "To listen to it as a new thing that had never been done before, you're like, will this work? Who knows."

But by the summer, things started to click. The music video for "Fat Lip" began getting more airplay on MTV and, by mid-July, made it to the top spot on *Total Request Live.* It would return to number one on *TRL* several more times throughout the summer, duking it out with NSYNC and the Backstreet Boys for the title of America's hottest music video.

Then, Sum 41 got another big break when they were invited to perform during the opening slot of MTV's televised twentieth-anniversary party on the first day of August. True to form, they decided to make the most of it.

"We're gonna be on MTV for five minutes," Jocz recalls the group saying. "Nobody is going to give a shit if we just go out and play our song. Let's do something a little different."

With MTV's help, the band recruited Mötley Crüe's Tommy Lee and Judas Priest's Rob Halford to join the stage with them as they performed a medley of "Fat Lip," the Beastie Boys' "No Sleep Till Brooklyn," Mötley Crüe's "Shout at the Devil," and Judas Priest's "You've Got Another Thing Comin'." The crowd was electric, feeding off the energy of the pop-punk youngsters and the star power of the '80s metal veterans. As countless viewers watched the live TV broadcast, the band showed off their larger-than-life stage presence and flexed their credibility by not only paying tribute to their influences but getting an unmistakable co-sign from two of the biggest stars of heavy metal's glory days.

"Getting Rob Halford and Tommy Lee on that stage garnered some kind of respect for us," McCaslin says now. "There were a ton of haters back then. That just came with the territory. But there were fewer after we did that. At that point, you had Blink-182 and Green Day and the Offspring, and no one in that genre had really dived into the metal thing. We've always been big metal fans, and hip-hop fans, and punk fans. People think of metal in a different way than they think of a pop-punk band, so I think bringing metal into the fold, people were like, 'Oh, they can play *metal.* That's tough!' I think the respect came from that."

When Sum 41 returned to the Warped Tour, everyone—well, everyone but them—knew things had changed. "The bands we knew were like, 'You guys are about to be superstars.'" Whibley said in a 2021 interview with *Billboard.* "We're like, 'What? What are you talking about?' They're like, 'You have no idea what's about to happen.'"

Suddenly, Sum 41 wasn't just successful—they were, indeed, superstars. Within weeks, "Fat Lip" was being played everywhere. The song broke out of MTV and into the stratosphere. It charted in twelve countries, hitting No. 1 on the U.S. Alternative Airplay chart and the top 10 on the U.K. singles chart. By the end of August, *All Killer No Filler* was certified platinum.

Following the summer of 2001, Sum 41 continued to be MTV favourites. Just in time for a new school year, they dropped a new music video for "In Too Deep," a parody of a scene from the Rodney Dangerfield movie *Back to School.*[17] In the video, the scrawny members of Sum 41 arrive at a pool lined with palm trees in sunny California to compete in a diving competition against a team of muscular, tanned, Speedo-wearing jocks. In its most iconic moment, Baksh rises out of the water, godlike, to rip his guitar solo in an homage to Slash of Guns N' Roses. The music video became an instant classic of its own, further establishing Sum 41 as poster boys of a pop-cultural movement defined by teen movies, pop-punk

17 Sum 41 asked Dangerfield to make a cameo in the music video, but he respectfully declined.

jams, and rock 'n' roll idolatry. "In Too Deep" would go down as arguably Sum 41's most popular song, and with it, the band proved that they weren't just riding a wave—they *were* the wave.

Very quickly, Sum 41 cultivated a fervent fan base that fully bought into their "fuck you" attitude and would gleefully attend their live shows to display the Sum 41 salute: four fingers extended on one hand and the middle finger on the other. "It's great to see punk rock with personality," Blink-182's Tom DeLonge told a *Rolling Stone* writer while backstage when Sum 41 was opening for them at a gig in Toronto that drew a reported ten thousand people. The band members' previously hesitant parents showed up to their local shows in their cars now with custom licence plates: SUM41DAD, SUM41MUM, and SUM41ROX. Whibley's mother even followed them on tour, including a memorable flight to Japan where they "drank the plane dry and kept getting kicked out of first class," as she later told the Canadian Press. Sum 41 had burst out of the quiet streets of Ajax and sought salvation in drunken debauchery and devilish destruction—now, they were being handsomely rewarded for it.

OVER THE COURSE OF 2001, Sum 41 went from opening for bands like Blink-182, the Offspring, Reel Big Fish, and Good Charlotte to headlining their own world tours.[18] And as their

---

18 "Sum 41 had opened for us a few times, and then they were doing their first headlining tour just after 'Fat Lip' came out, and I remember the looks on their faces when the crowd was singing along," says Gob's Tom Thacker. "We saw a line down the block and went, 'Holy shit, this is happening.' At that point I was like, 'This is fucking crazy. *Good luck.*' You pass the torch."

shows got bigger and bigger, so did their hijinks, which they continued to document on Jocz's video camera.

The band would initiate a new tour manager by knocking on their door in the middle of the night and spraying them with a fire extinguisher. If one of them had a canister of shaving cream or silly string in his hand, nothing was safe. In one incident, the guys put a six-inch-long human turd into a plastic bag and threw it at the door of another hotel room, a mythical stunt they called "The Poo-iss in St. Louis." They loved going to strip clubs—all kinds of nudity, really, including their own. Some of their pranks were more innocuous; during an Edgefest tour stop in Quebec City, the band covertly filled Aquarius' company minivan with snack-sized bags of Doritos—one of the festival's sponsors that year—that came tumbling out when Renaud opened the door.[19] They loved trashing hotel rooms and tour vans. Wherever they'd go, Sum 41 would in all likelihood leave a trail of destruction and maybe a few puddles of piss, puke, or worse.

"The craziness escalated because we're travelling the world, and we have a label saying they want more of it," McCaslin adds now. "So we're like, 'This is great. We can trash a place, not pay for it, and everyone's happy with us.' It's like your parents telling you to skip school."

Over the next few years, though, Sum 41 would transform into a different band than the one that exploded onto the world stage with their youthful anthems in the summer of 2001. They were still reckless, stupid kids, but they were growing up fast.

---

19 "If they started making fun of you or joking around with you, you knew they liked you," says Renaud. "They were really funny. You kind of wanted them to pick on you because they were so good at it."

* * *

IMMEDIATELY FOLLOWING SUM 41's sudden rise to stardom, the world would change dramatically. When Seann William Scott, fresh off his returning role as Stifler in *American Pie 2*, introduced Sum 41 as the musical guest on *Saturday Night Live*, it had only been three weeks since the attacks of September 11, 2001, had shaken America—and the world—to its core. It was a case of cultural whiplash for the ages: an actor known for his roles as a party-hard doofus hosted a comedy sketch show featuring a band of party-hard doofuses, in front of a nation still mourning the deadliest terrorist attack in history. In that moment, *SNL* was seen as a welcome source of comfort and unity, and Sum 41 played their part in that, bouncing across the stage playing the fun, carefree tunes "Fat Lip" and "In Too Deep" in front of millions of late-night TV viewers.[20] The aftermath of 9/11 would, of course, result in an incredibly tense political climate spurred by George W. Bush's War on Terror, and in the years to come a starkly anti-Bush form of politically charged punk rock would emerge in strong opposition to the Republican president's ensuing foreign policy.

The group of Canadian troublemakers best known as pranksters and party animals may have been the last people one would have expected to rise to that occasion, but Sum 41 showed a surprising amount of maturity in a few short years, refashioning themselves into a band that could write serious songs about

20 Chevy Chase was backstage for the episode, and Jocz recalled that Chase let himself into Sum 41's dressing room to meet the band and made his way through the crowd by shouting, "Hot soup!"

heavy topics while still retaining the irrepressible, fun-loving attitude that had drawn fans to them in the first place.

Sum 41's second album *Does This Look Infected?*, released in late 2002, showcased a more traditional and noticeably darker version of punk rock that played up their admiration of Social Distortion, Metallica, and New York hardcore, while playing down their influences from SoCal pop-punk and the Beastie Boys. "The thought was to kind of become a new band almost," Whibley told Stereogum. "It was just like, 'Let's throw everything out the window. I'm gonna scream over this next song, and it's gonna all be dark, minor chords, and it's got more of a metal kind of guitar riff throughout it. Completely different thing.'"

The new musical style also showcased the seriousness of the band's musicianship, which had always been there but was generally overshadowed by their onstage antics. Whibley's lyrics tackled a range of grown-up topics, like war ("Still Waiting"), HIV ("The Hell Song"), and teen suicide ("My Direction"). The band still had plenty of fun as they continued to live up to their reputations as party animals,[21] and put out characteristically goofy music videos for "Still Waiting" and "The Hell Song"—the latter of which topped *TRL* in March 2003—but critics and audiences were quick to note how much their music had matured in just eighteen months.

Two years later, they'd take that philosophy even further. In mid-2004, Sum 41 embarked on a humanitarian mission in

---

21 "There was still a lot of fun being had, but things were streamlined a little bit," Renaud recalls of that time. "It became a little bit more locked down. They had, to me, their best tour manager, Jeff Marshall, who was able to handle himself. He commanded respect, he had everything organized, and he knew how to take care of people. He had everything in a certain order to keep the train on the tracks, because it can easily derail."

the Democratic Republic of the Congo, where they planned to film a documentary with War Child Canada about the deadly civil war that had ravaged the Central African country for six years. But a week after their arrival, the band would suddenly be hanging on for their lives when fighting erupted between the Congolese army and rebel forces outside the Orchid Hotel where they were staying. "All hell broke loose," McCaslin says. "Everyone was hitting the ground as gunshots erupted. It sounded like it was next door. Helicopters flying overhead. There were mortar rounds exploding around the hotel." Sum 41, the film crew, and a group of about forty hotel guests hid together for hours before they were rescued by a U.N. peacekeeper from Canada named Chuck Pelletier, who helped load everyone into armoured tanks and evacuate them from the conflict zone.

That fall, Sum 41 released their third album *Chuck*, named in honour of Pelletier. Though most of the album was written and recorded before their harrowing experience, *Chuck* nonetheless revealed a band with a darker edge, deeper thought, and greater maturity. The record expanded their use of elements of hardcore punk and heavy metal, but also introduced a softer side that leaned into tender alt-rock ballads. All of that was apparent on the lead single, "We're All to Blame," a song that operates in fitful bursts of rapid-fire thrash-metal riffing and slow, serene choruses, constantly shifting between gears. The only song on *Chuck* that was written during and after the Congo trip, "We're All to Blame" is a scathing rebuke of global greed and corporate power and how it fuels war, fear, and death.

By then, Sum 41 seemed impossibly far removed from the party-hard summer anthems like "Fat Lip" and "In Too Deep" that had turned them into household names just three years earlier. The politically charged and emotionally evocative songs on *Chuck* were virtually unrecognizable from the carefree party punk of *All Killer No Filler.* And yet they were still commercially viable. *Does This Look Infected?* had charted in a dozen countries and was quickly certified gold, while *Chuck* replicated that success and became Sum 41's highest-charting album to-date in the U.S. and Canada. (It was unseated by 2007's *Underclass Hero*, Sum 41's all-time highest-charting album in North America, though its total sales were lower.) "We're All to Blame" and the power ballad "Pieces" became staples of rock radio as *Chuck* went on to sell more than five million copies.

FURTHER LISTENING

NO WARNING

Hometown: Toronto, Ontario
Years active: 1998–2005, 2013–present

Formed under the name As We Once Were, this Toronto-based group released some early demos before rebranding as No Warning, signing with the American hardcore label Bridge 9 Records and releasing their debut album, *Ill Blood*, in 2002. The hard-hitting, mosh-fuelling recording entrenched them in the hardcore scene of the early 2000s, and their audience continued to grow as they toured with veteran acts like Hatebreed, Madball, and Cro-Mags. By 2004, they had signed with the same manager as Sum 41 and released their second album, *Suffer, Survive*, on the Linkin Park-founded, Warner Bros.-owned imprint Machine Shop Records. The band broke up a year later, and the members went on to join other bands, including Fucked Up and Terror, while vocalist Ben Cook launched a solo project called Young Guv. No Warning eventually reformed and released a couple of singles followed by their 2017 comeback album, *Torture Culture*.

BY THE MIDDLE OF the 2000s, Sum 41 had become a powerful force that could be mentioned in the same breath as Green Day, Blink-182, and the Offspring as one of the biggest punk bands in the world. They had released three commercially successful albums in four years that sold millions of copies, they had scored more than a dozen internationally successful rock-radio singles, they had become fixtures of MTV and MuchMusic, and they had done it all while pursuing a creative direction that was arguably less viable among mass-market audiences than when they had started. In their first few years, Sum 41's songs had appeared in major movies like *Dude, Where's My Car?* and *Spider-Man*, and the band had collaborated with the likes of Ludacris, Iggy Pop, Slayer, Ja Rule, DMX, and Tenacious D, ensuring their cultural ubiquity extended beyond their own albums and singles. Whibley even had his first run-ins with the Hollywood celebrity tabloids when he briefly dated Paris Hilton in 2003.[22]

While that first half of the 2000s was the peak of Sum 41's mainstream popularity, the band's appeal was enduring enough that they went on to release a total of eight studio albums, a handful of live albums and DVDs, and a greatest hits compilation while touring around the world several times over. There were plenty of ups and downs—including the departure of Baksh and Jocz (and, after nine years, the return of Baksh), and Whibley's struggles with alcoholism that hospitalized and almost killed him in 2014—but Sum 41 remained stalwarts of rock music for nearly a quarter of a century until they said farewell with a final worldwide tour that ended in early 2025.

When Sum 41 first broke out of small-town Ontario to reach superstardom back in 2001, they had done what only a small group of Canadian musicians had done before, becoming bestselling recording artists not just in their home country, but all over the world. At a time when punk rock's role in pop culture was mostly limited to a few American bands

22 This was shortly before *The Simple Life* debuted in December 2003 (and before the infamous sex tape), but Hilton had already been well-known to tabloids as a model and socialite since the mid-'90s.

from California, Sum 41 became Canada's first internationally acclaimed punk band. They came out of seemingly nowhere—to this day, most people couldn't place Ajax on a map—and then they were everywhere.

As it turned out, Sum 41 was just the beginning. Within a few short years, Canadian kids a lot like them from small towns a lot like theirs would follow quickly behind them as the sound and spirit of punk rock became a seemingly unstoppable pop-cultural force. In fact, just as "Fat Lip" was dominating MTV to become a countercultural anthem for teenage misfits, a similarly rebellious young girl from a town just down the highway was a short way from becoming one of the biggest pop stars in the world.

3

AVRIL LAVIGNE

It's music's biggest night in early 2003. After a teleprompted introduction by rapper Busta Rhymes and actor Jamie-Lynn Sigler, the camera pans to a band led by a teenager with pin-straight, dirty-blond hair. She's wearing dark eyeliner and a jet-black trench coat with studded lapels and sewn-on patches showing a peace sign, a skull and crossbones, and a middle finger. The four slightly older guys in the band—dressed in garishly colourful suits—tear into the guitar riff, power chords, and driving beat of "Sk8er Boi," a song that's instantly recognizable now that it's had a good run as one of the biggest hits of the past year in more than twenty countries.

Most of the audience at New York's Madison Square Garden is seated, but right in front of the stage there's a crowd of about fifty people bouncing up and down in a total frenzy. For the first few seconds, Avril Lavigne seems a little reserved, maybe even a bit nervous. After all, she's young, this is the Grammy Awards, and her performance is being broadcast live to nearly twenty-five million viewers. But as she sings the song's first verse, she becomes more animated and her voice fills with the snarky attitude she's come to be known for. Just before she launches into the first chorus, Lavigne rips open the trench coat to reveal the words ROCK ON that she's crudely spelled out on the inner lining of the jacket using white gaffer tape.

Lavigne is nominated for five Grammys, but regardless of the results, she's already written herself into the history books. Since the release of her debut album, *Let Go,* less than a year ago, she's released three top-ten singles that have been in constant rotation on the radio and MTV. By the end of 2002, *Let Go* had sold more than four million copies in the U.S. alone, making it the biggest debut of the year.

But Lavigne's impact on pop culture can't really be measured in sales numbers or industry accolades. The singer's spunky music, androgynous fashion sense, and youthful rebellion have brought the sound, style, and attitude of punk rock into the mainstream in a big way, inspiring millions of teenagers around the world to wear camo pants and striped neckties, take an interest in skateboarding, and finally gather up the courage to tell off their parents. She's such a star that talent scouts are already on the hunt for "the next Avril."

All of this from someone who's still a teenager herself. As she pogos around the Grammys stage in her Chuck Taylor All Stars, Lavigne is just eighteen years old. Just a few years ago, before she became the "queen of pop-punk," she was a kid growing up in a small Ontario town where she enjoyed hockey and skateboarding, and where she sang in church with a voice that would make her one of the bestselling Canadian artists in history.

IN 1984, AVRIL LAVIGNE was born in Belleville, Ontario, an unassuming, middle-class city located roughly halfway between the provincial capital, Toronto, and the national capital, Ottawa. The middle child of John Lavigne and Judy Loshaw, she was named after the French word for April, a nod to John's francophone upbringing. When little Avril was five years old, the family moved to nearby Napanee, a small town of about five thousand people that's surrounded by farmland, waterfront, and cottage country. In the quaint town filled with Victorian homes, heritage buildings, and churches, the Lavignes lived in a two-storey brick house that backed onto a farmer's field. A family of devout Baptists, they went to church on Sundays at the Evangel Temple at the end of their block.

Like many Canadian kids, Avril Lavigne grew up playing hockey. She learned how to skate not long after she learned how to walk, and by the time she was ten she was playing for the boys' team. On the rink, she showed that she could hold her own as the only girl in a room full of guys; she was named MVP two years in a row, and the feisty winger wasn't afraid to battle hard for the puck and even get into scraps with her much taller and larger opponents. She was also active on the track-and-field team—setting a district record in the triple jump—and she pitched for the high school baseball team. But her real focus was music, and her parents had noticed her talents as early as when she was two years old.

As siblings do, her older brother and younger sister would heckle her for constantly singing around the house, but her parents were always supportive. Her mother persuaded their church to start a children's choir, and that's how Lavigne first started performing. She and her classmates at Cornerstone Christian Academy—a private evangelical school that she began attending in Grade 4—held recitals at many of the local churches. When she was ten, she was asked to sing a solo in a Christmas cantata, and the family started getting requests for young Avril to sing at more events around town and suggestions that she enter local singing competitions.

Meanwhile, John Lavigne—a musician himself—had bought his daughter a microphone so she could sing karaoke at home. Next, he bought some guitars, a keyboard, and a drum kit to turn the family's basement into a music room. "That's where I spent all of my time after school," Avril said in a 2003 interview with *NBC News*. "I remember my dad saying to me, 'You need to be down there for five hours.' I'd be like, 'Mom, that's too much!'"

Not that she would have preferred to spend that time on homework. By her own admission, Lavigne was "really bad" in school. She would doodle in her notebook and carve things into her desk, and she was known to get kicked out of class for being disruptive.

But in music, she excelled quickly. She had leading roles in three of Cornerstone Academy's annual spring musicals, performing for audiences of more than five hundred people. As a teenager, she started performing country songs at singing competitions and county fairs. When she was fourteen, she got a big break when she entered a contest run by a radio station in nearby Kingston where the winner would get to sing with Shania Twain, who was at the height of her fame that year after just releasing her 1997 album *Come On Over*. Lavigne won the contest and joined Twain on stage at the Corel Centre, home of the NHL's Ottawa Senators. There, she stood confidently in front of twenty thousand people as they performed a duet of "What Made You Say That." After the performance, she professed to Twain that she wanted to be "a famous singer" one day.

"This little girl came up and was so impressive," Twain later recalled in an episode of her podcast, *Home Now Radio*. "And she said that her dream was to become a singer and that's what she did. Really awesome. I'm proud of her."

Soon afterward, Lavigne started working with local folk musician Stephen Medd, who had spotted her while she was singing at a community theatre a few years earlier. Medd wrote a song called "Touch the Sky" specifically for Lavigne to sing, so she headed into a studio in Kingston one day in 1999 and recorded it flawlessly in front of Medd, her father, and producer David Archibald. Released on a compilation album called *The Quinte Spirit*, it was the first song recorded and released by Avril Lavigne. From there, things progressed quickly.

JUST BEFORE CHRISTMAS 1999, a music manager named Cliff Fabri saw Lavigne perform at a Chapters bookstore in Kingston, where she sang karaoke versions of country songs like Faith Hill's "It Matters to Me" and LeAnn Rimes's "How Do I Live." After that, Fabri became Lavigne's first manager. In the young singer, he saw a career model that combined the small-town folksiness of Sheryl Crow and the independence and attitude of Fiona Apple. He also figured there were lessons to be learned from Alanis Morissette, the breakout megastar from Ottawa who released two dance-pop albums in her teenage years and then found her stride as an angsty, tough-talking alt-rocker with the Billboard-topping *Jagged Little Pill* in 1995.

Fabri made a VHS tape of Lavigne singing karaoke in her parents' basement and sent it to people he knew in the music industry. One of those people was Mark Jowett, co-founder of the Vancouver-based company Nettwerk Music Group, who had been working with another singer managed by Fabri. When Jowett watched the tape of fifteen-year-old Lavigne wearing a black bandana and singing Sixpence None the Richer's "Kiss Me" and Sarah McLachlan's "Adia" in her basement, he immediately saw the potential and took the tape to his business partner Terry McBride.

"Just watch it," Jowett told him. "There's something about her."

Soon afterward, he met with Lavigne, her parents, and Cliff Fabri in Toronto. They struck a development deal to produce some demos for the label. "She was quite shy, but really good-natured," Jowett says now. "She had a great voice, and she was such a natural performer."

In the summer of 2000, Jowett sent Lavigne to New York to work with Peter Zizzo, a songwriter and producer who had already made hits with Céline Dion and Jennifer Lopez. They initially started working on a song Zizzo had written, but Lavigne was adamant that she wanted to write her own songs. Together, they co-wrote an original called "Why."

If the demos turned out well—and they *were* turning out well—Nettwerk would sign Lavigne to a proper record deal. That was Jowett's plan, anyway. Before they got to that point, a big-time American record executive caught wind of the young singer and was so dazzled that he was willing to bet a million dollars she'd be a star.

KEN KRONGARD WAS SO new to the A&R game that he hadn't yet learned any of the unwritten rules. For one thing, you don't listen to unsolicited material. But if for whatever reason you *do* listen to unsolicited material, you don't bother to take the time to write the person back, telling them you're passing on it. There are just too many wannabe stars and too little time.

Krongard broke all those rules. He listened to unsolicited material, and if he passed on it, he'd write back to explain why. And when the phone rang, he'd answer it.

Krongard was working as a junior A&R rep at Arista Records, the New York–based major label that had been widely hailed for breaking Whitney Houston and Barry Manilow and was reaping the rewards of the R&B stars on its subsidiary LaFace Records, but by the end of the '90s had few stars on its roster outside of soft-rock acts like Sarah McLachlan, Crash Test Dummies, and Dido. It needed a game changer.

Krongard got a call one day and, as he always did, he picked up the phone. On the other end was Cliff Fabri looking to pitch one of his clients in Canada. Krongard had actually been looking at Canada as a market for new talent, since most scouts weren't looking there—he figured that was how an unproven industry guy like him could gain an advantage—but had missed out on the Sum 41 sweepstakes and was still looking for his first big signing. So, in June 2000, Krongard flew up to Toronto and met Avril Lavigne for the first time.

"She had this charisma," Krongard recalls. "Somehow she just dominated the room."

A few months later, as the autumn leaves fell in New York, Krongard got another call from Fabri inviting him to sit in while Lavigne and Peter Zizzo worked on some early demos. At the Manhattan studio, he couldn't believe what he was hearing from a girl who had just celebrated her sixteenth birthday.

"I remember being in a trance," he says. "I had no idea it was going to be *that* good."

He picked up the phone right there in the recording studio and called his boss.

At that point, Krongard barely knew his boss. Earlier that year, BMG had fired Arista's founder, Clive Davis, after twenty-five years as president and CEO. The parent company replaced him with Antonio "L.A." Reid, a proven star-maker who in 1989 had co-founded the Arista subsidiary LaFace Records, where he had signed and developed an impressive roster that included Usher, Toni Braxton, TLC, and Outkast. Krongard had barely spoken a few words to Reid when he called his office.

"L.A., please don't argue with me. You've got to come down here, please."

Reid listened to the pitch and told Krongard he'd be there in a week. Krongard cursed to himself. He booked flights and hotels for Lavigne, her parents, and her manager for a return to New York the following week, where they would gather again at Zizzo's studio and wait for Reid to show up.

"I was nervous, Cliff was nervous, the producer was nervous, the kid who brings coffee was nervous," Krongard says. "And Avril could not give a fuck."

Finally, Reid arrived at the studio and wordlessly took a seat with his arms crossed. The head of Arista was in a "rotten mood," as he later admitted.

"She started singing, and within half a line, his face just dropped," Krongard says. "It changed completely. The song ended and he was jumping up and down, all smiles. To his credit, he got it immediately."

A few minutes after Reid left, the phone rang. "That girl's incredible," Krongard recalls Reid telling him. "She's the best I've heard in a long time, maybe the best ever. Sign her immediately." Then he hung up.

NOW, THERE WERE TWO record labels interested in Lavigne. It was a situation that Mark Jowett describes as "delicate." Nettwerk had gotten there first, but they had also been working with Arista as the managers of Sarah McLachlan and Dido, and they didn't want to jeopardize that relationship. Reluctantly, they stepped aside.

In November 2000, Avril Lavigne signed a contract with Arista Records worth a reported $1.25 million, including a publishing advance of $900,000. At sixteen years old, she was a millionaire.

Lavigne dropped out of high school in Grade 11 and moved to New York to commit fully to developing her music career—an easy decision for a struggling student who couldn't wait to get out of the classroom. From the beginning, though, she found it challenging to find her footing as an artist. Most people saw her differently than she saw herself. Krongard was no longer around to advocate for her—he was laid off only a couple of months after Lavigne signed to Arista—and the bosses at the record label apparently saw their new talent as the next Faith Hill, the breezy voiced blond who had become one of the biggest country stars of the '90s and beyond thanks to hit singles like "This Kiss" and "The Way You Love Me."

Back home in Napanee, Lavigne had evolved from a shy, hymn-singing church kid into a rebellious teenager who was rumoured to have skipped class and taken part in her share of drinking, smoking, and general unruliness that was a thorn in the side of her devoutly religious parents.[23]

"My last couple of school years, I started skateboarding, and I hung out with skaters and the punks. It was like my group," Lavigne told the *Globe and Mail* in 2003. "I was a little prep from the Christian school, and then when I got into high school, I changed. I became my own person—who I am."

That person was starting to see herself in rock 'n' roll. But it took a while for others to see it, too. In her first several months in New York, Arista hooked Lavigne up with nearly a dozen professional songwriters to work on material for what would become her debut album. To her, none of them were the right fit. Lavigne had gotten into Green Day, Blink-182, Nirvana, NOFX, and System of a Down—punk and metal bands that were in rotation among a typical skateboarding clique—but she felt that Arista still saw her as an angel-voiced country girl who was destined to climb the pop charts.

---

23 Lavigne once said her mother wouldn't even let her sing the Deana Carter song "Strawberry Wine" because she was too young to be referencing an alcoholic beverage.

After those unsuccessful sessions in New York, Lavigne headed to Los Angeles to work with a songwriter and producer named Clif Magness. The Texas-born musician had established himself in the music business in the early '80s when he co-wrote hits for soap opera star Jack Wagner and pop vocal group Wilson Phillips, and he won a Grammy Award in 1990 for his work arranging the Quincy Jones song "The Places You Find Love."

By the time she arrived in Los Angeles, Lavigne was worn out. As Magness remembered it, the singer burst into tears the moment she entered his studio.

"What's wrong?" he asked.

"They keep trying to make me Faith Hill," she cried.

"Well, what do *you* want to do?" he said. "What do you like? Let's do that."

Lavigne was given creative control over the songs she'd write with Magness—and the difference was staggering. In their first session, the pair wrote "Unwanted," a bona fide rocker that was far removed from the sunny, country-pop stylings of Faith Hill. "Unwanted" was a dark and brooding song filled with heavy, distorted guitars, pounding rhythms, and lyrics about feeling angry, neglected, and misunderstood.

When Magness finished mixing the track, he played it back for Lavigne. She loved it. But would her record label?

IF LAVIGNE HAD IT her way, the whole album would've sounded like "Unwanted." But Arista wasn't happy with this new and unexpected style, according to Lavigne. The label wasn't looking for angsty alt-rock. They were looking for crossover pop hits.

"Arista was drop-dead shit afraid that I would come out with a whole album that sounded like 'Unwanted,'" Lavigne told *Rolling Stone* in 2003. "I swear they wanted to drop me."

After the sessions with Magness, the label turned to the Matrix, a three-person songwriting and production team comprising Scott Spock and the husband-and-wife duo Graham Edwards and Lauren Christy. At that point, the Matrix's biggest credit was a Christmas song by Christina Aguilera, but their name was getting around in Los Angeles industry circles. Their three-headed approach with varied backgrounds had the potential to help Arista finally crack the code with Lavigne.

The Matrix thought they knew what to do when they walked into their first meeting with the singer. But they met a completely different person than the one they were expecting.

"This kid had melted toothbrushes up her arm, her hair was in braids, and she wore black skater boots. She didn't seem like the Faith Hill type," Christy later told *Sound on Sound* magazine. "After talking to her for about an hour, we cottoned on that she wasn't happy but couldn't quite figure out where to go."

Lavigne showed them "Unwanted" and told them *this* was what she was interested in doing. The Matrix knew they needed to find a middle ground between the marketable teen pop star Arista thought they had signed and the hard-nosed punk that Lavigne obviously wanted to be.

"She was not happy," Spock told *Mix* magazine. "She said, 'I don't want to do this—I want to rock!' We didn't know that she was this skater, punky type of girl. So we said, 'Okay, let's come up with a premise, then you come back tomorrow and we'll write a song.'"

The following year, that song would make her a global icon.

RELEASED IN MARCH 2002, "Complicated" was a smash hit. Listening to the first few seconds, it's clear the song is a showstopper: the guitar chords burst out of the speakers and Lavigne's voice is filled with the teen angst that defines her generation. The song earnestly captures the state of mind of a typical teenager, a boiling mixture of anger, confusion, frustration, and betrayal that someone would ever commit one of the most heinous of all teenage crimes: being an uptight, two-faced, stinking phony. The song made it to No. 2 on the Billboard Hot 100 and ended up spending more than seven months on the U.S. singles chart. It was also a hit in Canada and internationally, reaching the top ten in more than twenty countries.

But it was the music video for "Complicated" that cemented Lavigne's legacy. In the public's first introduction to the young singer, they saw a free-spirited kid, a rocker with an attitude, and an anti-fashion icon decked out in a tank top, a loose-fitting necktie, and baggy cargo pants with a chain wallet. In the video, Lavigne and her bandmates terrorize a shopping mall by pranking shoppers and security guards, jumping into a kiddie pool, crashing a toy monster truck through the hallways, and committing other sorts of mild mayhem that recreated the fantasies of every bored teenager in suburban America. If you weren't watching closely, it could have passed for a Blink-182 or Sum 41 music video.

By most accounts, "Complicated" is a straightforward early-2000s pop song—it's a Matrix co-write that was designed specifically for pop audiences, not the kind of edgy hard rock that Lavigne had been pursuing with Magness—but Lavigne made sure everyone knew what she was really about. The music video was a clear signal that the singer's taste for punk rock and adolescent hijinks was edging out the role of the good-clean-fun pop star she was supposed to fill. Lavigne had been put in a box, and she was doing her best to break down the walls from the inside.

When Lavigne's debut album *Let Go* arrived a few months later in June 2002, it debuted at No. 8 on the Billboard 200 and peaked at No. 2, fuelled by the unstoppable force of "Complicated." In September, the album's second hit single, "Sk8er Boi," further developed Lavigne's reputation as a "skater-punk princess" thanks to its punchy guitar riffs, chunky power chords, ultra-catchy chorus, and lyrics about the titular skater boy who's spurned by the high school *It girl*, but gets the last laugh when he ends up "rockin' up MTV." With "Sk8er Boi," Lavigne firmly planted her flag on the side of the rockers, the skaters, and the punks, in stark opposition to the jocks, the beauty queens, and the preppy kids—all in the form of a pop-punk banger not far off from "All the Small Things" or "In Too Deep."

By the time the power ballad "I'm with You" arrived as the third single in November—giving Lavigne three consecutive hits—*Let Go* had sold nearly four million copies and established a new archetype for the teen pop star in the twenty-first century.

In the music press, Lavigne was called the "anti-Britney." In contrast to the low-coverage outfits, choreographed dance routines, and rampant lip-syncing accusations of the other female stars of the day like Britney Spears, Christina Aguilera, and Beyoncé, Lavigne was seen as just an average teenager. She was seen as more *real*.

"You could take every aspect of the Britney persona and look for the polar opposite in Avril," New York radio programmer Tom Poleman told *Entertainment Weekly*. "Whereas Britney was more glamour and less reality-based, Avril is much more the regular kid. For boys, she seems more attainable; girls can see themselves living more like her, dressing the same, being attracted to the same boys."

For her part, Lavigne rejected the "anti-Britney" narrative from the beginning. "I'm just being myself. I just describe myself as 'Avril Lavigne,'" she told the *Globe and Mail*. "I don't want to say I'm this or I'm that. I'm much more than two words. Normal people don't walk around sticking labels on themselves."

The massive success of *Let Go* showed that the world had fallen in love with this girl who did what she wanted, dressed how she wanted, and said what she wanted. Lavigne was named Best New Artist at the MTV Video Music Awards and earned eight Grammy nominations in the two years that followed. *Let Go* was the biggest debut album of 2002 and the year's third-highest-selling album in America. Within a year, it was already certified six-times platinum in the U.S.

Let Go gave Lavigne the power to stand up and flip the middle finger to anyone who tried telling her how to do things. Lavigne's collaboration with the Matrix had yielded the album's three hit singles—Christy, Edwards, and Spock contributed to five of the songs on *Let Go*, including "Complicated," "Sk8er Boi," and "I'm With You"—but those early songs Lavigne wrote with Magness still called to her.

"I don't feel like 'Complicated' represents me and my ability to write," she told *Rolling Stone* a year after the single was released. "But without 'Complicated,' I bet you anything I wouldn't have even sold a million records. The songs I did with the Matrix, yeah, they were good for my first record, but I don't want to be that pop anymore."

In March 2003, Arista released the dark hard-rocker "Losing Grip" as the fourth single from *Let Go*, after Lavigne pressed the record label to choose it over the bright and airy "Anything but Ordinary." It was an act of defiance as well as a sign of what was to come: Lavigne wanted to be a rockstar, not a popstar—and this time, she was ready to fight.

"A lot of people didn't want to listen to me, but I spoke up until they did," Lavigne told *Rolling Stone*. "And I can always say, 'Screw you guys if you're not gonna work with me.' If they're not gonna listen to me, I'm not gonna do things. Try and make me—I'm not gonna."

BY THE TIME AVRIL Lavigne celebrated her eighteenth birthday, her life had changed dramatically. The singer's seemingly out-of-nowhere rise to fame had made her a hometown hero in Napanee, where locals celebrated their one-time neighbour's massive success and journalists from both the Canadian media and the international press swooped into town to write ground-level profiles of this little-known Ontario town that birthed a pop superstar.[24]

As Lavigne and her band bopped around the stage of the

---

24 The principal of Lavigne's high school claimed she was getting up to twenty calls a day from journalists.

Grammy Awards in early 2003, hundreds of Napanee residents gathered in the school gym to watch the show together in a celebratory event hosted by a MuchMusic VJ and featuring merch giveaways and performances by local bands. Many of the attendees were young girls, some of whom wore reproductions of Lavigne's firetruck-red Napanee Minor Soccer Club jersey—which proudly displayed the logo of the team's sponsor, the local Home Hardware, on the chest, and a giant number 2, Lavigne's jersey number, on the back—after she had worn the original on *Saturday Night Live* a month earlier.

All across town, billboards and roadside signs congratulated Napanee's homegrown pop idol. The local newspaper published a weekly "Avril alert" along with a sixteen-page supplement the weekend of the Grammys. The owner of the singer's favourite pizza joint was overwhelmed with orders for the "Avril special," a pie with pepperoni, mushrooms, and green olives.[25] Classmates sold Lavigne's school yearbook for hundreds of dollars on eBay, and some people were buying locally harvested rocks for $1.50 apiece. The mayor even met with a boy from Argentina who had come all the way to Napanee to visit Lavigne's hometown.

Elsewhere, Lavigne was an instantly recognizable celebrity who now had to disguise herself whenever she went out in public. In New York or Los Angeles, she'd mostly be left alone, but she couldn't be out on the street just about anywhere else without being noticed by fans or paparazzi. When she landed at the Singapore airport for a short tour of Asia, there were hundreds of people there to greet her, and fans threw gift bags

---

25 Bill Kosmopoulos, the then fifty-four-year-old owner of La Pizzeria, kept a bagful of newspaper clippings behind the counter of his restaurant with all of Lavigne's interviews.

into her car as she rushed to separate herself from the mob. Everywhere she would go, her fans would stake out hotel lobbies day and night for a chance to meet their favourite singer.

Lavigne loved that she had achieved her dream of becoming a professional singer. But she didn't love the promotional side of it, nor did she particularly love the idea of being a celebrity or a role model. She made few attempts to hide that fact. Journalists would repeatedly mention that she looked bored and distracted during interviews—or worse, moody and visibly annoyed—a fact that Lavigne would freely admit when asked.

"To understand me you have to meet me and be around me. And then, only if I'm in a good mood—don't meet me in a bad mood," she told a *Maclean's* journalist in a hotel room in Buffalo. She went on to announce that she in fact had a headache and was hungry and jet-lagged, which, of course, made her interviewer instantly nervous. "I find the promotion—all the interviews, photo shoots, the press—the annoying part," Lavigne added.

This brutal honesty endeared her to the public, who saw her as the embodiment of the typical teenager: often sulky but also easily excitable, frequently naive, occasionally rude, always authentic, refusing to put on an act for anyone, brushing off any perceived slight or mild annoyance with a dismissive "*whatever.*" Lavigne's managers knew they couldn't—and *shouldn't*—stop her from being herself, so they didn't try.

By the spring of 2001, Lavigne had parted ways with Fabri—a split that neither party discussed publicly—and signed with Nettwerk's management team, a good-karma moment for the company that had stepped aside to let Arista sign Lavigne in 2000. Nettwerk co-founder Terry McBride flew from

Vancouver to meet with the Arista team in their New York headquarters. McBride recalls being handed a marketing plan that he describes now as "thicker than the Bible." He glanced at it and dramatically hurled it into the air.

"Do you know who this girl is?" he asked the room. "She's seventeen years old and she looks at her feet when she talks, and you want to give her media training?"

McBride continued, "Every other seventeen-year-old being asked the same question over and over again is going to look at their feet. We *need* her to look at her feet. We need her to act her age. Why? Every seventeen-year-old will relate to that. You're putting her in as a pop artist. She's not a pop artist. She doesn't listen to pop music. She listens to *these* bands, not *those* bands. Your whole marketing plan is wrong. If you can capture the authentic seventeen-year-old girl—being a little shit, which is what everybody does—it'll catch fire."

So, Lavigne was given a licence to be herself. She unknowingly freaked out the execs at Arista when they saw her pulling chewing gum out of her mouth and twisting it around her finger while she was being interviewed on MTV's *Total Request Live.* She got annoyed about a journalist who used the term "inferiority complex" because she didn't know what it meant. She'd be buzzing with energy one second and then totally crash out the next, her tastes—music, fashion, boys, etc.—changing by the minute.

Sometimes parents—mostly mothers—would come up to Lavigne and thank her for being a good influence on their daughters by "not dressing like Britney," which just irked her even more. "Oh yeah, 'The anti-Britney, the anti-Britney,'" she told *NBC News.* "Everybody just thinks because, you know, the whole pop thing, 'Show off your belly, dance around with your background dancers, lip sync' whole deal thing was really popular for a long time. I'm not made up and I'm not being told what to say and how to act, so they have to call me the anti-Britney, which I'm not. I think that's very rude and very mean. I think it's a dumb game. It's just the media putting up like those labels."

"Well, it's not just the media," host Jane Pauley replied. "It's a business. You're the product. In order to sell the product, you've got to put some kind of label on it."

"Yeah, see, that's what I don't like," Lavigne retorted. "I don't wanna feel like a thing and I don't wanna feel like a product—and that's what comes with pop music."

All Lavigne really wanted to do was get onstage and sing to her fans. When she wasn't doing that, she just wanted to hang out with her band, a group of guys she could call friends, mentors, and down-to-earth allies as she adopted the lifestyle of a touring musician, teetered on the edge of adulthood, and navigated through a new world of pop stardom and all of the pains and pressures that came with it.

NETTWERK ASSEMBLED A BACKING band for Lavigne by scouring the Ontario punk-rock scene for young dudes who had the look, the chops, and the personality to keep up with the world's newest pop-punk icon. Rhythm guitarist Jesse Colburn and drummer Matt Brann came from the same Ajax punk scene that had birthed Sum 41, while bassist Charles Moniz had played with the Burlington, Ontario, hardcore legends

Grade.[26] Lead guitarist Evan Taubenfeld, the lone American in the group, hailed from Baltimore, where he had a band called Spinfire until he met an A&R rep from Arista and was invited to audition. These were a bunch of guys in their late teens and early twenties who played in punk bands, had spiky, dyed hair and piercings, rode skateboards, and dressed themselves in blue jeans and band tees. They fit right in with Lavigne.

"She's young, her music's young, [so] we needed a band that would fit well with who she is as a person," manager Shauna Gold told *Maclean's*. "Maybe they're not top-of-the-line studio musicians, but they still play really well and have the right energy and the right look."

Among the band, Lavigne was like a little sister. To her, they were "my boys." They'd tease one another with lighthearted smack talk, they'd calm her down when she picked fights she may or may not have been able to win, and they'd cuddle up with one another with friendly affection. The band's offstage life consisted of mostly harmless fun and games, like skateboard rides through the carpeted hallways of a hotel, re-enactments of professional wrestling moves, or a Charlie Chaplin–inspired competition to see who could click their heels the most times in one jump. Colburn and Moniz, both vegetarians, influenced Lavigne to take up the diet herself. Lavigne and her band still took part in their fair share of underage drinking, but it was tame compared to the usual clichés of rock 'n' roll debauchery. If you watched them together, you'd think they were siblings or lifelong friends, not a group of people who had only known

---

26 Brann played in a band with Sum 41's Jason "Cone" McCaslin, while Colburn played in a band called Closet Monster alongside Lavigne's original bassist, Mark Spicoluk. Spicoluk played in Lavigne's band for most of 2002 before he was replaced by Moniz.

one another a few months and who were, technically speaking, coworkers. Lavigne was especially close with Taubenfeld, who was closest to her in age and began writing new songs with her early on.

Given their backgrounds, Brann, Colburn, Moniz, and Taubenfeld were integral to Lavigne's musical education. Her bandmates gave her a crash course in punk rock. For her eighteenth birthday, Moniz gave her CDs by AC/DC, the Clash, and Me First and the Gimme Gimmes; Brann gave her Nirvana's *Nevermind*; and Colburn gave her albums by the Smashing Pumpkins and the Pixies. Her iPod was loaded up with Blink-182, Dashboard Confessional, Third Eye Blind, Oasis, Marilyn Manson, and System of a Down, and she went out and bought a CD by the Ramones so she could finally learn what all the fuss was about. During an encounter with the Goo Goo Dolls, singer Johnny Rzeznik bought her a disc by one of his favourite bands, the Replacements.

That Lavigne was learning so much so quickly only fed into her critics' narrative that she was a poseur who was plucked from obscurity by her major-label overlords and fashioned into a corporate product engineered to sell records. Journalists, fans, and even fellow musicians questioned Lavigne's credibility. Actually, "questioned" isn't the right word, given the viciousness of her detractors on message boards, blogs, and zines. These often-anonymous haters wouldn't mince words when they wanted to tear Lavigne down, whether it was a direct assault on her artistic integrity or collateral damage in a strike aimed at another target. Lavigne's name became shorthand for the perceived archetype of a money-hungry industry plant co-opting the aesthetics of punk rock to make an easy buck.

"Lavigne is sickening to me," seethed Iann Robinson of MTV *News*. "She's everything that's wrong with music today. She's a manufactured voice. She claims she's punk, but she doesn't even know who the Ramones are." Celebrity gossip blogger Perez Hilton was a particular thorn in her side, having hurled such insults at her as "hack" and "douche." Lavigne said she once got into a bar fight with a stranger who told her she had "ruined punk rock."[27] Maybe the most even-handed criticism came from *Rolling Stone* writer Jenny Eliscu: "She's hardly punk, but you've got to start somewhere."

Lavigne handled this one-sided war on her credentials as well as any nineteen-year-old would. "Punk is a touchy subject," she told *Entertainment Weekly* in one of several interviews in which she addressed her many critics. "A punk is a person who's always getting in trouble and doing things they're not supposed to. Yeah, I do that… Then there's punk as a way of life, and punk rock as an aggressive form of music, which is very political, and I never said I was that. People are like, 'Well, she doesn't know the Sex Pistols.' Why would I know that stuff? Look how young I am. That stuff's old, right?" To her point, many of the punk bands that were emerging at the beginning of the twenty-first century weren't directly influenced by the genre's pioneers such as the Ramones and the Sex Pistols—they had grown up on '90s bands like NOFX, Pennywise, and Bad Religion. Most teenagers weren't even listening to much of the first-wave stuff. Old people were.

---

27 "Some girl came up to me and started it," Lavigne told *TIME* magazine. "She said, 'You ruined punk rock.' I said, 'What?' Then she said it again. So I kicked her and punched her, and she got tossed out of the bar. The pathetic thing is, I heard she wanted an autograph, too."

Lavigne's crew stood tall behind her. "If she was a marketing thing, I wouldn't be in the band. None of us would," Colburn told the *New York Times*, his bandmates by his side, nodding in agreement. "Avril isn't punk, but she never really pretended to claim to come from that scene," Taubenfeld said later in an interview with *Ultimate Guitar*. "She had pop-punk music and the media ended up doing the rest."

And sure, Lavigne hadn't hauled amps in and out of dive bars and community halls to play twenty-minute sets for a dozen local kids, and she hadn't driven around the continent in a beat-up, barely running, old passenger van, but she couldn't help but be a product of circumstance. This was a sheltered kid from a religious family in a small town who found her way to rock and rebellion in her teens, the same time that just about everybody does. Plus, her label certainly hadn't intended for her to make the type of music she ended up making—she was the one who convinced her co-writers to let her rock out.

"There are no guys in suits that can manufacture artists like Avril Lavigne," L.A. Reid said himself in a *Rolling Stone* interview. "I wish there were. God knows the record business needs them right now." MuchMusic VJ George Stroumboulopoulos agrees, noting that doing the exact opposite of what you're expected to do is punk in and of itself. "Avril showed up wearing capri Dickies, Chucks, and a tank top with the tie over it. Avril was dressed like somebody who didn't have a lot of money, who could thrift," he says. "That was very punk to me, that she wasn't doing the traditional pop star young girl thing that we had seen time and time again."

And if one were to say Lavigne's music was too poppy, she'd have been the first to agree. By the time she completed the Try to Shut Me Up Tour, a six-month, seventy-date run that took the singer and her band to arenas across North America, Asia, the U.K., Europe, and Australia with support from Simple Plan, Gob, Swollen Members, and Our Lady Peace, Lavigne was already sick of playing "Complicated."[28] She was also starting to vary her look, disgruntled by the idea of her wardrobe being viewed as a costume or a product.

"I can see how it could, for some people, look like the label made me up—this chick who wears a tank top and a tie," she told *Maclean's*. "Whatever, I think the image is way too fucking pop. It doesn't show my whole realness and my rock, edge side."

By late 2003, Lavigne was ready to make a statement of her own, and it was going to be made on her terms. It was going to be as moody, edgy, and hard-nosed as she felt inside. And it was going to show the world that she was an unstoppable force that was here to stay.

EXPECTATIONS WERE HIGH WHEN Lavigne unveiled her second album, *Under My Skin*, in the spring of 2004. In the two years since *Let Go* had shipped to music stores, the album had sold more than twelve million copies worldwide and the Try to Shut Me Up Tour had drawn hundreds of thousands of screaming fans to concert arenas around the world. The singer had been nominated for eight Grammy Awards across two awards seasons, she had graced the cover of *Rolling Stone* magazine,

---

28 On that tour, she regularly padded out her set with a cover of Green Day's "Basket Case" and Bob Dylan's "Knockin' on Heaven's Door," on top of the songs from *Let Go*. In May 2003, she made a stop in L.A. to play a version of Metallica's "Fuel" for the *MTV Icon* tribute to the legendary metalheads.

and she had entered the living rooms of North America with multiple TV appearances on the late-night circuit, including *The Tonight Show with Jay Leno*, *Late Show with David Letterman*, and *Saturday Night Live*.

Now, Lavigne had been tasked with making a follow-up to *Let Go* that would live up to her fans' expectations, her industry bosses' sales quotas, and above all, her own quest for creative self-determination. The widely celebrated but also viciously mocked young star set out to quash the idea that she was a marionette of the music industry; she wanted to assure everyone that while they didn't have to like her songs, they couldn't call her inauthentic. This time, Lavigne refused to work with professional songwriters, perhaps not coincidentally after a public disagreement with the Matrix over the share of credit on their earlier hits. She had already started writing new songs with Taubenfeld while they were on the road touring *Let Go*, and three of those songs would eventually make it onto *Under My Skin*. For the others, she would rely on collaborations with other artists she knew and trusted with her vision. She hand-selected Canadian singer-songwriter Chantal Kreviazuk and her husband, Our Lady Peace singer Raine Maida; American songwriter and producer Butch Walker, who had worked with Gob on their major-label debut *Foot in Mouth Disease*; former Evanescence guitarist Ben Moody; and big-time rock producer Don Gilmore.

Lavigne was clear: she was going to be a rock artist, and this was going to be a rock album. Between the dark, grungy hard rock of "Take Me Away," "Together," and "Forgotten," the upbeat pop-punk of "He Wasn't" and "Freak Out," and the melodic, softer-edged alt-rock of "Don't Tell Me" and "My

Happy Ending," Lavigne delivered on her long-kept promise to rock out while still offering up a feast of irresistible pop hooks. *Under My Skin* not only revealed Lavigne's true identity as an artist but it showed that her success wasn't an anomaly that had been lab-produced by faceless suits at a record company.

Under My Skin shot straight to No. 1 on the Billboard 200 and spent a total of sixty-six weeks on the U.S. chart. It also peaked at No. 1 in at least eleven other countries. The album went on to sell more than ten million copies worldwide. By the time she reached her twentieth birthday, the girl from Napanee had two hit records. But Lavigne still had at least one more milestone to reach—a chart-topping single.

THE SUCCESS OF THE singles from *Under My Skin* made sure Lavigne's voice continued to be heard around the world. And the year-long, 150-date Bonez Tour made sure Lavigne herself was physically present in cities around the world. Meanwhile, the tabloid press did its best to bring the singer's private life into the public realm. For a while, there wasn't anything really juicy; she tended to dodge questions about boyfriends and had a brief, minimally publicized relationship with her guitarist Jesse Colburn, who left the band in 2004.[29] But then she gave the paparazzi something really good.

In the months following the release of *Under My Skin*, rumours began to swirl about a romance between Lavigne and Sum 41's Deryck Whibley. The pair began dating around mid-2004 and were engaged about a year later. In June 2006,

---

29 Colburn was replaced by another Canadian punk musician: former Gob bassist Craig Wood.

the couple got married in a private ceremony in California. The celebrity press loved it: One of the world's biggest pop stars had found love with a bad-boy punk who was himself one of the biggest rock stars of the day (and who even had his own tabloid pedigree, having previously dated Paris Hilton). The Canadian press was particularly ravenous, covering Lavigne and Whibley as if they were members of the Royal Family. The couple's wedding in Montecito, a town just northwest of Los Angeles, was a "short, classy ceremony with the sound of helicopters droning overhead carrying photographers trying to get a shot," a source told the CBC. Until their 2009 divorce, this pair of small-town Canadians led a life together as the pop-punk power couple.

Less than a year into that highly publicized marriage, Lavigne would remind everyone of the real reason they should be paying attention to her. In early 2007, Lavigne released "Girlfriend," the lead single from her third album, *The Best Damn Thing*. A bubblegummy, pom-pom-waving, almost frustratingly catchy hit that still channelled the brash, bratty pop-punk Lavigne was known for, "Girlfriend" rocketed to No. 1 on the Billboard Hot 100, giving Lavigne her very first chart-topping single in the U.S., while also topping the charts in a dozen other countries. "Girlfriend" was one of the biggest songs of 2007, and its peppy, ultra-catchy chorus was basically inescapable for the remainder of the decade. *The Best Damn Thing* reached the top 10 of the album charts in twenty-four countries. It was not only a commercial hit but a milestone of self-expression. These were fast, crunchy, energetic songs that felt indebted to her "Sk8er Boi" heritage, trading in moody rockers for upbeat anthems and ushering in a new wave of girl power. Lavigne sounded confident and empowered as she fully embraced the "pop-punk princess" title that had been bestowed upon her by the media.

By the end of the decade, Lavigne had sold tens of millions of records, released multiple smash-hit singles around the world, and become one of the most significant figures in pop music—a larger-than-life superstar from humble beginnings who was obsessively admired by millennial teenagers around the world.[30]

IN THE YEARS IMMEDIATELY following *Let Go*, major labels began tripping over themselves to sign teenage girls with rock-music inclinations, hoping that these artists, like Lavigne, would define a generation of young women without much effort. In the early 2000s, Lavigne was hardly the only teenage girl with a strong singing voice and an interest in moody guitar rock, and several of them, like fellow Ontarians Skye Sweetnam and Fefe Dobson, had already made inroads in the music industry by the time Lavigne released "Complicated." While Lavigne's success had primed outlets like MuchMusic, MTV, and pop radio for these other artists' sounds and aesthetics, the endless comparisons made it difficult for them to stand on their own. In 2003, Sweetnam and Dobson were featured in an MTV *News* article titled "Don't Call Me Avril," which surveyed them

---

30 Lavigne became so famous that she was even subjected to a fan theory that she died in 2003 and was replaced by a body double named Melissa Vandella, a claim that has been broadly publicized despite its absurd premise and the dubious evidence used to support it. It's ridiculous, but it's also illustrative: generally speaking, you don't get to have a conspiracy theory about your supposed death and secret replacement unless you're a really big deal.

and two other up-and-coming female singer-songwriters and their struggles to assert their identities in the wake of "Avrilmania." In the article, Sweetnam is quoted as saying, "People just want to compare you so they can measure your style against something else," right before the writer says Sweetnam "looks like she could be Avril's sister."

Even Katy Perry, who would go on to become one of the bestselling musicians of all time, found herself bombarded with attempts to mould her into a Lavigne clone. As Perry bounced around between major American labels while trying to find her sound, she worked with Butch Walker and the Matrix. When the A&R agent who signed Perry to Capitol Records, where she would finally find mainstream success, pitched Perry to his boss, he told him, "Oh my god, I've found the next Avril Lavigne meets Alanis Morissette."

Young women in the music industry are often still needlessly pitted against one another, but Lavigne's enduring influence has, over time, opened the door for more women to flourish in pop-punk, whether that means incorporating alt-rock guitars into Top 40 radio hits

FURTHER LISTENING

SKYE SWEETNAM

Hometown: Bolton, Ontario
Years active: 2002–present

The year that Avril Lavigne took the world by storm, a fourteen-year-old Ontario girl named Skye Sweetnam began working on her debut album, *Noise from the Basement*. By the time it came out in 2004 with a *Let Go*-like approach to a range of pop, rock, and punk sounds, she drew attention to the Avril comparisons via her song "Hypocrite" so critics didn't have to. Sweetnam amassed plenty of attention for the cleaner material: Shakespeare-slamming "Billy S." was all over Canadian radio and MuchMusic; she sang the theme songs for shows like *Radio Free Roscoe*, *Wayside*, and *The Buzz on Maggie*; and she opened for Britney Spears on the Onyx Hotel Tour in 2004. But she really shined in *Basement*'s punkier moments, like "Number One," "Shot to Pieces," and a cover of Blondie's "Heart of Glass," and that's eventually the direction she leaned into. After her second album, *Sound Soldier*, was not released in the U.S., she founded alt-metal band Sumo Cyco in 2011, channelling her childhood love of Rage Against the Machine, Metallica, and Faith No More.

or tearing it up every night in the indie-rock touring circuit. In recent years, Lavigne's influence has been publicly cited by major pop stars, including Billie Eilish and Olivia Rodrigo, as well as ascendant indie-rockers like Soccer Mommy and Snail Mail.

Lavigne has sold more than forty million albums, becoming one of the bestselling Canadian artists of all time, while *Let Go* is one of the world's bestselling albums of the twenty-first century. She's toured with pop-punk bands like Bowling for Soup, Simple Plan, Not by Choice, Gob, and Silverstein, and she influenced an entire generation of artists who are now indisputably seen as punk or punk-influenced.

After spending the 2010s eschewing punk and coming into her own as a pop artist—albeit a rock-influenced one—Lavigne leaned harder into a traditional pop-punk sound than she ever had on 2022's *Love Sux*, co-produced by Blink-182's Travis Barker. It was, in a way, a homecoming—Lavigne returning to the sounds and inspirations of her earliest works in a world that had been shaped by those works. This time around, there was no one who would dare question her authenticity. If they did, they'd have two generations of fans to fight off.

4

SIMPLE PLAN

On a bright, sunny day in Midtown Manhattan, excited teens stream into a courtyard just south of Central Park to surround a pop-up stage. Some stand shoulder to shoulder in the crowd, others survey the proceedings from a raised platform, while the luckiest among them flank the stage from the side, just feet away from the action. They're there to see Simple Plan, one of the world's hottest pop-punk bands, shooting live footage for a new music video. One of the kids in the crowd is Roxy Ryan, a drummer for a punk band in Long Island, who cut class to go into the city and hand her idols her band's demo tape.

Right on time, the five members of Simple Plan file onto the stage and launch into their song "Vacation" while the throng of teens and a couple of suited-up music executives dance along. Ryan makes her move, slinking past security and onto the stage carrying a handful of purple jewel cases. But before she can give them to the band, she's foiled by the sudden appearance of her high-achieving identical twin sister, an overzealous truancy officer, a perma-scowling crime boss, and a hairless dog with a microchip in its stomach. The Ryan sisters jump off the stage and are crowd-surfed to safety.

In this scene from the 2004 movie *New York Minute*, starring Mary-Kate and Ashley Olsen, Simple Plan are the guests of honour. Arriving right at the end of the Olsen twins' decade-long cultural dynasty, the movie serves as a time capsule of who was considered famous enough to earn a showcase in a $30 million Hollywood feature starring two of the most bankable young stars of the day. It's telling, then, that Simple Plan is the band whose very presence serves as the main motivator for Mary-Kate's character. The producers haven't invented a fake band like in *Almost Famous* or *Freaky Friday*. They've hired a real band with actual draw, one that teenage girls around the world would believably skip school to see, a band that the Olsen twins are actually fans of. For Simple Plan, it's a massive flex of how quickly they've become a standout in the crowded pop-punk field with their clean guitar riffs, catchy melodies, and straightforward lyrics about adolescent life's petty frustrations.

Simple Plan doesn't care if people call them sellouts for being in *New York Minute*. They've already been called sellouts for touring with Avril Lavigne, for recording the theme song to *What's New, Scooby-Doo?*, and for landing hit after hit with their polished pop-punk sound. What many of their haters don't realize is that the members of Simple Plan aren't just a bunch of slightly edgy teenagers cobbled together by some big-shot American music industry executive bent on gentrifying punk music. They're bona fide punk scholars from the suburbs of Montreal who spent their teenage years paying their dues in the dive bars and minivans of the punk underworld, waiting for the world to catch on to their accessible songwriting and incredibly hooky melodies. Now that's happened, and they're being rewarded with millions of fans, including the Olsen twins.

Not bad for Quebec's biggest export since Céline Dion.

THROUGHOUT HIS ENTIRE CHILDHOOD, Pierre Bouvier had a rebellious streak. When he was just six years old, he started skateboarding around the suburbs of Montreal, grinding on any curb he could find and pissing off security guards. When he was a little bit older, he started snowboarding, which pissed off the skiers. At Collège Beaubois high school in Montreal's West Island, he took to wearing band tees under his uniform—Metallica, Guns N' Roses, you know the type—which might have pissed off the teachers, had they known about it.

"That counterculture of being a snowboarder or being a skateboarder puts you on the verge of being hated," Bouvier says now. "That's where that whole 'us against them' mentality began."

Before long, his T-shirts attracted the attention of his classmate Charles-André Comeau, better known as Chuck. Comeau was a little nerdier than Bouvier and significantly more studious, but he would always make the time to further his musical education when he wasn't studying for his next test. "School was the number-one thing. I had to have good grades," says Comeau. "And I was good in school. I wouldn't say it came naturally, but I was willing to work hard."

On paper, the two didn't have much in common. Bouvier was a rebellious slacker and the son of a truck driver-turned-broker, while Comeau was an overachiever whose parents were a lawyer and a PR director for a major university. But they bonded over their love of music and became inseparable.

In 1992, they and their friend Jean-Sébastien Boileau formed their first band together on the recommendation of one of their teachers. Bouvier had been playing the guitar since childhood and had the least trace of a French-Canadian accent (courtesy of his anglophone grandmother), so he became the frontman, while Comeau played drums and Boileau played bass. The boys were obsessed with grunge bands like Stone Temple Pilots and Soundgarden, so they called the band Stone Garden. They rehearsed regularly in the Comeau family's basement, bashing out covers of songs by their favourite bands.

Around this time, Bouvier's obsessions with music and snowboarding collided in a big way. He became enamoured with a series of snowboarding VHS tapes, watching them over and over again in his family's home on Île Bizard. He was transfixed by the shaky handheld footage of snowboarders bursting from the peaks in a squall of powder and catching some air or driving around in their trucks in search of the next slope to conquer. He was doubly transfixed by the background music: the chugging chords and driving drums of modern California punk bands like Bad Religion and the Offspring, which quickly overtook grunge and heavy metal as the soundtrack to his life.

Bouvier was hooked by the music's message of overthrowing mainstream society and corporate overlords. For his whole life, he felt like he had been told what to do, and punk became his latest defence against the doldrums. Bouvier brought his new musical discoveries to his bandmates, who responded in kind.

Comeau was a hockey player, not a skater or snowboarder, but he took to punk all the same. One night in 1993, he was listening to CHOM-FM, an English-language rock station based in Montreal. Just as he was falling asleep, the DJ put on "American Jesus," the lead single from Bad Religion's recent album, *Recipe for Hate*. The buzzing guitar riff, Greg Graffin's confident vocals, and the Greek chorus of backing singers immediately embedded itself into the now wide-awake teen.

Bouvier and Comeau became part of an ever-growing cohort of young Quebeckers obsessed with the new wave of punk bands coming out of California in the early '90s. They became regulars at L'Oblique, a record store in Montreal's hip Plateau neighbourhood, building CD collections filled with the latest albums from bands on Epitaph and Fat Wreck Chords.

Stone Garden was over. Bouvier, Comeau, and Boileau quickly rebranded into a punk band just like their new heroes. They started calling themselves Roach and wrote nearly a dozen songs about the issues that pissed them off, like police brutality, the corporate machine, and racism. One of Bouvier's older brothers was in a rock band called Feedback, and he and a friend who worked in a studio hauled a sixteen-track recorder and microphones into the Bouvier family basement to record Roach's first EP. The result was thirty-six minutes of lo-fi punk rock called *Insecticide*, bearing songs like "Cops Are All the Same," "Tell Off Your Boss," and "Racism Suckkks." The band made two hundred copies and drained all of the ink from Papa Bouvier's giant photocopier to print the inserts.

The tapes turned the members of Roach into the coolest kids at school, and they started playing house parties and even a few Montreal clubs, as long as they were accompanied by their parents. Each show brought them one step closer to feeling like their heroes—which was a lot closer than they realized.

IT SHOULD HAVE BEEN obvious how huge punk rock was going to be in Montreal. First off, it is French Canada's biggest city, and guitar-heavy rock with simple English lyrics had been breaking the language barrier since prog rock in the '70s and metal in the '80s.[31] Second, Quebec's long, bitter winters and sloping hills created a thriving snowboarding culture, and the same videos that Bouvier watched on repeat brought the new wave of California punk into thousands of Quebecois households, even in the province's deeply francophone areas. Skateboarding, snowboarding, and punk rock in Quebec turned into a thriving culture for live music, and punk bands would regularly make the trek north from California, even in the dead of winter, to play to jam-packed, unruly crowds of excited French Canadians throughout the province in places like Montreal, Quebec City, Trois-Rivières, and Sherbrooke.

"Quebec in general was a mecca for Canadian pop-punk," Bouvier recalls. "Bands like Lagwagon, Strung Out, and early Blink-182 were blown away by how popular those shows were. And they would go out there and sell a bunch of shirts and make a ton of money for what their bar was at the time."

---

31 Pink Floyd's 1977 concert at Montreal's Olympic Stadium directly inspired their next album, *The Wall*, while Emerson, Lake & Palmer's concert at the same venue that year was their biggest headlining show ever. Meanwhile, the metal band Voivod emerged from the north of the province in 1982 to draw worldwide attention to the province's metal scene, which eventually led to Montreal being deemed a "city of excellence" in heavy metal by its own city council in 2019.

In November 1994, Bouvier and Comeau saw NOFX, Face to Face, and Ten Foot Pole play downtown at the Spectrum. For a dollar, Comeau bought the *Fat Music for Fat People* compilation album featuring bands from Fat Wreck Chords, the label started by NOFX's lead singer, Fat Mike. ("I ended up buying albums from pretty much every band on that compilation," says Comeau.) People were moshing and stage-diving for hours, turning the venue into a gigantic steam room. "It was like nothing I had ever seen before," Bouvier recalled to *Kerrang!* magazine in 2016. "I spent some time in the mosh pit getting smashed around, but I soon realized that what I really wanted was to be up on that stage."

It didn't take long. When a local band had to drop out of a gig opening for Face to Face, Roach was tapped to replace them. In their first show as a quartet—Comeau's neighbour Philippe Jolicoeur had recently joined as lead guitarist—on Valentine's Day in 1995, the Spectrum was absolutely packed, and Roach took the stage as the first of four bands. They looked like kids because they *were* kids, but seconds after Jolicouer punched through the opening chords of "It's Your Fault," a wave of moshing broke out in the crowd.

Nick Farkas, one of the show's promoters, was blown away. "This is way, way, way better than anything else out there," he remembers thinking. "The kid could sing," he adds. "They weren't very tight or anything, but you could tell that it was more interesting than anything else that was coming out, for sure."

Farkas's business partner, Paget Williams, agreed. "They could play, they were ambitious, they had drive, they were organized, and they had a goal," Williams says now.

Farkas and Williams decided to take the band under their wing. The duo ran a concert promotion company, Greenland Productions, and were looking for local bands to open for the SoCal titans they were bringing to town. Three weeks after the Face to Face gig, Roach was back at the Spectrum playing Greenland's Sno Jam festival, opening for their idols Lagwagon, Strung Out, and Ten Foot Pole. After the set, Comeau watched the bands play from backstage while studying for his history test the next day.

That April, Greenland hooked up Roach with local producer Rod Shearer, who recorded the band's second release, a four-track cassette called *Concerned*, on Farkas and Williams's label, 2112 Records. The release coincided with Roach's rebrand: after getting served an injunction from another Canadian band called Roach, the Quebec boys changed their name to Reset. Now having switched up their sound, lineup, and name, the band was fully locked in to show touring bands what Montreal punk rock was all about.

IN THE EARLY DAYS, Reset's age and inexperience set them apart. Comeau was so used to the specific setup of his drum kit that he would bring it to gigs and get upset when he wasn't allowed to set it up—a major faux pas in the fast and furious world of live music, where a shared kit is the norm. On Reset's first tour, four dates in Ontario and Quebec opening for Fat Wreck Chords punks Good Riddance, the band showed up in Bouvier's dad's RV, towing a Mercedes, which drew incredulous looks from the other bands, who had been driving around in beat-up vans.

But while it took the teens a few months to learn the rules of the road, their love of punk rock and open admiration for their tourmates quickly endeared them to the scene. "I think they could see how genuine we were in our interest in this kind of music," says Comeau. "Our love really came from the heart. We wanted to belong and wanted to be a part of it, and we really wanted to fit in. We didn't act like we were better than anybody else. We were just stoked to be there."

Throughout 1995 and 1996, Reset cemented themselves as rising stars in Montreal's punk scene, opening for Pennywise—one of their biggest inspirations—and Blink-182, who were in the middle of a massive major-label bidding war. Reset's band members graduated high school, and they decided to forgo CEGEP, Quebec's junior college system—except for Comeau, who, on his parents' urging, went to the prestigious private school Collège Jean-de-Brébeuf, the alma mater of former Canadian prime minister Pierre Trudeau and his son, Justin.

In the summer of 1996, right before Comeau started CEGEP, Farkas and Williams gave the band some money to record their debut album with Rod Shearer at Le Studio in Morin-Heights, a small town tucked away in Quebec's Laurentian Mountains. Once recording was complete, they were flown out to Los Angeles for a ten-day trip to mix the record at Westbeach Recorders, the studio founded by Brett Gurewitz of Bad Religion.

In February 1997, Reset's debut album, *No Worries*, was released on 2112 Records. A heartfelt blast of SoCal-style punk rock, the album riffled through big-picture issues like labour exploitation, environmental activism, and settler colonialism. They celebrated the release by selling out the Spectrum for a headlining gig and booking their first cross-Canada tours opening for Ten Foot Pole and MxPx. The band felt confident these tours would help them continue to take their punk rock crusade to a higher level. But in reality, they would spell the beginning of the end for the Reset that they knew.

COMEAU CONTINUING HIS STUDIES spoke to larger issues within Reset. Comeau's parents weren't sold on the idea of their teenage son flying to California to make a punk-rock album, to say nothing of the tours and late-night gigs. Comeau wasn't the only academically minded member of the band—bassist Boileau left to go to university after releasing *No Worries*, paring down Reset to a lean, mean three-piece, with Bouvier taking over bassist duties—but there was always a tension between Comeau's studious leanings and the free-spirited nature of being in a punk band.

And while Bouvier and Comeau had been bandmates for five years, nothing prepared them for life on the road. Over two tours in 1997, the differences between the two became exacerbated. "To me, part of the appeal of being a musician was the lifestyle," Bouvier says. "We go out there, we play, we drink some beers, we have fun. We're punk rockers." But Comeau didn't drink or smoke, and it didn't take long for their different lifestyles to wreak havoc on the band's dynamic. To Bouvier, Comeau was "just this nerdy guy that was more into pushing the band." He felt that Comeau's drive for success was getting in the way of having a good time.

Over the course of Reset's tour with MxPx, Comeau was the odd man out, constantly fighting with his bandmates about increasingly petty matters. Things came to a head in Edmonton, on the penultimate night of the tour, when after yet another argument, Comeau left the band's hotel room in a huff. When he came back, he overheard his bandmates talking feverishly. Then he heard Bouvier—his friend of six years, bandmate for four—deliver the final blow: "We need another fucking drummer."

That was it. Comeau was tired of being the only one to take things seriously. He had fought tooth and nail against his straitlaced parents to skip out on university to pursue his dream of being a rockstar, but at this moment, none of that mattered. The dream was over.

Comeau burst into the room and stared his bandmates dead in the eyes.

"I heard you guys," he said. "Don't bother kicking me out. I'm done."

Maybe he expected his bandmates to be caught off-guard and start backtracking. Or maybe it was just some dumb prank they were pulling on him, like the night before in Calgary when Reset's roadie ambushed him as he was getting out of the shower, yanking the towel from his torso and shoving him into the hallway, naked and panicking.

But this time, there were no laughs. Bouvier and Jolicouer had made their decision, and Comeau had made up his own mind. The next day, Comeau played the last set of the tour at the Starfish Room in Vancouver's Downtown South and then said goodbye to MxPx and to his now former bandmates. The band bought him a plane ticket to Montreal, and he left Reset and his dreams of rock stardom behind.

Bouvier and Jolicoeur were left to drive their gear back across the country while they figured out their next steps. They were going to find a new drummer, write some new songs, and continue on the slow but steady path to punk stardom. It was 1997, and the possibilities for uptempo, politically minded punk rock felt endless—labels like Fat Wreck Chords and Epitaph were churning out new classics every few weeks.

"I was more of the musical driving force behind the band, and in my mind, I was like, 'That's all we need. We just need the music. Everything else doesn't matter,'" says Bouvier.

Bouvier and Jolicoeur soldiered on. They found a new drummer, a guy from Vancouver named Adrian White who moved to Montreal to join his new bandmates, and in 1998 the trio recorded Reset's second album, *No Limits*, in Vancouver with Greg Reely, who had worked with a wide range of local artists that included Sarah McLachlan and Skinny Puppy. Near the end of *No Limits*, released in early 1999, Bouvier eulogized his relationship with Comeau on "Friend." But, like many public declarations of having moved on, there was some regret lurking beneath the surface. With Comeau gone, Reset had lost their main business driving force. "The band became a little more stagnant because Chuck wasn't making phone calls and wasn't doing all this stuff that I wasn't really used to doing," says Bouvier. "We needed someone to be more of a manager, and he wasn't there anymore."

With nobody to pick up the phone, Reset was going in circles. Bouvier had returned to his old dead-end jobs, working at a chicken restaurant and driving trucks for his dad. He felt like a washed-up has-been at the age of eighteen, and he considered going back to school. He thought his days of being a hotshot musician were behind him. He would say to himself, "I don't know if I want to do this anymore. I feel like I'm wasting my life."

* * *

WITH HIS MUSICIAN DAYS behind him, Comeau had earned a prestigious direct admission to McGill University's law school program, one of only twenty-five students to be offered a spot straight out of CEGEP. He was following in his dad's footsteps, but a part of him missed the band life. It wasn't long before he was roped back in.

Jeff Stinco, a high school friend, reached out to Comeau after hearing about his split from Reset. Early jams were successful, and they slowly began to assemble a new band, recruiting fellow Collège Beaubois classmate Sébastien Lefebvre to play guitar.

One night in 1999, Bouvier and Comeau ran into each other at a Sugar Ray show at the Metropolis in downtown Montreal. It was the first time they'd seen each other since the MxPx tour. Over the din of the crowd, the two agreed to put the past behind them and talked about the music they'd been working on recently.

"I've got this new band," Comeau said. "You should check it out."

Then, he added a little white lie. "We're lining up some Hollywood soundtracks," he said. "Actually, some major labels are interested."

"Wow, really?" Bouvier said, intrigued.

Shortly after, he stopped by the old jam space and listened to Comeau's new band. By this point, the speed-demon punk rock that the boys had grown up on had given way to a tighter, poppier style. Blink-182, with whom Reset had become friendly after playing together in Montreal, had perfected the art of melodic pop-punk, earning a hit single with "Dammit" and ushering in a new era of punk rock. Comeau's new crew had also started listening to WBTZ, or "The Buzz," a radio station based out of Burlington, Vermont, that championed bands like Everclear and Eve 6 who had sidestepped the West Coast punk rock craze in favour of beefier, grungier alt-rock. It all added up to music that was hookier and more melody-driven than Reset had ever been. It was a band that might actually attract the major-label attention that Comeau was claiming. But they were missing one important piece. "I wanted to find a singer that I thought would be better than you," Comeau told Bouvier. "But I never found that guy." As a parting gift, Comeau gave Bouvier a cassette of some songs that his new band had recorded.

Later that week, Bouvier was on another drive for his dad when he popped Comeau's cassette into the tape deck. Over the course of twelve hours, Bouvier played the tape over and over again, humming to himself, spitting out words, melodies, ideas. Once he got back, he marched over to Comeau's basement, where the guys had met for another rehearsal.

"I did it," Bouvier said. "I found your chorus."

He picked up a guitar and sang a sweet, sad little melody about the unrequited longing of a lovesick teenager. Simple and sincere, it cut right through the punk-rock power chords with an instantly memorable pop hook—exactly what the band needed.

Comeau and Stinco looked at each other, and then back at Bouvier. They'd found their lead singer.

And, though it wouldn't happen for a few years, that song,

"I'd Do Anything," would turn out to be their breakthrough single.

EVEN BEFORE THIS NEW band had a name, they were amassing diehard fans. First was Patrick Langlois, a buddy of Comeau's from CEGEP. When Comeau got kicked out of Reset, Langlois encouraged him not to give up on music. And when Comeau teamed up with Stinco to form a new band, Langlois already had stars in his eyes.

"Your new band is gonna be so much better than Reset and it's gonna be booked for the Warped Tour and I'm gonna work for you guys," he told Comeau one night.

Langlois had been a regular at Montreal punk shows since he was a preteen. Despite his love of music, Langlois had no interest in being a musician himself; instead, he wanted to work alongside his favourite bands, and he decided that Comeau's new project was his ticket to the big time. And Langlois knew exactly how they were going to make it big.

Through his concert-going adventures, Langlois had become a massive Blink-182 fan. From the moment he got his driver's licence, he would drive to any of the band's shows within six hours of Montreal. In the spring of 1999, Langlois found out that Blink-182 was playing a college show in Upstate New York and immediately called Comeau with a plan.

"There's this show in Albany, and we should go," he told his friend.

"I can't," said Comeau, defeated. "I have an exam that day."

"No, let's go, man!" Langlois spat back. "You can see Mark and give him a demo of your new band."

Langlois's offer hit deep. Comeau was enjoying his time in law school, but he still saw it as a way to break into the music industry. He had always told himself that if his band didn't work out, he'd be a music lawyer, an agent, or a manager. "I had fallen in love with music so profoundly that I couldn't see myself doing anything else," he says now. "But truly, ninety-nine percent of my dream was to be in the band."

While his classmates took their exam, Comeau hopped in Langlois's car and headed down to Albany. As they wandered around the festival grounds, they spotted Blink-182's bassist, Mark Hoppus, hanging out by the bike racks. Comeau quickly made his move.

"Mark! It's Chuck from Reset!"

"Oh, hey!" said Hoppus. "Come backstage, let's hang out."

Comeau and Langlois headed backstage and hung out with Hoppus, guitarist Tom DeLonge, and their new drummer Travis Barker. Comeau talked about his new band and handed over their demo that he conveniently had on him, and Hoppus talked about Blink-182's upcoming album, *Enema of the State*, which they were releasing a month later.

"Oh, we'll be in Montreal in two weeks to do some promo for the record," Hoppus added. "What's your number? Let's hang out and get sushi before the show."

Two weeks later, Comeau and Langlois joined Blink-182 at Kaizen, a gourmet sushi restaurant in downtown Montreal. They went to MusiquePlus—MuchMusic's Quebecois equivalent—for a live recording, and to the rock club Foufounes Électriques[32] for an autograph-signing session. At the end of

32 Quebec French for "Electric Asscheeks."

the night, Hoppus gave Comeau an advance copy of *Enema of the State*. From the first listen, Comeau knew the album was revolutionary.

"Holy shit," he said to himself. "This is going to change everything."

When Comeau met back up with Blink-182 the next day, he couldn't contain his excitement. "It solidified the idea of what we could accomplish as a band, what the possibilities were—it changed instantly when I heard that record," Comeau says. "We know this style of music, we understand it, we've been doing it for several years with little variation. But if we put out a great record, the sky's the limit. We can achieve all our dreams of touring the world."

Hoppus hadn't just given Comeau a copy of the album—he had given Comeau hope.

Enema of the State was, as Comeau predicted, an instant hit, and it was as much a game-changer for pop-punk at large as it was for Comeau's conception of what a pop-punk band could achieve. A few months later, after *Enema of the State* had sold close to a million copies in the U.S. and more than one hundred thousand in Canada, Comeau received an email from Hoppus:

> Let me tell you how stoked I am on it. "Anything" is honestly one of my ten favourite songs of all time right now. Seriously. I have that song on repeat on my CD player and have listened to it about ten times in a row. I will honestly do anything that I can to get the word out.

* * *

HOPPUS'S ENDORSEMENT WAS GREAT news for Comeau. For Bouvier, it represented something a little more dire: he was still a member of Reset and hadn't had the heart to tell them about his new band with Comeau. To make things more complicated, Reset had just landed a massive opportunity that represented a second wind for the stagnating band. In late 1999, they were booked to play at the latest evolution of Sno Jam, a massive outdoor concert called Jam des Neiges 2000, to be televised on MusiquePlus the following March. Plus, both Reset and Comeau's new band rehearsed on the same street on one of les Îles-Laval, a small archipelago between the Island of Montreal and Île Bizard—Comeau's new band rehearsed at his parents' house, and Reset rehearsed six doors down, at Jolicoeur's place. Sometimes, when Bouvier had back-to-back rehearsals, he would drive away from Jolicoeur's house, park around the corner, and scurry over to Comeau's to avoid suspicion. While Comeau's new band was trying to build their repertoire, Bouvier was only partially committed—gigging, rehearsing, and partying with Reset was occupying a lot of his free time. If he was going to properly devote himself to music, he'd have to choose one or the other.

It was a tough decision for Bouvier. Reset was the band he had started as a teenager and was the source of all his musical education. They had a reputation, two albums' worth of songs, and a massive gig lined up. But he felt the band's style of music was increasingly becoming a thing of the past. Plus, Reset had barely made any money from their album sales. On the other hand, the new band had never played a gig together and didn't even have a name. But they were more of the moment in 1999, representative of a new wave of punk rock that, like the best pop music, could be played on the radio and on MTV.

"Blink is starting to blow up, and the style of pop-punk became less like Pennywise, and more like poppy songs that have punk-rock energy," says Bouvier.

Blink-182 and MxPx had already moved toward radio-friendly pop-punk, and newer bands like Good Charlotte and Sum 41 were starting to find success with this new sound, as well. Even Face to Face, the first California band that Reset opened for, had moved from skate punk to alternative rock on their latest album, *Ignorance Is Bliss*.

To Bouvier, Reset felt like the past. This new band could be the future.

Finally, in late 1999, Bouvier quit Reset. He was ready to take a chance with Comeau's new band and, just as crucially, he was ready to take another chance on his friendship with Comeau. "He wasn't a skater, he wasn't a snowboarder, he didn't like partying, he didn't like drinking with buddies, he didn't like going out, but he really liked being in a band," says Bouvier. "He was really into all the bands that I was into, he knew all the lyrics, we had this common interest, and through that we had fun. We didn't have fun doing the activities that I would do with other people. We had fun playing a show together, we had fun writing a song together, we had fun planning the next step. In some ways, we are polar-opposite personalities, but we find common ground with our love for this band and our love for the music. I think he always saw it, but now I'm mature enough to realize, what he brings to the table has worth, and I *need* it."

With Bouvier fully invested, Comeau got to work holding up his end of the bargain: to turn his lie—that the music industry was interested in this nameless idea of a band—into reality.

AS THE NEW MILLENNIUM HIT, the band moved swiftly. They recorded a four-track demo with a local engineer, Graeme Humfrey, while Comeau cold-called every name in the *Yellow Pages of Rock*, an annual publication filled with the contact information of everyone in the music industry. To add some legitimacy to the band, Comeau posed as the band's manager, calling himself Chuck Talbot, using his mom's family name.

On January 22, 2000, the band played their first gig in nearby Saint-Jean-sur-Richelieu, opening for Montreal hardcore band Bald Vulture, who had once opened for Reset. Days earlier, Humfrey hastily gave them the temporary band name A Simple Plan, named after a movie he had just seen. The band decided to drop the *A* and go by Simple Plan—just temporarily, of course, until they came up with a better name. They never did.

Around this time, Simple Plan got in touch with Coalition Music, a Toronto-based management company best known for managing nationally successful rock acts Our Lady Peace and Finger Eleven. If the company's co-owners, Eric Lawrence and Rob Lanni, had it their way, their involvement with Simple Plan would have been over before it even began. They had made their name on the strain of alternative rock that replaced grunge in the mid-'90s and had avoided the initial rise of pop-punk entirely. "I don't like pop-punk. I don't like that stuff," Lawrence recalls thinking at the time. "It's not the shit that I listen to in my kitchen. My era's different, and I'm working with what I love."

Their younger colleagues helped them come around. A pair of recent hires, Devi Ekanand and Julian Gruhl, were closer to pop-punk's target demographic and persuaded their new bosses to take a chance on Simple Plan. Coalition invited Simple Plan to their studio in Toronto, and the co-founders were sold. "That's when it dawned on me that, whether I love the music or not, there's something about this band," says Lawrence. "There's something about the way that they're guiding themselves, their desire to have their music be heard by anybody that they can get to hear it, anywhere on the planet."

Coalition signed Simple Plan to a management deal in the spring of 2000. A short while later, Lawrence was listening to the local rock radio station, 102.1 The Edge, when he heard a familiar voice: it was a demo of a Simple Plan song, "I'm Just a Kid." The DJ, George Stroumboulopoulos, had a policy on his show: people could personally hand him a CD of a new punk band and he'd play a song on the air after only a ten-second spot-check, though he'd always warn them, "If it sucks, I'm going to pull it off in the middle of the song."[33] Lawrence knew Stroumboulopoulos through the music industry and called him up instantly.

"George, we're working with that band," he said. "Do you like them?"

Stroumboulopoulos minced no words: "This song is a fuckin' smash."

Coalition hooked Simple Plan up with Lanni's brother, Arnold, who was coming off a Juno nomination for Producer

---

33 "I just thought I was some 'defender of the faith' in punk rock, so it was the [comedy] bit of a fucking jackass," Stroumboulopoulos says now. "But I still stand by it, because you have to have taste, right?"

of the Year for his work with Our Lady Peace. Simple Plan settled in at Arnold Lanni's Arnyard Studios in Toronto to work on some new demos that their managers would use to try to lock down a major-label record deal. But, true to their scrappy DIY upbringing, the band wasn't going to let their managers do all the work.

Through his endless cold-calling, Comeau had already piqued the interest of Andy Karp, an A&R rep for Lava Records, an offshoot of Atlantic Records in New York that had put out records by Matchbox Twenty, Kid Rock, and Sugar Ray. (He had pulled the ol' "Chuck Talbot" trick on him, which actually earned Karp's begrudging respect.) Karp liked the demo Comeau had sent, so he visited Toronto in September 2000 to see Simple Plan perform at a showcase. He liked them but didn't love them, and he told the band that having Bouvier sing and play bass made them look too much like Blink-182.

As Simple Plan was trying to figure out their next steps, they were reminded of Reset's performance on the Jam des Neiges broadcast earlier that year. Bouvier's replacement on bass and vocals was a guy named David Desrosiers, from the easternmost part of Quebec. Simple Plan was impressed and decided to persuade Desrosiers to jump ship to become *their* bassist, even after Desrosiers's hesitation about leaving Jolicoeur with yet another position to fill.

The band's goal was to sign to an American label, but by the end of 2000, they decided they would settle for the next best thing: a Canadian label. After some interest from Sony Music Canada, Simple Plan was ready to sign a deal. They had been made a verbal offer, but before the paperwork was signed, Sony's international executives triggered a massive reorganization. The new leadership reneged on the offer.

Devastated, Simple Plan was back at square one. But they still had one last card to play.

PATRICK LANGLOIS, COMEAU'S FRIEND from CEGEP, had landed a job with Aquarius Records to give the label some internet presence. Langlois, ever the dreamer, ended up trying to build a record label of his own, Role Model Records, which he and his colleague Matt Drouin pitched to Aquarius's owner, legendary Montreal concert promoter Donald Tarlton. The two upstarts were inspired by the label's deal with Sum 41, in which a Canadian label released their music at home and a major label released it in the rest of the world. They wanted to build Role Model on that method.

Langlois figured that Role Model would sign Simple Plan, Tarlton would help Simple Plan become a worldwide success, and everybody would get rich and famous—until, eight months of planning and one term sheet later, Coalition rejected Role Model's offer, hoping to land a major-label deal directly.

Months later, Langlois was back at it trying to help his buddies make it big. Through his work at Aquarius, he learned that Andy Karp was coming to Montreal from New York to check out Rubberman, a local alt-rock band signed to Aquarius with hopes of following in Sum 41's footsteps as an international export. Langlois, who shared Comeau's penchant for bending the truth, came up with an idea: Simple Plan was going to throw a show the same night as Rubberman, invite Karp, blow his mind with the new lineup, and get signed.

Simple Plan's managers got in touch with Karp directly and invited him to the show; he said yes, so the band and their team drove home to Montreal from Toronto. To cover their tracks, they booked the show under the alias Touchdown. They rented a Montreal venue called Club Zone, promised the owner that he could keep all the door money, invited all their friends, plied them with lyric sheets so they could sing along, and hoped for the best. Rubberman was scheduled to go on at 9:00 p.m., so Simple Plan—er, Touchdown—scheduled themselves for 10:30 p.m.

The night of the shows, Langlois was out for dinner with Karp, sneakily texting updates to Comeau the entire time. Close to 9:00 p.m., Comeau's phone vibrated with bad news from Langlois: "Fuck, we're still at the restaurant, there's no way Karp is there on time. You guys can't get on stage yet." Meanwhile, Simple Plan's friends started pouring into the venue, and before long, the bar was running out of alcohol. Ten thirty came and went, and the Club Zone owner kept pushing Simple Plan to start performing.

Comeau's phone vibrated again with another text from Patrick, this time, with good news: Karp was on his way. Within moments, Simple Plan stormed the stage. Karp showed up to a five-piece band confidently playing a commanding set of catchy pop-punk songs to a packed house of drunk locals hollering along to every word.

Karp had thought Rubberman was fine, but he thought Simple Plan was incredible. After the set, he invited the band and their managers back to his hotel room a few blocks away. There, after a few rounds of drinks, Karp looked at the band and dropped the bomb: "We want to do a deal."

The band kept their cool, but the moment they spilled onto the streets of late-night Montreal, they erupted with cheers and high fives.

"It was such a feeling of, like, 'We *told* you!'" Bouvier says. "We knew we had something. We weren't crazy. And all those 'no's and all those disappointments were now like... we're gonna get a record deal."

WITH A WORLDWIDE RECORD deal in hand, Simple Plan headed back to Lanni's studio in Toronto to turn their demos into a debut album.

In the studio, Bouvier and Comeau looked to capture everything that made Simple Plan different from what they'd been doing with Reset. They had traded out the heavier sound of chugging power chords—what Bouvier calls "mosh pit fuel"—for a leaner version of punk rock that took inspiration from timelessly catchy songs by artists like Tom Petty. In doing so, Bouvier reframed his writing approach: rather than write an instrumental and then come up with a vocal melody, he'd start with the words instead. "My process since those days is to find a cool line and then let me sing it in a way that's going to feel memorable," he says. "I'll put a melody to those words that makes the line shine."

Lyrically, they moved away from Reset's overtly political content and tapped into something a little more heartfelt. While they still cared about subjects like police brutality, exploitation, human rights, and international conflict, they wanted to express themselves more personally and relate to others more profoundly through their music. These new songs were about relationships, breakups, family, friendships, and feeling down about yourself—not exactly the voice of a revolutionary, but a voice for any restless teenager or young adult like them.

"When we shifted our approach and started to write more about ourselves, the songs became more personal and it felt more like a true window to who we were as people," Comeau says.

The dynamic within the band was as communally productive and creatively fulfilling as ever, leading Simple Plan to put together an album's worth of songs that made them proud. But as it turned out, the recording process would be anything but smooth.

Arnold Lanni had high standards for the band and showed it in what they felt were less-than-tender ways. He was prone to taking off for a few days, telling the band to record themselves until he returned to edit and critique it. When he came back, he'd scrap those days' worth of recordings. The band kept trying, recording and re-recording all their songs, and even some new ones, but nothing was good enough. As the band would later recall, Lanni had an analogy that he liked to use: "Right now, I'm John McEnroe, and you guys can't return my serve."

Lanni would later defend his methods as a way of pushing the band to be better without them feeling like they were being micromanaged. "When I was a musician, I never wanted people looking over my shoulder," he told *Alternative Press* in 2017. "I'd want the producer to say, 'Here's the song. Here's what I'd like you to do. How much time do you need? An hour and a half? I'll come back in an hour and a half because that way, I'm not looking over your shoulder as you track it.' It was just to get them to chase what they wanted to chase. If you aim for a target and you don't hit the target, I have to at least mention it."

Even without the benefit of hindsight, Simple Plan understood that Lanni was trying to bring out the best in them. "Arnold Lanni is not someone that comes from pop-punk," says Bouvier. "I don't think he ever listened to a pop-punk record before he made a record with us. I don't think he thought it was all that great. I think he definitely thought *we* were great, but for him, he was making these amazing Our Lady Peace records that are completely different from what we're doing. And there is a musical subtlety, and there's a musical depth to those records that is way deeper than Simple Plan. He was thinking, 'There's this whole other spectrum of dynamic that you guys have never explored.'"

Despite their differences, Simple Plan and Arnold Lanni would end up finishing the record by early 2002, about a year and a half after they began. And soon, Simple Plan's debut album *No Pads, No Helmets... Just Balls* would make all of that time, effort, and frustration more than worth their while.

No Pads, No Helmets ... Just Balls, released on March 19, 2002, was preceded by the lead single "I'm Just a Kid," which got a nice boost when moviegoers heard it in the teen comedy *The New Guy* that spring. But it was the second single, "I'd Do Anything," that really got the momentum going that September. "I'd Do Anything" was, effectively, the first song that Simple Plan ever wrote—the chorus that Bouvier wrote on a twelve-hour drive as he mulled over joining the band, and the song that Mark Hoppus was obsessed with while Blink-182 enjoyed their first taste of worldwide success.

Hoppus was such a fan of the demo that he agreed to appear on the final version. Bouvier and Comeau flew out to San Diego with the master tape and recorded Hoppus's vocals in Studio West, where Blink-182 recorded parts of *Enema of the State*.[34] Afterward, Hoppus took Bouvier and Comeau back to his house. "It was like getting a glimpse into what could happen to us if we played our cards right, and if we worked hard," Comeau recalls.

"I'd Do Anything" was a hit, crossing over to the Billboard pop charts in the U.S. and charting in Australia and the United Kingdom. *No Pads, No Helmets... Just Balls* went gold in the U.S. in just under a year and platinum six months after that on the strength of the album's final singles, "Addicted" and "Perfect."

Written as an apologetic letter to Comeau's parents, who were disappointed that their son had dropped out of law school, "Perfect" was supposed to be like every other song on the record—melancholic and heartfelt by way of relentless guitar attack, riff after riff, line after line. But while the band was recording the song, Lanni suggested that, right as the chorus hits, they should cut the instruments so Bouvier's vocals could ring out unaccompanied. The band thought it was ridiculous at first, but they tried it anyway and decided to keep it. It became Simple Plan's biggest Billboard hit, peaking at No. 24 and lasting twenty weeks on the chart, and making everything Comeau had put his parents through worthwhile.

That accessibility had to be what the band's managers had been aiming for when they partnered them with Arnold

---

34 Hoppus also appeared in the "I'd Do Anything" music video, further increasing Simple Plan's pop-punk credibility.

Lanni. "Something happened that was magical that worked and that people responded to," says Bouvier. "I think it's the coming together of this guy that has no idea what pop-punk is and couldn't give a shit, and a band that's trying to hang on to it."

SIMPLE PLAN'S MASSIVE SUCCESS was bittersweet. Even today, more than twenty years since its release, *No Pads, No Helmets... Just Balls* remains a divisive entry in the pop-punk canon. Around its release, *Rolling Stone* gave the album two stars out of five, with reviewer Jon Caramanica calling it "bombastically produced blasts of snotty posing" and "clean, pleasant rebellion"—in essence, punk-inspired sounds devoid of political engagement. Granted, the *Rolling Stone* of 2002 was a far cry from the version of the publication that, fifteen years later, would publish an article titled "The 50 Greatest Pop-Punk Albums" and rank *No Pads, No Helmets... Just Balls* in thirty-third place on the merit that Simple Plan "excelled at making snappy, catchy, sweet tunes that feel like the big scenes they complemented in flicks like *The New Guy*, *The Hot Chick*, and *Confessions of a Teenage Drama Queen*," as written by Brittany Spanos.

And while they were a hit with the MTV crowd internationally—and the MuchMusic crowd at home—Simple Plan was not a hit with the Warped Tour crowd, who were the same type of young punks that Simple Plan had been. That crowd viewed the band as yet another manufactured product of money-hungry record executives looking to capitalize on the latest trends, completely unaware of where the band had come from.

In Canada, the reaction was even worse precisely *because* the crowds knew where the band had come from. The only thing worse than an industry plant was a sellout.

"In Canada, we almost had to stop playing because there's mud and bottles being slung, and I'm trying to dodge shit," says Bouvier. "We all had to get prepared for battle. And it hurt—not physically. I mean, a little bit. It broke my nose at one point."

Adds Comeau, "When we played Warped Tour in Calgary in 2003, I'd never seen so many bottles in one set. Literally, a guy had to use a shovel to take them off the stage. It was the most brutal show."

Even the perpetually enthusiastic and cordial Nardwuar the Human Serviette—the eccentric music journalist and punk rocker who was working with MuchMusic at the time—took shots at the band during their Warped Tour 2003 interview in Vancouver, gifting them a Public Image Ltd. T-shirt under the guise of wanting to "teach" them about punk rock, and asking them if they had heard of the concept "GGBB"—good guys, bad band. At one point, Bouvier turned the tables on Nardwuar, telling him, "We never called ourselves punks, why are you calling us punks?" Nardwuar had no choice but to admit, "Because, I don't know, everybody else calls you punk."

Bouvier gets it, but it didn't make it feel any better at the time. "It was hard, especially for Chuck and me because we had come from the Fat Wreck Chords world," he says. "We even saw it with Blink-182. They were a cool pop-punk band, and then they blew up, and then people were like, 'Oh, Blink-182's fucking lame.' We saw that times ten because, let's face it, Simple Plan is even more poppy than Blink-182. It was really hard, but we kind of used it as that chip on our shoulder. It sucked and it was heavy, but it was always accompanied with really awesome success. It was difficult, but the pill was easier to swallow because things were going well, because the record was selling, because we were selling out shows, because we were doing signings at record stores and it was fucking mayhem."

Even as they continued to be antagonized by crowds, Simple Plan returned to Warped Tour year after year, earning the respect of their fellow musicians even when their fans wouldn't follow suit. "On Warped Tour, we'd go on stage and—especially in Canada—we'd get everything thrown at us," says Bouvier, "and then we'd go backstage and go have lunch, and I'm getting high fives from the guys from Rancid and Bad Religion and NOFX, and I'm friends with these people."

Simple Plan had decided to embrace the pop side of pop-punk, and that was no more evident than when they agreed to open for Avril Lavigne—who had her own legion of harsh critics—on a month's worth of shows in 2003. Simple Plan saw it as a make-or-break moment for their ever-elusive punk credibility.

"Our first record, it did well, we have some respect," says Bouvier. "But we understand that, by taking certain things like going to pop radio, like going to MTV, that upsets some people. That upsets KROQ and the rock stations. We decided that if we go in front of people, if we open up for Avril Lavigne in front of all these young fans, as long as we keep being us, we can feel okay with it. People can hold it against us, sure. But we will know that we didn't do anything different. We just saw a gig that would put us in front of a lot of people, and these are humans. They're girls, mostly, but they deserve to listen to whatever they want. And we're going to do the same thing that we do when we play on Warped Tour, and we're just going to do it in front of different people. At the time, that was pretty ballsy. That was something that people didn't do. And it's also something that I'm glad has changed."

From there, Simple Plan continued to move forward with their heads held high. In 2004, they recorded their second album, *Still Not Getting Any...* with legendary record producer Bob Rock, who had produced every Metallica record from their self-titled in 1991 (a.k.a. the "Black Album") to *St. Anger* in 2003. While the relatively short time frame for writing and recording found Bouvier and Comeau backsliding into old habits—"Pierre would go out and party and get home super late and I'd call him, wake him up, and say, 'I don't care what you did last night, get down here!'" Comeau told *Modern Drummer* in 2004—their friendship persisted unscathed. By this point, they knew that Simple Plan depended on the two of them getting along.

"Chuck is very business-minded. Not like me, I'm kind of a slacker," says Bouvier. "I'm great at writing songs and I'm great at performing and I have all these talents, but as far as planning and having the drive, I'm just not there. That's not where my head is at. And his is." As for what Bouvier has that Comeau doesn't? "Talent, easy answer," Comeau says. "He's very talented musically. He's my favourite writer in the whole world. When we write together and we hit something, I get shivers twenty-five years down the road. We've worked with so many awesome writers now with the band, and there still hasn't been one person that has written something that has hit me the same way emotionally that I respond to a melody that Pierre comes up with. He's my favourite songwriter."

Still Not Getting Any... was released on October 26, 2004, on Lava Records, which by then was wholly owned by Atlantic. It debuted at No. 3 on the Billboard 200 after 139,000 copies sold in the U.S. during its release week, and it would go on to sell more than a million copies in the U.S. in just over two months. It debuted at No. 2 in Canada and also spawned worldwide radio hits "Welcome to My Life," "Shut Up!," and "Untitled (How Could This Happen to Me)." From then on, Simple Plan's success was pretty much locked in. Their third and fourth albums—*Simple Plan* in 2008 and *Get Your Heart On!* in 2011—and accompanying singles charted worldwide, and they continued to tour and release music throughout the 2010s. In 2020, "I'm Just a Kid"—their first-ever single—had a renaissance on TikTok as part of a trend where users would re-create childhood photos. Nearly twenty years after its initial release, the single finally went platinum in the U.S.

Today, Simple Plan have sold more than ten million albums, toured around the world many times over, appeared in numerous films and TV shows, performed at the Olympics closing ceremony, and won over the Warped Tour crowd after a near-record eleven summers with the travelling festival. Amid all their accolades and put-downs—millions of adoring fans countered by a sizable cohort of haters—Simple Plan will likely always, in one way or another, be those road-warrior kids from Montreal who took their childhood friendship and shared love of punk rock and worked as hard as they could to share it with the world.

5

BILLY TALENT

There's a lot of history in Germany's Festhalle Frankfurt. Built in the first decade of the twentieth century, it had the largest dome in Europe when it was completed in 1909, and later survived bombings by Allied Forces in the Second World War. In the '70s, it began to host rock bands like Led Zeppelin, the Rolling Stones, and Kiss, and it has since been the site of many famous concerts by groups like Depeche Mode and Rush.

It's here that Billy Talent is playing to almost fourteen thousand fans in November 2022, more than six thousand kilometres from home. They're filming the performance—a high-energy, twenty-one-song set spanning their six albums across three decades—for a live album to be released several decades after some of the greatest legends in rock history did the same thing in that same room. They're doing it in Frankfurt, not just for the novelty or the history, but because Germans love Billy Talent more than anyone else. Really.

Yes, the band gets plenty of love back home in Canada—and in Austria, Switzerland, and Hungary, where their albums regularly chart in the top ten. And their shows draw massive crowds in many other countries. But by far, the biggest ones are here in Germany.

What's most astonishing about it—beyond the fact that four guys from deep in the suburbs of Toronto are Germany's most beloved musical import since David Hasselhoff—is that the band themselves had called it decades earlier. Singer Ben Kowalewicz was somewhat of a provocateur during the band's earliest days, before they were even known as Billy Talent. At shows in the band's hometown of Mississauga, Ontario, when his onstage banter was particularly combative, he'd often say, "We're huge in Germany!" as if to taunt the crowd to take them more seriously, or to write off any tepid reactions or less-than-stellar performances as mere flukes. It was a throwaway joke, like an American high schooler claiming to have a girlfriend in Canada, but it ended up being a prophecy.

A third of the way through the Festhalle show, thousands of fans clap along to the hi-hat as the band gets ready to play "Try Honesty." It's a song they wrote twenty years before, back home in their unassuming suburban neighbourhood. Just before guitarist Ian D'Sa begins to play the opening chords—a twangy guitar riff that's become instantly recognizable in many parts of the world—Kowalewicz steps up to the mic at centre stage for a brief introduction:

"Let's go back to the very, very beginning, shall we?"

* * *

STREETSVILLE IS A NEIGHBOURHOOD that lies on the Credit River in the northwestern part of Mississauga, a next-door neighbour to Toronto and the seventh-largest city in Canada. It's a place that largely preserved its small-town character during and after the amalgamation of Mississauga in 1974, leading to its nickname "the village in the city." The historical community of Streetsville is full of quaint Victorian-era buildings that today are home to post offices, churches, cafés, and Irish pubs, as well as beauty salons, Subway sandwich shops, and a jerk-chicken joint.

Meadowvale lies just to the west; it's the kind of picture-perfect, family-friendly suburbia that's often idealized (or satirized) in movies. It's filled with tree-lined streets, single-family dwellings, and Catholic elementary schools—that is, until it abruptly ends at a perfectly straight line between the community and cornfields, as if a city planner many decades ago looked at a map, drew a big square, and said, "Build."

Back in 1990, when Ben Kowalewicz, Ian D'Sa, Jonathan Gallant, and Aaron Solowoniuk were teenagers, the combined area of Streetsville and Meadowvale accounted for a population of about sixty-five thousand. Life was safe, quiet, and relatively small. As high-schoolers, there wasn't a whole lot for them to do—at least, not much that they were especially interested in.

The four teens went to Our Lady of Mount Carmel Secondary School, a brand-new Catholic high school that was built in the late '80s to serve the new subdivisions in

Meadowvale. Like all good Catholic schoolboys, they loved rock 'n' roll, particularly the really devout, pious stuff like Nirvana, Rage Against the Machine, Soundgarden, the Beastie Boys, the Ramones, Descendents, and Green Day. And they all wanted to play in a band.

A naturally outgoing teenager with boyish good looks, Ben Kowalewicz grew up in a Polish-English household in Montreal before his family moved to Meadowvale when he was in Grade 10. At a house party one night in 1990, he met a guy named Trevor Bowman. A popular kid at school, Bowman had played with a group called the Screaming Hungarians that had recently broken up, so he was starting a new band, To Each His Own. Kowalewicz lied and told Bowman he played drums. He joined Bowman and a few other guys—including Jonathan Gallant, a hulking bass player with a deep voice, strong jaw, and football player's build—and faked it as a drummer as best as he could. But after a couple of months, he showed up to practice and there was another guy sitting at the drum kit. It was Aaron Solowoniuk, whom Gallant had met at a Metallica concert in Toronto. A tall kid of Polish-Ukrainian descent whose stern face betrayed his soft-spoken demeanour, Solowoniuk was, unsurprisingly, a much better drummer than Kowalewicz. That evening, Kowalewicz learned he was out of the band.

Not long after, though, Kowalewicz got a second chance: To Each His Own needed a singer. Kowalewicz had never sung before, but that clearly wasn't going to stop him from trying. He brought over his Fender R.A.D. guitar amp and a microphone bought at RadioShack, and he started singing. Soon, To Each His Own was the coolest band at Mount Carmel.

Meanwhile, Ian D'Sa, who started playing guitar when he was thirteen, had formed a band called Dragon Flower with a couple of other Mount Carmel classmates. A smart, kind-faced kid with dark hair that he would later style into an imposing pompadour that added an extra six inches to his already generous height, D'Sa was born to Goan parents in the English town of Southall, a suburb of West London known as Little India. The D'Sa family moved to Canada when he was three years old, settling in Meadowvale, a similarly suburban setting with a high proportion of South Asian immigrants.

At a school talent show in 1992, Dragon Flower played covers of the Tragically Hip's "New Orleans Is Sinking," Soundgarden's "Outshined," and Led Zeppelin's "Immigrant Song." The set went over well with the Mount Carmel crowd, but they were immediately upstaged by To Each His Own, natural performers who got the entire gym riled up. "We were like, 'Yeah, we slayed that!' And then these guys went on after us, and the whole audience was like 'Woooo!'" D'Sa recalls. "We weren't really performers like them."

The two bands wanted to play more shows together. But in their corner of Mississauga in the early '90s, there weren't many opportunities. They would have to put on their own shows, with a little help from an unlikely source.

English teacher David Rogers, a music fan in his mid-thirties with some experience producing rock shows, had recognized the abundant musical talent at Mount Carmel, and diplomatically approached his boss with a proposal to throw a Christmas variety show in the school cafeteria called Jingle Bell Rock. Rogers would handle all the details: printing posters, selling tickets, renting equipment—arranging liability insurance, of course—and providing some pizza and drinks.[35] They would sell tickets for five dollars, with all of the proceeds going to charity. After some hesitation, the principal gave him the green light.

"To our knowledge, it was the first time a rock concert had happened in the area, because the area didn't exist before," Bowman says. "No one else was doing what we were doing."

On the day of the show in December 1992, the school's principal showed up to see a bunch of shaggy-haired students lugging huge guitar amps and drum kits onto the stage and some five hundred sweaty kids funnelling into the cafeteria ready to start a mosh pit.

"This isn't just a musical variety show, is it?" he asked.

"It, uh, kind of evolved into a rock show," Rogers replied.

The principal shrugged. "Eh, I'm good with that."

A few months after the first Jingle Bell Rock, Kowalewicz, Gallant, and Solowoniuk decided to move in a different direction with their music and start a new band.[36] They needed a guitar player, so they asked the best guitarist at Mount Carmel. Before long, they were rehearsing in the basement of D'Sa's family home. They started out playing covers of Rage Against the Machine, and then eventually began writing their own songs. They called themselves Pezz.[37]

---

35 Rogers actually spent $1,200 of his own money to make the show happen. Fortunately for him, they sold enough tickets that he was able to recoup those upfront costs and donate the rest.

36 Bowman was so excited about To Each His Own that he got a tattoo with the band's name. Six months later, the band broke up. He says he once won a contest for the worst tattoo because of it.

37 Pezz was initially called the Other One, but the name didn't stick for very long.

Gob's original lineup in their first promo photo in the spring of 1994.
Courtesy of Gob

Theo Goutzinakis and Tom Thacker of Gob playing at the Piccadilly Pub in Vancouver in late 1998. *Courtesy of Gob*

Gob getting friendly with the zombie cheerleaders during the music video shoot for "I Hear You Calling" in 2000. *Courtesy of Gob*

Sum 41 celebrating the release of *Half Hour of Power* with a private show at Toronto's notorious strip club Zanzibar Tavern on June 19, 2000. *Credit: David Leyes*

Sum 41 and staff from their Canadian label Aquarius Records—Lenny Levine (top left) and "Parkside" Mike Renaud (top centre)—partying at the *Half Hour of Power* album launch. *Credit: David Leyes*

Avril Lavigne showing her usual snark on stage at Beachfest in Sunnyside Park in Toronto on September 2, 2002. *Credit: David Leyes*

Avril Lavigne, her band, and her management team backstage at Beachfest, celebrating *Let Go*'s double platinum certification in Canada. *Credit: David Leyes*

Pierre Bouvier and Chuck Comeau getting ready for a "juice break" during a Roach rehearsal at Comeau's family home circa 1993. *Credit: Jean-Sebastien Boileau*

Simple Plan playing an early gig in February 2001. *Credit: Patrick Langlois*

Pezz (later known as Billy Talent) rehearsing in Ian D'Sa's basement in Meadowvale in 1996. *Credit: Ian D'Sa*

Pezz hanging out backstage at Lee's Palace in Toronto in 1999. *Credit: Ian D'Sa*

Ben Kowalewicz and Ian D'Sa of Billy Talent killing time at the airport on the way home from their German tour with Beatsteaks in 2005. *Credit: Bowman*

Silverstein playing one of their first shows at a house party in Oakville on February 23, 2001. *Credit: Gordon Douglas Ball*

Silverstein show off their van before taking off on their first tour in May 2002. *Courtesy of Silverstein*

George Pettit leaping into the crowd during an Alexisonfire show at the Opera House in Toronto on September 16, 2003. *Credit: David Waldman*

Alexisonfire on a boat in the Toronto harbour before playing the Edgefest festival at Molson Amphitheatre on July 1, 2005. *Credit: Dustin Rabin*

Dan Kanter and Fefe Dobson on tour in the United States in support of her debut album circa 2003. *Courtesy of Fefster Inc.*

Fefe Dobson doing her best Sid Vicious impression during the *Sunday Love* era, circa 2005–06. *Courtesy of Fefster Inc.*

Marianas Trench rocking out at the Virgin Festival in Vancouver on May 21, 2007. *Credit: Adrian O'Brien*

* * *

IT WAS CLEAR EARLY on that Pezz had something special. "I was really jealous of them," Bowman says. "I went to their second or third practice, and they were already playing with a sound that no one else was doing at the time."

By the time Pezz played the second edition of Jingle Bell Rock in 1993, four unpopular guys who would hang out in the corner at house parties had become Mount Carmel's must-see band. "Pezz blew the doors off of any band on any bill I ever saw," Rogers says. "They owned it. No one wanted to follow them." Their classmates wanted to see a rock band, and in Meadowvale, they were that rock band.

Following the success of Jingle Bell Rock, Pezz began putting on their own DIY rock shows in places like the local Masonic lodge or Kinsmen Club. These were modestly sized community halls used for relatively quiet meetings of fraternal societies; they had certainly never hosted a rock show before. D'Sa would borrow his mother's chequebook to put down a $150 deposit, and he and Bowman would rent a PA system for the gig. The guys would collect hundreds of milk crates from local corner stores and supermarkets,[38] and they'd steal plywood from the many construction sites in their neighbourhood. Then they'd stack the milk crates, cover them with the plywood, and secure it all together with duct tape—voilà, they had a stage. They'd charge a couple of bucks or a canned food item at the door and pray that nobody broke anything so D'Sa wouldn't lose his mom's deposit.

---

38 "My basement was just filled with milk crates," D'Sa says. "We'd be jamming, and it would smell like rotten milk."

For a while, that's what every Pezz show was—a DIY spectacle, operating purely out of necessity.

"There was literally nowhere for a band like us to play," D'Sa says.

"You'd create something, and then people came," Kowalewicz adds.

The first real venue to take a chance on Pezz was a billiards bar called Stardust in a rough part of town in Mississauga's south end. The owner would push a bunch of pool tables together to turn them into a makeshift stage where mostly metal bands would play. The shows would get rowdy, and it wasn't uncommon for the cops to be called in to break up fights in the parking lot. "It was madness," Bowman recalls. "They'd give us pitchers for five bucks, and it got messy." The owner would often call the band the next morning to tell them he had money for them from the ticket sales; they had completely forgotten about it, happy with another job well done.

By the summer of 1994, the members of Pezz had graduated from high school and were ready to start venturing out of Mississauga. They got booked by the Hamilton-based record label Sonic Unyon to play their weekend festival called the Sonic Picnic at the horse raceway in Orangeville, a town just northwest of Mississauga. With a bunch of trendy Canadian rock bands on the bill, including Treble Charger, hHead, and Trigger Happy, it was the biggest crowd they'd ever had. After their set, a guy came up to them and asked if he could buy their tape. Pezz didn't have a tape. That's when it occurred to them that they should probably start recording some of their music.

Gallant bought a four-track recorder and D'Sa engineered their first sessions with a bunch of cheap microphones—again from RadioShack—so they could record their first cassette. It was a lo-fi, live-off-the-floor production that sounded pretty rough. To their young ears, though, it was amazing. They called it *Demoluca*, because their friend Jason Deluca had shown up at the house where they were recording and banged on the basement window until they let him in. Consisting of four original songs, the demo showcased Pezz's quirky style and featured Kowalewicz mostly rapping over chunky guitar riffs and a hard-hitting rhythm section. Listening to it, you can tell how much they loved Rage Against the Machine, but there are also noticeable elements that draw from bands like the Red Hot Chili Peppers, Jane's Addiction, and the Police.

In January 1995, six months after making *Demoluca*, Pezz visited Toronto's Signal 2 Noise studio to record a proper demo with Dave Tedesco, an engineer who had worked on projects by Headstones and Rainbow Butt Monkeys (later renamed Finger Eleven). Pezz re-recorded two of the tracks from their first cassette and added two more. Then, a year later, they recorded four more tunes live off the floor. They called the collection *Dudebox*.

With their new demo tape in hand, Pezz got busy mailing *Dudebox* to all the record labels and managers they could find. Without exception, the packages were returned to them unopened. As time passed and the rejection letters piled up, Pezz came dangerously close to fizzling out.

THE FIRST TIME D'SA got the feeling that he could actually do something with music was when he was watching *Going Coastal*, the MuchMusic program hosted by Terry David

Mulligan that introduced him to independent Canadian rock bands like Halifax's the Hardship Post and Vancouver's Mystery Machine. "These are independent bands from this country and they're getting played on TV and radio," he remembers thinking. "If these bands are doing it, why aren't we? We're from Mississauga, not the big city. We can do it, too."

But that didn't look like it was going to happen for Pezz. By the latter half of the '90s, they were in their early twenties and couldn't continue to justify the lifestyle of their teenage years. There wasn't a career to be had playing shows to high school kids at a pool bar or in the basement of the Masonic lodge. They needed to get real jobs.

D'Sa studied film at Ontario College of Art & Design in Toronto and then classical animation at Sheridan College in Mississauga, and he found work on the children's TV shows *Angela Anaconda* and *Birdz*. Gallant went to Ryerson University (now known as Toronto Metropolitan University) to get a business degree. Solowoniuk held down a desk job for a bit and then started working on an assembly line at the DaimlerChrysler factory in nearby Brampton. Kowalewicz bounced between a few jobs, including as an assistant at the Toronto rock radio station 102.1 The Edge.

"We had some turbulent times," says Kowalewicz. "We were on life support."

Still, Pezz continued to play any gigs they could get. And finally, after many years trying to make it on the Toronto club scene, they managed to wedge themselves into a spot. Thanks to a recommendation from Jeff Rogers, manager of Winnipeg alt-rockers Crash Test Dummies and the owner of Handsome Boy Records, they landed a recurring gig at Elvis Mondays, a free band showcase that had been hosted by promoter William New at the legendary El Mocambo every week since the early '80s. They became the go-to backup band: New would call Pezz on a Monday afternoon if a band had bailed on the gig, and the guys would load up their gear and drive downtown to play later that night.

"We were trying to break into Toronto for so long," D'Sa says.

From there, they met other local bands and finally managed to get booked at other popular rock clubs like Ted's Wrecking Yard and the Horseshoe Tavern. They booked a room at a rehearsal studio in the city and started rehearsing three times a week. Things were going well, and it looked like Pezz might actually amount to something. It was time to record a proper album.

In retrospect, it was naive of Pezz to think they'd have much success by simply cold-pitching their rough-sounding demos to everyone in the Canadian music industry. But to them, it was a sign that they should re-evaluate their sound. So, the songs that would appear on their debut album were different. They were *weird*, but the right kind of weird. Kowalewicz started singing instead of rapping, and his distinctively piercing voice stood out immediately—there was nobody else who sounded anything like him. D'Sa stepped up to the mic to harmonize, and his guitar riffs became less derivative of their big-league rock influences and far more innovative—they were knotty, tricky little numbers that leapt between punk and reggae, and that sounded like they should be played by two guitarists instead of just one. In between all that, Gallant and Solowoniuk sat in the mix perfectly, giving the songs the right amount of punch without trying to distract from the musical oddities that Kowalewicz and D'Sa were bringing to the forefront.

The band linked up with producer Brad Nelson and engineer Daryl Smith to record twelve songs at Great Big Music and Chemical Sound in Toronto. They called the record *Watoosh!* and released it themselves on July 23, 1999. An experimental blend of quasi punk rock and outsider art, the album was probably an even tougher sell than their earlier work. But it sounded like nothing else, and that was something.

As Pezz continued to slog it out in the local clubs, *Watoosh!* became a cult favourite in the Toronto indie-rock scene—but that was about the extent of its popularity. It did manage to attract the attention of a punk band in Memphis, but not in a good way. The band was also called Pezz, and they had been using the name since 1989. D'Sa got an email from a lawyer informing him that the Americans held the rights internationally, and that the Canadians had to stop using it immediately. Just as Pezz were beginning to make a name for themselves, they had to ditch that name.

Kowalewicz was working at a record shop at the time, and a kid came in with a VHS bootleg of the film *Hard Core Logo* and told him to watch it. Based on Michael Turner's novel of the same name and shot as a mockumentary similar to *This Is Spinal Tap*, the 1996 film follows a washed-up punk band—comprising singer Joe Dick, guitarist Billy Tallent, bassist John Oxenberger, and drummer Pipefitter—as they reunite for a disastrous tour of Western Canada. The film stars Headstones vocalist Hugh Dillon as Joe Dick and actor Callum Keith Rennie as Billy Tallent, and it features cameos by punk icons Joey Ramone,

Art Bergmann, and Joey Shithead.[39] Kowalewicz loved it.

The next time he was with the band, Kowalewicz suggested they rename themselves after one of the characters from *Hard Core Logo.* They didn't want to risk making the same mistake twice, though, so they dropped a letter to try to avoid another cease-and-desist letter. Pezz was now Billy Talent.[40]

UNLIKE MOST OF THEIR contemporaries, who were hitting it big in their late teens or early twenties, the members of Billy Talent were in their mid-twenties when their band started gaining ground at the turn of the century, which greatly impacted their approach to songwriting. "There was something appealing to writing about the underside, or the dark side of things. At that time there was a lot of pop and party music going on, like Limp Bizkit and stuff like that. You have an opportunity to write about things that matter, so why would you not take it?" says D'Sa. "The whole point of writing lyrics is to make people think about something long after the song has ended."

With these harder-hitting lyrics in place, Kowalewicz continued to evolve his vocal approach. He dropped the rapping entirely and stuck to singing, with the occasional scream. Where Pezz had been an eclectic fusion of disparate sounds that could pivot to something completely different at any time, Billy Talent delivered structured blasts of punk and post-hardcore, distilling the aggression of bands like Refused,

---

39 There's also a cameo by Terry David Mulligan, the Gob-adoring MuchMusic television host much loved by D'Sa.

40 The only downside: to this day, Kowalewicz still runs into people who think his name is Billy Talent. "It was a blessing and a curse," he says. "It's insane how long we've been debunking that."

Fugazi, and At the Drive-In into something more accessible. "It was definitely a rebirth," says D'Sa. "We were all excited. It felt like there was a focus, finally."

Centred within those loud, frenzied songs were clean and catchy melodies, and not just from Kowalewicz. D'Sa had played piano as a kid before picking up the guitar and always stuck to rhythm until he joined Pezz. He played around with riffs and licks in the Pezz years, but it wasn't until Billy Talent that he started developing his own signature style—spidery guitar lines that took care of the rhythm and the lead at the same time.

"When we were playing a lot of drop-D music like Rage Against the Machine, I started figuring out that I can play chords with one finger and noodle some lead melodies on the side, and it checks off both boxes, so I think that's where it came from," says D'Sa.

"All the unique chords he comes up with are different types of piano voicings," Gallant adds. "He lets the bass sit on the root and plays all the extensions of the chord on top of that. It's super unique, and nobody else plays like that."

Kowalewicz remained tight-lipped about his band while they polished their act, even to his colleagues at 102.1 The Edge—the idea of using his job as a way to get his band's foot in the door just felt tacky. But one afternoon in June 2001, Billy Talent came up in a conversation with Jen Hirst, a co-worker's friend who had popped by the station. Hirst had graduated from a music management program in Toronto and was up for an A&R position at Warner Music Canada. She had seen Pezz play at Ted's Wrecking Yard a few years earlier and was impressed by Kowalewicz's stage presence but not exactly enamored of their music. The gig had been in the middle of the band's identity crisis, caught somewhere between rap-rock and their funky punk sound, and their repertoire was all over the place. Kowalewicz assured her that things were different now and invited her to see Billy Talent play their next show.

When she checked them out, Hirst instantly recognized that this wasn't the same band she had seen at Ted's. Billy Talent was much tighter and more interesting than Pezz had ever been. Hirst became obsessed. She wanted that job at Warner, and she wanted Billy Talent to be the first band she signed. She told the band, "You're what I'm going to pitch as soon as I get to the label, and I'm going to do everything I can to get you a record deal." Not long after, Hirst got the job at Warner, and she immediately got to work trying to sign Billy Talent.

"I really dug my heels in," she says. "It wasn't really an easy sell to a major label at the time."

The label finally relented and met with the band, but they weren't about to offer them a record deal. Not yet, anyway. The company offered them a small amount of money on a demo deal to show them some of their new songs. It was something, but not enough. Hirst got the feeling that the company wasn't eager to make any sort of real commitment to Billy Talent. So, she took matters into her own hands.

"When I started to notice that the deal wasn't going to move forward, I thought, well, my loyalty is to the band and not to the label. So, I'm going to help them out as much as I can," she says. "I started hooking them up with everybody I knew."

Hirst started with Chris Taylor, the entertainment lawyer who represented Sum 41, Nelly Furtado, and Avril Lavigne. Taylor immediately saw their potential. Then, Hirst set them up with producer Gavin Brown, who had been the drummer of Toronto-based post-hardcore band Phleg Camp in the '90s and had recently moved into producing heavier rock bands like Danko Jones and Three Days Grace. Brown was working with Michael McCarty at EMI Music Publishing Canada to find unsigned bands to develop, so he came by Billy Talent's rehearsal studio to find out what Hirst's excitement was all about.

Phleg Camp had been heavily influenced by post-hardcore acts like Fugazi and the Jesus Lizard and had worked with underground rock guru Steve Albini. When Brown heard the chaotic sounds of songs like "Try Honesty" and "This Is How It Goes" and saw Kowalewicz's commanding presence that reminded him of a young Iggy Pop, he knew exactly what Billy Talent needed to get where they wanted to go. As soon as he left their rehearsal space, he called McCarty: "Hey, let's move on this."

McCarty didn't take much persuading. He had been watching the recent spate of punk bands in the U.S. signing to major labels and selling hundreds of thousands of records, and he was particularly interested in the example set by At the Drive-In, the post-hardcore band from Texas that made their major-label debut with *Relationship in Command* in September 2000. When At the Drive-In broke up six months later, at the height of their popularity, McCarty saw an opportunity in the void they left behind.

"I was watching that scene," he says. "In my mind, I was looking for At the Drive-In but with better songs. Gavin came into my office and said, 'Check this out.' He put the recording on, and I said, 'Oh! That's At the Drive-In but with better songs!'"

Brown went back to Billy Talent's rehearsal space, this time with McCarty. Sure enough, McCarty was wowed. "They played like they were onstage at Maple Leaf Gardens," he says. "It was unbelievable. It was electrifying. There's no holding these guys back. They're over the top. Ben was repeatedly throwing himself against the door. It was just incredible."

Afterward, they went to a local tavern to talk business over burgers and beers.

"So, what's the story with Warner?" McCarty asked them.

"Well, Jen loves us, but she can't get her boss to pull the trigger."

"Okay, well, I want to sign you."

McCarty offered Billy Talent a publishing contract on the spot. "All of a sudden we went from a $2,000 demo deal to a $150,000 development deal," D'Sa says. The agreement was that they'd record some proper, quality demos—using EMI's money and studio space—and then use those demos to land a record deal.

It didn't take long for things to start moving. Warner had just gone through a regime change, and the new brass was more open to signing Billy Talent. But McCarty was hesitant. First, he wanted to make sure Hirst would still get credit for signing the band. Second, he didn't want a Canadian label to sign the band internationally, because he felt it would limit their reach. He had gone through the same thing a few years earlier with Sum 41 when they signed to the U.S. major Island Def Jam along with a Canada-exclusive deal with Aquarius Records. McCarty suggested partnering on a demo deal whereby Warner Music Canada and EMI would split the cost. They'd give Warner's American division first dibs on the record, but if they didn't

FURTHER LISTENING

FLASHLIGHT BROWN

Hometown: Guelph, Ontario
Years active: 1995–2007

In the late 1990s, Flashlight was a ska-punk trio from Guelph, Ontario, a college town an hour west of Toronto, who moved to the big city in hopes of being Canada's answer to Goldfinger. For their first few albums, things were pretty standard: they signed to Montreal label Stomp Records, toured the country, had a video on MuchMusic, and had to change their name to Flashlight Brown after a cease-and-desist from another band called Flashlight. But in the early 2000s, their fortunes started to change. In the wake of major-label deals by Sum 41 and Simple Plan, Flashlight Brown teamed up with Rob Cavallo—Green Day's go-to producer—and signed to Hollywood Records for their fourth album, *My Degeneration*, an upbeat blast of party-hardy punk rock. The partnership led to a set at Lollapalooza and an appearance on the soundtrack to *Rugrats Go Wild*, the big-screen team-up of popular American cartoons *Rugrats* and *The Wild Thornberrys*. But it wouldn't last. Weeks before Hollywood was to release their fifth album, *Blue*, Flashlight Brown abruptly left the label, citing "extreme differences of opinion." That was basically it—the band stopped playing gigs in 2007, except for a one-off in 2011 with Ian D'Sa from Billy Talent on guitar.

bite, they'd shop it around to the rest of the major labels.

That was the plan, anyway.

In early 2002, Billy Talent recorded six demos with Brown at EMI's in-house studio, and their songs sounded better than they'd ever heard. "It was the first time we sounded like a unique band," says D'Sa. "This was Billy Talent." But they'd barely gotten a chance to show anyone the new recordings before a couple of scouts from Los Angeles rolled into town and kicked off a full-blown bidding war.

WITH EMI AND WARNER on board, the hunt for the right American label partner for Billy Talent was on. McCarty had roped in Steve Hoffman, an artist manager based in Toronto whose company was best known for managing Rush, to attend a rehearsal and see if he wanted to start managing the band. It was already late in the evening, but Hoffman asked Billy Talent to stick around a little longer—he had an idea. A pair of A&R reps for Atlantic Records, Tom Storms and Kevin Williamson, were visiting from

Los Angeles, and Hoffman thought they'd be into the band. Hoffman invited them to the jam space.

"Hey, get out of bed and come see this band," Hoffman said over the phone.

"What the fuck are you talking about? I've got *Forensic Files* on," Storms said.

Throughout the '90s, the success of Nirvana, Pearl Jam, and Soundgarden, who had all been plucked from the Seattle grunge scene, had shown the bigwigs in the music industry that it was worth scouting unknown bands in overlooked markets. This was a strategy that Storms and Williamson could get behind. In Los Angeles, they had been in the race to sign several soon-to-be rock legends like Rage Against the Machine, Korn, Weezer, and the Wallflowers, but they'd missed out on all of them. If they were going to sign the next chart-climbing rock act, they needed to get there first.

"We were signing stuff out of fucking garages," Storms recalls.

Something told the Atlantic reps there could really be something here. So, at the stroke of midnight, Storms and Williamson arrived at Billy Talent's tiny rehearsal room in Toronto. As soon as the band started, it was obvious why this couldn't wait.

"They clicked on their amps and played a couple songs, and it was like, *fuck*," Storms says.

"When they hit their first note, it was the exact same feeling that I had when I saw Rage in a rehearsal room in the San Fernando Valley," says Williamson. "You'd almost fall back in your chair, that's how powerful it was. At the time, I was working with Jewel and Sugar Ray, so Billy Talent was a pleasant kick in the ass."

The next morning, Storms and Williamson called their bosses at the Atlantic office. They wanted to sign Billy Talent, and they wanted to do it right away.

"It wasn't, 'You've gotta see this,' or, 'This is something to keep an eye on,'" says Williamson. "It was, 'We've gotta close this. These guys are fucking amazing. I don't care what we have to do—this is a must-have band.'"

Atlantic had an edge. All they had to do was sign Billy Talent quickly, before other labels knew what they were missing. "By the time we got back to L.A., everybody had found out about it," says Storms. "The word had gotten out, and it was a frenzy."

Taylor, the band's lawyer, helped them parlay Atlantic's interest into a sweepstakes. For two months in the summer of 2002, Billy Talent was flown out to New York every weekend to be wined and dined by representatives from American major labels. In all, there were six U.S. record companies that wanted to sign them—plus Hirst and her team at Warner Music Canada still wanted the band.

"A decade of no one giving a shit and being told constantly that you're not going to make it," says Kowalewicz. "Next thing we know we're being flown to New York, staying in a nice hotel, going out for dinner, and somebody else is paying."

Now that the word had gotten around, things changed for them in Toronto, too. That summer, it was finally more than just Trevor Bowman and a few other friends at their shows; there were strangers lined up down the block to see Billy Talent.

When it came time to make a decision, Billy Talent and their backers landed on a deal they felt would make everyone happy. They signed a co-venture agreement with Atlantic Records and Warner Music Canada, whereby the American label would represent the band internationally, with Storms and Williamson as the band's A&R duo, and their Canadian counterpart would handle things domestically, with Hirst at their side.

"Atlantic has the rock background and they've been known to break cutting-edge rock bands," D'Sa told Jam! Music in 2003. "We're a little bit different. We're not your average rock band. And everyone from the guy working the door to the top of the company seemed really enthusiastic about the music and seemed really genuine."

"We're not the most accessible band," Kowalewicz adds now. "We're a very weird band. I have a very strange voice, Ian is a very unique songwriter and guitar player, and Jon and Aaron have their own odd ways of playing. When you glue it all together, it makes this weird Voltron-type thing. We needed somebody to see the beauty in that."

A year later, people around the world were going to.

"TRY HONESTY" WASN'T JUST Billy Talent's debut single—it was their mission statement. Kowalewicz's theatrical vocals exploded into piercing screams at climactic moments; D'Sa's guitar lines were melodic and memorable; the lyrics were both heartbroken and macabre; and Gallant and Solowoniuk delivered a sturdy, driving foundation. All these future trademarks of Billy Talent's sound were front and centre the moment they entered thousands of households by way of TV and radio in July 2003.

"We just took the energy and worked on the accuracy, trying to get that kind of post-punk feeling with modern radio accuracy," says Brown, who produced the track—and the rest of Billy Talent's self-titled major-label debut—at the Factory in Vancouver. "The other thing was a belief to put art on the radio. Can we capture the At the Drive-In vibe but put it on the radio?"

They undeniably did. "Try Honesty" immediately obliterated any notion of how mainstream heavy music could get. It spent eleven weeks on *Billboard's* Alternative Airplay chart in the U.S., peaking at No. 24, with additional placements in the U.K. At home in Canada, it was an absolute smash.[41] In a pre–"Try Honesty" world, "nobody was getting that heavy on the radio," says George Stroumboulopoulos, who racked up plays for the song on 102.1 The Edge in Toronto. Its music video, featuring the band playing in an abandoned psychiatric hospital, was a fixture on MuchMusic for months, eventually taking the top spot in the *MuchMusic Countdown*, the channel's weekly roundup.

Though "Try Honesty" was very much in the vein of the rest of the album in a way that a single *Watoosh!* track couldn't have been, given the band's then-frenetic approach, *Billy Talent* was still a varied look at making sense of paranoia and frustration by way of controlled chaos, offering enough pop tautness to make the big, screaming moments really land without needing to overdo it. *Billy Talent* appealed to the kids who were perhaps intimidated by hardcore punk, but also had just enough of the genre's hallmarks to entice fans of those sounds. If the term

41 Canadian rock radio didn't publish charts between November 2000 and April 2004, but if they had, "Try Honesty" and follow-up single "The Ex" would have almost certainly appeared. All twenty-six Billy Talent singles since then have charted, including seven No. 1 songs.

"pop-hardcore" rolled off the tongue half as well as "pop-punk," perhaps that's how people would have referred to Billy Talent's sound.

While tracks "Try Honesty" and "The Ex" were lyrically straightforward songs about betrayals and breakups, the album also featured nuanced, thoughtful takes on domestic terrorism ("River Below"), sex work ("Standing in the Rain"), suicide ("Nothing to Lose"), and a friend's struggles with multiple sclerosis ("This Is How It Goes"). The band backed up their tunes with visceral, artfully graphic videos directed by Sean Michael Turrell that embodied their subject matter. The video and radio campaign for "Nothing to Lose," an unsparing song inspired by the suicide of an Ontario teenager in 2002, doubled as a fundraising effort for Kids Help Phone, a Canadian charity that operated a youth crisis hotline, while the clip for "River Below" depicted an ex-military man building and detonating a bomb while the band played in a garage across the street.

Billy Talent was a massive hit. In Canada, it sold nearly eight thousand copies in its first week alone, hitting fifty thousand by November 2003 and one hundred thousand the following March. The band also became a fixture at Canadian music award ceremonies as both performer and nominee. They received three nominations at the 2004 Juno Awards, winning New Group of the Year; six nominations at the 2004 MuchMusic Video Awards for "Try Honesty," winning MuchLOUD Best Rock Video; and nine nominations at the 2005 MuchMusic Video Awards—five for "River Below" and four for "Nothing to Lose"—taking home Best Video overall and MuchLOUD Best

Rock Video for "River Below."[42] They toured all over Canada, the U.S., and the U.K. with Sum 41, Buzzcocks, Alexisonfire, MxPx, Simple Plan, and the Darkness, and performed lengthy stints on Lollapalooza 2003 and Warped Tour 2004.

"It was so unbelievably unobtainable and so silly that I didn't, at the time, let it register with me," says Kowalewicz. "But the thing I remember most is how proud my family was of me, and our friends were of us."

By the time the band was done promoting *Billy Talent*, they had firmly established themselves in their home country as a distinct force with a robust slew of successes.

In the U.S., it was a different story. When "Try Honesty" first launched, it looked like Billy Talent was poised to be as big of a hit in America as they were about to become in Canada. Alternative rock and college radio stations were beginning to pick it up, as was MTV2. Storms and Williamson were confident that the momentum was just beginning, and that everyone was going to buy into the hype, as the staff at Atlantic had. "There was such a huge buzz on the record in the company, and people loved it. The poster of the cover was in everybody's office," Storms recalls. "The first week of radio was really good, we got a lot of big stations. We were close to getting KROQ, which was the ultimate add in L.A. at the time, and Seattle and a bunch of other markets."

But 2003 was a difficult year for the music industry. Over the preceding five years, peer-to-peer file-sharing software had heralded the rise of music piracy, making it significantly easier

---

42 There was no award for Best Red Carpet Vehicle at the MuchMusic Video Awards, but if there had been, Billy Talent surely would have won—the band arrived at the awards ceremony in 2005 riding a Second World War–era Sherman tank.

for listeners to download music for free. This giant hole in the jumbo jet that is the modern music industry sucked out millions of dollars of profits, and that April, Apple launched iTunes in an attempt to plug it. Right as Billy Talent was starting to release their music, the turbulence was hitting Atlantic Records hard. Near the end of the year, a group of investors purchased Warner Music Group for USD$2.6 billion, prompting several rounds of layoffs and ultimately merging Atlantic with fellow Warner-owned label Elektra.

"It was a really tough time," says Storms. "We went through an organizational and ownership change at Warner Music, and it was just bad timing. Shit happens, but it was really unfortunate."

Williamson had moved to another Warner label, Maverick Records, and Storms and the other remaining Atlantic staff were overworked and dealing with critically low morale. Billy Talent got lost in the shuffle, and the album fared modestly. It peaked at No. 194 on the Billboard 200 a few weeks after release, and it also landed at No. 11 on the Heatseekers Albums chart of artists who had yet to crack the top 100 of the Billboard 200.

"The label put out 'Try Honesty' and then more or less dropped us, so there was nothing to help promote us," says Kowalewicz. "And so the U.S. just never really took to us."

But there was a place outside of Canada where fans would flock to Billy Talent in droves—Germany, the very place Kowalewicz had claimed would make him famous a decade earlier.

* * *

IT'S IMPOSSIBLE TO SAY exactly why Germans take so strongly to Billy Talent. Sure, Germany has a particular skew toward hard rock and heavy metal, with a higher ceiling than most countries for bands who scream atop demonic riffs, but Billy Talent sounds nothing like Rammstein and the *Neue Deutsche Härte* ("new German hardness") subgenre they spawned, nor would they be booked for Wacken Open Air, one of the world's largest heavy metal festivals. And while Billy Talent put in the work in their early major-label years, grinding it out across Germany in two hundred- and three-hundred-capacity venues, they grinded it out in the U.S., too. In truth, the German love affair with Billy Talent was happening before the band even stepped foot in the country.

It started at the headquarters of Warner's Central European division in Hamburg, in the office of Ole Kirchhoff, head of the rock department at the Warner subsidiary East West Records. Kirchhoff was fielding a pitch by Mark Botting of Scott Welch Management for Audiovent, a recent Atlantic Records signee led by three guys whose brothers were in Incubus. At the end of the meeting, Botting handed Kirchhoff a demo CD featuring a half-dozen early mixes of Billy Talent's recordings with Gavin Brown.

Kirchhoff played the CD as soon as Botting left his office. He loved what he heard, which he describes now as a mixture of the punk sensibilities of bands like Black Flag and Refused with guitar riffs that reminded him of AC/DC. Within hours, he had played the demos for his colleague Niels Andersen and for Bernie Schick, from the tour promoter FKP Scorpio, who just happened to be Kirchhoff's next meeting that day.

"The three of us agreed instantly—which we never do—that we should give it another chance," Kirchhoff recalls. "It wasn't even the finished recordings, it was just some demos, but we all agreed that we should proceed."

Warner had just begun the endless cycle of mid-2000s major-label restructuring, and the labels were increasingly beholden to global priorities. Billy Talent—a new band from Canada whose snarling vocals did not foretell much mainstream success—were very much not a global priority. "We three said, 'Fuck the priority lists! This is what we want to do,'" says Kirchhoff. Knowing that the higher-ups at Warner's European branch and FKP Scorpio weren't planning to support Billy Talent, the trio hatched a plot: they each told their bosses that the other company was interested. Kirchhoff pitched Billy Talent to his boss's boss, who approved, in part because Kirchhoff had promised that FKP Scorpio had confirmed a German tour. Meanwhile, Schick told his employer that Warner would be releasing Billy Talent's album in Europe, which allowed him to book the tour that Kirchoff had claimed to his bosses was already a done deal. To keep costs at a minimum, Schick put in some money privately and Andersen offered to drive the tour van.

Schick worked on the German leg of what became Billy Talent's first European tour, which also took them to festivals in England, the Netherlands, and Belgium just weeks before *Billy Talent*'s release in September 2003. He booked the band to start out at the Terremoto Festival—the intended successor to German alt-rock institution Bizarre Festival that ended up being a one-and-done—and then continue on with their new German allies for a series of shows at small clubs across the country for the annual VISIONS Party Tour, run by the monthly music magazine *VISIONS*, which came with its own built-in audience.

The Terremoto Festival took place at the Weeze Airport, a former air force base in Germany's Lower Rhine region, with Billy Talent in an opening slot on the festival's third stage. Schick recalls a crowd of about fifty people gathering in the rain to watch Billy Talent perform, ballooning to five hundred by the end of the set. "People could hear the sound, and said, 'I need to go, I need to listen,' and that's exactly what happened."

After their set, Billy Talent went backstage to load up their Sprinter van when they noticed a group of intimidating-looking men with long hair and leather jackets beelining toward them. The band looked at each other with fear in their eyes, thinking they were about to get mugged. The men were, of course, Kirchhoff, Schick, and Andersen, who exploded into smiles the moment they met the Canadian band.[43]

"They were losing it," says Miska Csepreghi, Billy Talent's high school friend who accompanied them on tour as their videographer and merch vendor. "They embraced *me*. And I'm like, 'I just shoot the camera! I sell merch! I'm nobody!' They were losing their minds."

The trio were Billy Talent's first German superfans, but they would not be the last.

The VISIONS Party Tour gave Billy Talent an exhilarating introduction to German audiences. Even in smaller cities like Dortmund, the crowds were teeming with energy from start to finish, with fountains of sweat pouring out of everyone in the venues. "It was so hot that putting another body up on stage would have been too much," says Csepreghi, who was often

43 To commemorate that first encounter, the band and their German team got matching tattoos of an umbrella with the text "DE03"—"DE" for "Deutschland" and "03" for the year.

relegated to filming from the crowd instead. "The guys were drenched from head to toe. It was like they had all had a bath." From the time the band arrived at the venue until long after their sets ended, Billy Talent were swarmed by dozens of fans eager to get their autographs and pay them compliments. At that point, they had only released one single and hadn't even performed in Canada since they released it. Before they had any major accolades back home, they already had swarms of new fans in Germany.

"It was at that moment that I realized I would love to see Billy Talent play these shows for the rest of their lives, because of the amount of energy, the amount of sweat, the amount of excitement that was in the crowd, and it was literally from day one," says Csepreghi. "They were blown away. They all got off stage and they're like, 'What was that? Where was that coming from?' I've respected the German music scene ever since that moment because it proved that they love music, and they will defend it until the day they die."

Billy Talent returned to Germany for a few dates in November 2003, tacked on to the end of a late-fall U.K. tour, but the catalyst for their longstanding success in the country occurred the third time they played there, opening for German alt-rock band Beatsteaks at the end of March 2004. Beatsteaks had just released their fourth album, *Smack Smash*, buoyed by the lead single, "Hand in Hand," their first radio hit. *Smack Smash* would peak at No. 11 on Germany's Offizielle Top 100 albums chart, and Beatsteaks would go on to win *VISIONS* Magazine's Album of the Year and the MTV Europe Music Award for Best German Act.

Beatsteaks were at the top of their game, and with their

radio success came a massive increase in fans. Schick was confident those fans would also dig Billy Talent. Musically, Beatsteaks were more in line with brawny, soccer-chant-friendly rock contemporaries like Franz Ferdinand and the White Stripes than Billy Talent's angsty, cerebral punk, but what the tourmates-to-be had in common was riff-laden tunes and singers who weren't afraid to scream a little bit if it served their arena-rock ambitions.

Initially, Billy Talent wasn't going to do the tour. "We were tired and wanted to start working on the next album," says Gallant. But Schick insisted they do the shows, pitching in his own money and offering to manage the tour himself. When they got out on the road, Schick was proven right: Beatsteaks fans loved Billy Talent.

"That was the tipping point in Germany," says Gallant. "When our next record came out, we had every one of their fans buying the record. That was a huge win."

As Billy Talent loaded out of Die Röhre, a five-hundred-capacity venue in Stuttgart, Bowman—who was handling videography and the merch table for that tour—said goodbye to the staff.

"See you guys on the next tour!" he said.

"We are never going to see you again," the venue owner replied. "The band is too big."[44]

Over the next couple of years, Billy Talent would come to learn how true that was. And despite their struggles with their American label—and a deeper, more existential source of adversity still to come—they were going to rise above.

---

44 Case in point: in 2005, German magazine *Rock Hard* ranked *Billy Talent* No. 453 in their book *The 500 Greatest Rock & Metal Albums of All Time.*

* * *

IN 2005 AND 2006, Billy Talent returned to Vancouver with Brown to record *Billy Talent II*, a more calculated and dynamic body of work that found them settling into the sound they explored on *Billy Talent*. As the band put the finishing touches on the album with mixing engineer Chris Lord-Alge in California during March 2006, Solowoniuk—the stoic drummer anchoring his chaotic bandmates on and off the stage—wrote a letter to the band's fans. For years, he had been keeping quiet while his bandmates spoke in vague terms about Kowalewicz's friend with multiple sclerosis, whose battle with the nerve disorder had inspired the song "This Is How It Goes." Finally, Solowoniuk was ready to admit the truth: *he* was the friend who had been battling the condition for close to a decade.

"It's been a crazy journey since then, being in this band and this song being written about 'our friend' who was struggling with MS, and then us touring that whole first album and being asked that question in interviews and us talking about 'our friend' and how 'he's doing okay,'" says Solowoniuk. "And then, when *Billy Talent II* came out, I just felt it was time to start talking about it more, and that led to so many beautiful, amazing things happening in my life, and being able to help many other younger people dealing with MS as well."

When Solowoniuk was twenty-three, right after he started working at the DaimlerChrysler assembly line and while Pezz were finally getting ready to record *Watoosh!*, he started experiencing a painful buzzing in his legs. After a year of inconclusive MRIs, a sudden bout of eye pain confirmed the suspicions of Solowoniuk's neurologist: the drummer had multiple sclerosis, a chronic autoimmune disease affecting the brain, spinal cord, and optic nerves. Solowoniuk told his bandmates the next day in D'Sa's bedroom and then took some time off to process the news. His doctors encouraged him to leave the band and quit playing the drums to avoid aggravating his illness, but Solowoniuk refused. Treatment—an indefinite series of three needles each week—was successful, and he was able to rejoin the band in time to record *Watoosh!* At times, the only trace of Solowoniuk's condition was that the band toured with a mini-fridge filled with medication.

"Aaron plays the drums for a reason: he likes to be in the back," says Gallant. "I think that was probably half of the reason he didn't want to talk about that." But with the band's profile growing larger, and with increased prevalence of MS diagnoses in children, Solowoniuk wanted to use his newfound platform to raise awareness. In his blog post, he wrote,

> I guess the reason I'm telling you this is because I didn't let something like MS get in the way of me becoming who I was suppose[d] to become. I suppose the reason I kept it a secret for so long is because I thought it could get in the way or even help me achieve some of my goals out of pity. That's the last thing I wanted. Please share this story with anyone you think it would help. There are a lot of people young and old that are fighting some sort of disease and thinking that they can't win. You really can win if you believe in yourself.

In December 2006, Billy Talent hosted the first F.U.MS benefit show at the Opera House in Toronto, with all proceeds going to the Multiple Sclerosis Society of Canada; the next year, Solowoniuk started a scholarship program for Canadian youth whose families have been affected by MS, yielding more F.U.MS fundraiser concerts and establishing a German branch of F.U.MS. "What he's done and managed to accomplish when everything was telling him not to, and what he did is just really fucking remarkable," says Kowalewicz.

As intense and dark as the band's music can be, charity and community awareness has been a part of their mission since their first show, Jingle Bell Rock in their high school cafeteria. "We played shows for Anti-Racist Action back in the '90s; we've tried to help out whenever we can," says D'Sa. "The amount of charities that we're aligned with and that we try to raise awareness or money or whatever it is for, it just feels good," adds Kowalewicz.

FURTHER LISTENING

ILLSCARLETT

Hometown: Mississauga, Ontario
Years active: 2001–present

Three years into a career of Sublime worship, illScarlett lived the stuff of legends: they set up a generator in the parking lot of the Barrie, Ontario, stop of the 2004 Warped Tour and played to the fans in line. Festival founder Kevin Lyman invited them to play the post-show barbeque for the bands that night and offered them a proper spot on the tour the next summer. By 2007, illScarlett had signed to Sony BMG Music Canada for their album *All Day with It* and had a pair of minor radio hits, the reggae-rocking "Life of a Soldier" and ska-punk smash "Nothing Special." They took it slow after releasing their self-titled album in 2014, barring an anniversary tour for *All Day with It* in 2019, but in 2023 they released their first new recording in nearly a decade: a cover of Elton John's "I'm Still Standing."

BY THE TIME THE band was prepared to release *Billy Talent II*, the Atlantic Records that had signed them a few years earlier was long gone, and the band had given up hope of breaking through in the U.S. "The A&R at Atlantic said she didn't hear any Green Day singles. That was her criticism of the album," recalls Gallant.

In Germany, the reaction was the complete opposite. "When we heard the second album, we knew it—I said to them, 'This one is going to go to No. 1, and if it goes to No. 1, we'll all get a tattoo,'" says Kirchhoff. "I lost. We all got a tattoo. Shit!"

Between the success of lead single "Devil in a Midnight Mass" on German radio and another triumphant run of shows in Germany weeks before the album launch—this time headlining eight-hundred- to one-thousand-capacity venues—*Billy Talent II* was destined for success. Though the band would fly to Toronto to launch the album properly with a live *Intimate and Interactive* session on MuchMusic, their now-solidified German fan base purchased the album in droves, launching it to No. 1 on the album charts and selling more than one hundred thousand copies before the end of the year.[45] The record also hit No. 1 in Canada and charted in several other countries, including No. 4 in Austria, No. 46 in the U.K., and No. 134 in the U.S. (beating their previous performance on the Billboard 200 despite their struggles in the American market).

Billy Talent II was everything you'd want a second album to be. It proved that nothing about its predecessor was a fluke, with more socially conscious lyrics—this time tackling topics like the opioid crisis ("Fallen Leaves") and the Iraq War ("Worker Bees")—and also with dialled-down aggression on tracks like "Surrender" and "The Navy Song," exposing new sides to the band while also increasing the impact of heavier moments. Its singles are among the most enduring in the band's back catalogue: "Devil in a Midnight Mass" is a scorching indictment

---

45 *Billy Talent II* would remain on the German albums chart for sixty-seven consecutive weeks, by which time the album had sold two hundred thousand copies and contributed to a sales bump for the first album, *Billy Talent*.

of sexual abuse in the Catholic Church that opens the album with a signature D'Sa guitar riff so distorted it sounds like a stun gun, while "Red Flag" is a rousing call to arms for the next generation to overthrow existing regimes and enact widespread, meaningful change.

The success of *Billy Talent II* proved that the band's formula had staying power. From there, they continued to build their stronghold not just in Canada but in several international markets. Billy Talent went on to release four more albums that consistently climbed the charts in Germany, Switzerland, Austria, Belgium, Finland, Australia, Ireland, and the U.K., including No. 1 records in four of those countries. Solowoniuk remained the band's drummer until 2016 when he experienced a symptom flareup, but he has continued to accompany the band on tours whenever possible. The band has sold more than four million albums globally and continues to play to massive crowds in Canada, in Europe, and around the world.

When Billy Talent exploded out of Mississauga in the early 2000s, they showed that with enough perseverance, an unusual group of punk kids who had been rejected and ignored in their own

FURTHER LISTENING

CANCER BATS

Hometown: Toronto, Ontario
Years active: 2004–present

Not long after forming in Toronto's underground, Cancer Bats signed with Alexisonfire's label Distort and released their debut album, *Birthing the Giant*, in 2006. With a sound that was roughly equal parts hardcore punk, heavy metal, and blues rock, they became a fixture of the hardcore touring circuit of the day and helped establish a subgenre that would come to be called "southern hardcore" as it gained popularity in the latter half of the decade. The Bats' second album, 2008's *Hail Destroyer*, featured guest spots by members of Rise Against, Billy Talent, and Alexisonfire and earned major accolades, particularly among a growing audience in the United Kingdom. Still going strong, Cancer Bats have released seven full-length albums—three of which charted in the U.K.—and earned five Juno nominations, remaining stalwarts of the heavy music scene in Canada and well beyond.

backyard could make the jump to international acclaim. They showed that a Canadian band playing a weird type of rock music could find an audience around the world, that a band with as many haters as Billy Talent could convert millions of people into fans, that an angsty band who sneered and screamed at the top of their lungs could become a fixture of cable TV and mainstream rock radio. Looking back now—and even then—it seems completely implausible that any of this happened.

And yet elsewhere in Southern Ontario, it was going to happen again.

6

SILVERSTEIN

Shane Told has just been offered his first recording contract, and it's a big one.

Earlier that year in 2002, scouts from Atlantic Records had come from Los Angeles to see his band, the Livid, rehearse at their guitarist Chris Schembri's house in Mississauga, and after financing some demos, they've decided that the Livid is worth a five-album commitment. The deal will come with a cash advance of $250,000, plus extra for recording, video, tour support, and equipment. Altogether, it's a major-label contract worth almost a million dollars. Told is just twenty-one years old.

The Livid formed five years earlier in 1997. They're a hard-rock band that fits into the popular post-grunge sound of the era, with thick, muscular guitars and brawny vocals, but also with a sensitive side that can belt out the occasional acoustic ballad. By now, major labels have moved on from finding the next Nirvana and are instead on the hunt for the next Nickelback or the next Creed. If not that, they'll happily settle for another Staind, Default, Puddle of Mudd, or Incubus. The Livid fits the profile.

But as Told looks at the offer from Atlantic, he feels indifferent. He only joined the band recently because Schembri is his best friend and they needed a bassist. The truth is, though, this just isn't really his thing. He spent his teenage years singing and playing guitar in a fast-paced punk-rock band called Jerk Circus, which modelled itself after the popular SoCal acts of the '90s. Jerk Circus gained a bit of underground notoriety in the local punk scene, but by now they've mostly fizzled out. In its place, Told has turned his attention toward his new project, a band inspired by '90s emo and metal acts.

Told is into underground punk music, and the Livid is playing mainstream radio rock. This financially lucrative, life-changing recording contract offered by Atlantic Records is a piece of paper that he doesn't really want to sign. Fortunately for him, Told doesn't have to be the bad guy. Soon, the Livid's singer will quit the band to continue at medical school, and Atlantic will pull their offer.[46] With the Livid's prospects out the window, Told no longer faces a dilemma. He'll see things through with this new band: Silverstein.

46 Meanwhile, Atlantic would move on to another band from Mississauga. On the same day the label's A&R reps were in the area to meet with the Livid, they scouted Billy Talent.

BY THE LATE '90S, an unofficial rivalry had formed between young people in Toronto and young people in "the 905," a collection of smaller suburban cities west of Toronto and along the northwestern shore of Lake Ontario.[47] At the time of the 1996 census, Brampton, Mississauga, Oakville, Burlington, and Hamilton combined to make a population of approximately 1.4 million, and their numbers were rapidly growing every year. In most cases, you wouldn't need to drive more than thirty minutes to get from one city to another. Because of this, a music scene had formed that was bigger than the sum of its parts. There were Brampton bands, Mississauga bands, Oakville bands, Burlington bands, and Hamilton bands, but they all played together and, in some cases, shared members. Toronto had its own music scene, and the 905 had theirs. In fact, one of Oakville's most notable punk bands in the late-'90s even titled their first and only album *Nevermind the Suburbs*.

That band was Jerk Circus, the skate-punk band formed in 1994 by middle-schooler Shane Told and his classmates Joe Rozsa, Brian Robinson, and Andy Lewis. The four bandmates initially bonded over their shared love of Black Sabbath, but soon started getting into punk-rock bands like Green Day and the Offspring. When Lewis, the drummer, acquired a copy of NOFX's *Punk in Drublic* on CD in 1994, they became obsessed with fast songs with catchy melodies, and started listening to similar punk bands like Strung Out, Lagwagon, and Rancid.

As Jerk Circus began to take form, the guys would sign out the bass guitar from their school's music room every day, because Robinson didn't have one of his own—in fact, he

---

47 The region got its nickname from its area code.

had never played before—and Told stepped up as the band's lead singer, even though he got off to a rough start. The band performed at a Grade 8 talent show, and later that year, Told's classmates peppered his yearbook with comments like "Too bad you can't sing."

"I guess I wasn't very good," he concedes. "It was an uphill battle for me."

Throughout their high school years, Jerk Circus evolved into a successful local band: Told found his voice, Robinson became one of the most impressive bassists in the region, and the band gained a sizable following of young punks in the 905 scene. On the last day of high school in 1999, Told ran into his friend Ray Tombran at a graduation party.

"You're not going to university, are you?" Tombran asked him. "You know you're just going to end up playing music."

But just as they were establishing themselves, the members of Jerk Circus were getting pulled in other directions. They were talented musicians, and others in their local scene had taken notice: Robinson and Lewis were recruited by a group of guys a few years older than them—including Tombran—to form a new band called the Fullblast. The local punk scene loved the Fullblast right away, and the band started getting way more gigs than Jerk Circus ever had. That left Told and the other remaining members in the dust.

"I was bummed out," Told says. "This was something I had been working on since I was twelve years old with these guys. But I decided, 'Well, maybe I can do something else.'" So, he set about starting a new band. "The Fullblast sounded basically the same as Jerk Circus," he says. "I wanted to start something completely different."

By 2000, Told's tastes had begun to shift away from the SoCal style of skate punk that he felt was getting a little old and maybe even a little too mainstream. Told had grown tired of seeing Blink-182 T-shirts on high school classmates who weren't otherwise into punk rock. Instead, he'd turned his attention to another underground movement of bands like Knapsack and the Get Up Kids that were playing a style of punk rock that was more introverted, more angsty, more emotional. Some people were calling it "emo."

In the beginning, emo meant something different from what it does today. When the style first emerged out of the hardcore punk scene in Washington, D.C., by pioneering acts like Rites of Spring and Embrace, it represented a version of hardcore that scaled back the aggression to introduce more melodic, sombre instrumentation and emotional, introspective lyrics—hence the name "emotional hardcore," then shortened to "emocore," then shortened again simply to "emo." As wistful English post-punk acts like the Smiths and the Cure were taking a firm hold of the alternative rock landscape throughout the late '80s, emo was making its way around local punk scenes in America. It was melodramatic music with themes of heartbreak, nostalgia, and general despair, but it was also very much still hardcore punk, and that's what the bands themselves continued to call it.[48]

By the '90s, though, a new wave of emo bands began incorporating softer, more melodic elements of indie rock and pop-punk into their sound, transforming the subgenre into a

---

48 The term "emo" and its derivatives were reviled by the artists themselves. Ian MacKaye of Embrace (as well as Minor Threat and later Fugazi) referred to the "emocore" label as "the stupidest fucking thing I've ever heard in my entire life."

more popular movement that stood apart from the hardcore punk underground. Bands like Jawbreaker and Jimmy Eat World signed to major labels, while other bands had significant success on indie labels, like Lifetime, the Promise Ring, and the Get Up Kids. Still, by the end of the '90s, emo remained largely an underground phenomenon. Much larger, sure, but underground nonetheless. In just a few years, though, that was about to change.

JOSH BRADFORD HAD BEEN playing guitar in a ska-punk band called Questionable Sushi that found moderate success in their local scene in Burlington, a city roughly the same size as nearby Oakville. On the side, he and his classmate Richard McWalter, also a guitarist, had been working on some new material that was just what Told had in mind. He met Bradford and McWalter on the 905 Board, a popular message board for the region's music scene, and joined them in early 2000, taking on lead vocals and bass guitar. They just needed a good drummer. Told logged on to the 905 Board again and saw a post from a user called xPaulx: "Emo drummer available." xPaulx was seventeen-year-old Paul Koehler, who was younger than Told, Bradford, and McWalter, but already playing at their level. The four of them wrote new material in Bradford's parents' basement in Burlington, working on a sound that reflected their shared love of this new underground movement.

At the band's first few practices, they worked on a handful of new songs that didn't have any lyrics yet. To improvise, Told would randomly pick up books and magazines that were lying around the house and sing their words into the mic. One day, he read from *Where the Sidewalk Ends*, a poetry collection by Shel Silverstein, the renowned children's author who died less than a year earlier in May 1999. After practice, the four bandmates talked about how they had all read that book when they were younger, connecting with the clever poetry, quirky illustrations, and theme of rebellion. They didn't discuss the book again until a few weeks later when their first show was fast approaching and they still didn't have a name for their band. Told noticed the book lying on the floor. "Silverstein," he said.

IN AUGUST 2000, SILVERSTEIN released their first set of music, a six-song EP called *Summer's Stellar Gaze.* The songs were clearly indebted to the '90s wave of emo, complete with upbeat punk rhythms, arpeggiated guitars, and teary-eyed vocals. The band also added a violinist to the recording sessions to give the tunes an extra layer of sentimentality—an artful bit of additional instrumentation that stood out amidst a subgenre of rock music that consisted almost entirely of guitar, bass, and drums. With their first EP, Silverstein was doing what a lot of other bands had already been doing, but they were doing it quite well.

The band's lineup continued to solidify. In December, they added bassist Billy Hamilton, a fan they found on the 905 Board, which freed up Told to focus solely on his singing, giving him more vocal control and improving his stage presence. McWalter had been studying engineering out west in Victoria, British Columbia, and by the end of his first year in the spring of 2001, he had decided to stay. McWalter was replaced by Told's childhood friend Neil Boshart, who had been playing in the Oakville metal band Maharahj.[49] A year later, in April 2002, Silverstein released a second EP called *When the Shadows Beam*. Boshart's history as a metalhead showed in the band's songwriting, as Silverstein had begun to develop a darker, harder-edged sound. And now that the band was playing with more heavy, high-gain metal riffing, Told started not only to sing but scream over the louder, more aggressive parts, particularly on the standout track "Bleeds No More."

From there, Silverstein started looking for a record label to release their debut album. They made press kits using two different demo discs: "light" and "heavy." They loaded up the "light" demo with two or three softer songs that landed more on the pop-punk side and sent that demo to labels like the California-based independent imprint Drive-Thru Records, which at that point had released albums by New Found Glory and Dashboard Confessional. Meanwhile, the "heavy" demo had a couple of their more aggressive songs with screamed vocals; these they sent to labels like the Chicago-based Victory Records, known for its roster of hardcore bands including Earth Crisis, Snapcase, and Integrity.

By the early 2000s, Victory Records was arguably the single biggest and most influential operation in the American hardcore scene. To Silverstein, Victory felt like a long shot. Then again, Victory had already signed one band from Burlington. Why not another?

49 Maharahj formed in 1997 and released an EP and two albums on Now or Never Records, the New Jersey–based independent label best known for launching the Dillinger Escape Plan.

GRADE DIDN'T BECOME ONE of the biggest hardcore bands in the world, but they influenced many that did. Formed in Burlington, Ontario, in 1994, the band released its first two records on small American indie labels and began to earn acclaim among the hardcore scene as they pioneered a sound that some would call "melodic hardcore." But it was Grade's third album, 1999's *Under the Radar*, that secured their legacy.

For *Under the Radar*, Grade went to Justin Koop, who had been making a name for himself as a producer of rock, metal, and hardcore bands. In 1991, Koop was hired as the in-house producer at the Music Gym, a rehearsal studio in Burlington that rented rooms to local bands in need of a place to play. Located in a warehouse space just off Ontario Highway 403 that connects the city to the other nearby population centres of Mississauga, Oakville, and Hamilton, the Music Gym was effectively the headquarters of the 905 music scene.

"The studio was pretty small, but we had enough to do records," Koop says. "Bands would come in from nearby high schools, they'd rehearse, and they'd jump in the studio. Sometimes we'd do a record in a night. It was a revolving door of bands, all the time."

FURTHER LISTENING

GRADE

Hometown: Burlington, Ontario
Years active: 1994–2002

When Grade released their first album, *And Such Is Progress*, in 1995, they were a maelstrom of menacing guitars and Kyle Bishop's throat-shredding screams. But by the time they launched their magnum opus *Under the Radar* in 1999, they managed to make room for melody without sacrificing any of their edge. Within the hardcore scene, *Under the Radar* was a hallowed, boundary-pushing record. Largely because of it, Grade is often credited with pioneering a sound that blended the aggression and intensity of metallic hardcore with the melodic melodrama of emo and pop punk. More specifically, Grade is recognized for popularizing the idea of both screaming and singing—a style that would soon be basically inescapable. Grade released their final record *Headfirst Straight to Hell* in 2001, then disbanded a year later, though they've reformed occasionally for live performances since 2006 and released singles in 2010 and 2014.

Koop had been making some demos with the Burlington rock band Finger Eleven, who were working on material for their second album *Tip*, to be released in 1997 on Mercury Records. Those demos turned out well enough that they were making the rounds, and Koop became known among the region's rock bands for dialling in killer guitar tones in his recordings. "All the bands were guitar-driven bands, so as soon as they heard me getting good guitar sounds, the guitar players would be like, 'Oh, we have to record with him.'"

That's when Grade came in.

"Grade had a great name for themselves. They were influencing a lot of bands. They were the first hardcore band that was blending the screaming vocals with guitar melodies," Koop says. "As far as I know, they were one of the first bands doing that. I hadn't heard that before. We all just sat around like, 'Is this good?' We weren't even sure."

One person who thought it was good was Tony Brummel at Victory Records, who heard the demos they recorded with Koop and signed them to a multi-album deal. Grade went back into the studio with Koop to record the rest of the album and make their Victory debut.

Especially after *Under the Radar*, there were bands all over the continent that wanted to make music like Grade—particularly in their own hometown of Burlington. There were perhaps no bigger fans of Grade than the five members of Silverstein, who looked at their local hardcore heroes the way a young hockey player looks at Wayne Gretzky.

In 2002, a year after releasing their final record *Headfirst Straight to Hell*, Grade disbanded. In their final years, the group had recruited drummer Charles Moniz, known in the 905 scene as a member of the pop-punk band the Pettit Project. Jerk Circus had played a lot of shows with the Pettit Project and Told and Moniz had become good friends. After Grade's breakup, Moniz was looking for a new band. Told, who had recently been splitting his time between Silverstein and the Livid—the Mississauga band that had just missed out on a major-label deal with Atlantic Records—asked Moniz to fill the Livid's drummer vacancy. The arrangement didn't last, but it put Told and Moniz in a room together for long enough that they got to talking about Silverstein's efforts to land a record deal.

"We're sending out some demos," Told said.

"Are you sending one to Victory?" Moniz asked.

"Yeah, you know, Victory . . . it's a huge label," Told said. "I don't know . . . I don't expect much."

"Well, you know what, I'll call them and have them check it out."

For Silverstein, Victory was the best-case scenario. It had been the biggest hardcore label for the better part of the '90s, and they were still going strong. Better yet, they had Grade.

Days after Silverstein sent their demo to the Victory offices in Chicago, Koehler got a phone call from Tony Brummel. Within a couple of weeks, the label boss was in Toronto having breakfast with Silverstein. Brummel loved the demo, and he wanted to sign them right away.

"Tony from Victory loved Grade more than anything," Koehler says. "In his eyes, Grade was one of the most important bands. Maybe he thought we could be the new Grade. He would often share his love of Canada and of Grade, and I think we fell right in line with that."

Silverstein left the meeting feeling elated. Then came another offer—but this one wasn't for Silverstein.

WITHIN DAYS OF SILVERSTEIN'S meeting with Brummel, Shane Told was working at his summer job when he got a call about yet another potentially life-changing opportunity. The artist management team at Nettwerk was putting together a band for seventeen-year-old Avril Lavigne, who had just exploded out of Napanee, Ontario, to make the biggest pop debut of 2002 with *Let Go.* Lavigne's managers wanted to surround her with bandmates who liked the same music and had the same style, so they were recruiting musicians from punk bands across Ontario. They asked Told if he would be interested in playing bass for Lavigne's band.

Silverstein hadn't signed anything with Victory. They'd had a good meeting, but it wasn't a done deal. "It probably took like ten days, but at that time in your life, it feels like forever," Koehler recalls. Told was given the choice between joining the backup band for an international superstar or signing a recording contract with the biggest name in hardcore as the frontman of his own band.

Told knew in his heart that he wanted to see it through with Silverstein, so he turned down the Lavigne offer.[50]

Within a few months, Lavigne's album and its three hit singles would become mainstays on MTV, pop radio, and the Billboard charts, and the singer and her backing band would

---

50 Told repaid Moniz's favour by referring him to Nettwerk. Moniz played bass for Lavigne's band between 2002 and 2007. He has since won seven Grammy Awards as an engineer for Bruno Mars and Adele.

embark on a massive concert tour, playing a total of seventy shows across North America, Asia, Europe, and Australia that grossed, on average, $300,000 a night. Meanwhile, Billy Talent—the band that Atlantic Records signed after the Livid's deal fell through—was getting ready to head into the studio to record their major-label debut album.

At age twenty-one, Told had walked away from two huge opportunities to play in a band that would have been working under a deep-pocketed American major label. He was betting on Silverstein.

"I love this music, and I love this band," he told himself. "I have to see this through."

WITHIN WEEKS OF TOLD turning down Nettwerk's offer, the paperwork arrived from Victory. Silverstein signed their first recording contract—a four-album deal with a budget of $10,000 for their first record—in the fall of 2002. It was a modest sum, relatively speaking, but it was more money than the band had ever seen. Told was going to succeed or fail on his own terms.

By then, emo was starting to break into the mainstream market. Saves the Day's *Stay What You Are* and Dashboard Confessional's *The Places You Have Come to Fear the Most* had each sold more than one hundred thousand copies in a year, and Jimmy Eat World had bounced back from their major-label misadventures with *Bleed American*, which turned out to be a massive commercial success that yielded the crossover pop hit "The Middle."

Still, Silverstein wasn't anticipating that kind of success.

Those bands hewed closer to pop-punk, which was already a market-tested product; Silverstein, meanwhile, leaned into the heavier side of emo that incorporated metal and hardcore. "That sound was way more commercial than our band," Told says. "There was no *screaming* on the radio."

But Brummel, their label head, must have seen what was happening. While Victory was known as a powerhouse in hardcore, and *only* hardcore, there were signs that emo could reach a much bigger audience. Before picking up Silverstein, Brummel had signed Thursday and Taking Back Sunday, and Victory was already seeing the returns. Thursday's second album *Full Collapse* in 2001 and Taking Back Sunday's debut *Tell All Your Friends* in 2002 both sold more than one hundred thousand copies by early 2003.

Brummel wanted to show off Victory's new signing. He didn't give Silverstein any orders about what songs they should record, where they should record them, or how the album should sound. He just told them to make a record and make it quickly.

FOR SILVERSTEIN, THEIR CHOICE of producer was easy. They wanted a guy they knew, a guy whose studio was right down the street, and a guy who, most importantly, had worked with Grade. So, they went to the Music Gym to work with Justin Koop.

Silverstein had just six weeks to record their debut album, a tight timeline for a band that had existed for barely two years before they were picked up by Victory, and whose band members were barely into their twenties. But when Silverstein headed into the studio in January 2003, Koop was pleasantly surprised to find that the young group actually knew what they were doing. "They were very tight. They had arranged their songs maturely for their age. They self-edited themselves very well. They were very aware of how they wanted their songs to sound and how they wanted them arranged beforehand. I was impressed by that," Koop says. "They knew what they wanted, and they were going for exactly what they wanted. They wanted to be on Victory Records, they wanted that same fan base that Grade had, they wanted to come up right behind them and do what they were doing, and I think they did that quite well."

Silverstein went into the studio with ten songs. Culling four of the most memorable songs from their second EP and adding a half-dozen new ones, the band started to sound less like their '90s idols and more like something new. On songs like "Giving Up" and "The Weak and the Wounded," they exemplified the quiet-loud dynamic that would become a defining characteristic of 2000s emo: twinkly guitar tones and plaintive melodies would be suddenly interrupted by an onslaught of power chords and metallic riffing, and Told's pop-minded harmonies would be punctuated by throaty screams. Older cuts like "Red Light Pledge" and "Bleeds No More" felt a little less refined by comparison—evidence that Silverstein's songwriting abilities were improving so quickly that only a year made a noticeable difference—but with enhanced production from Koop and stronger performances from the band, they had more than enough punch to become standouts.[51] Silverstein even got

51 "Bleeds No More" includes a recording of Told's then-girlfriend saying, "You're the worst thing that ever happened to me," a line from the Chuck Palahniuk novel *Fight Club*. The band was obsessed with *Fight Club* and wanted to sample Helena Bonham Carter's delivery of the line in the 1999 film adaptation, but they didn't want to get sued for copyright infringement.

a co-sign from their quasi-mentors by enlisting Grade vocalist Kyle Bishop for a guest feature on the album's finale.

Towering above them all, though, was "Smashed into Pieces," a song that would kick off their debut like an emo wrecking ball. After Koehler revved up with a fast-paced snare roll and Boshart and Bradford followed with a pair of suspenseful guitar riffs, the band came crashing in as Told screamed and sang his way through hard-rocking verses and a sweetly sad chorus, all of it aching with sincerity in every note, every chord, every crash of the drums. The song sounded desperately heartbroken but also thrillingly kinetic—a platonic ideal of what "emo" should signify. And if the intensity of angst, earnestness, and heartache was a huge part of emo's appeal (and it was), Silverstein conveyed all of that succinctly with the album's title, *When Broken Is Easily Fixed.*

At the beginning of April 2003, Victory announced that Silverstein's debut album would be released the following month. The label promoted it with "Smashed into Pieces" and "Giving Up," both posted online the week of the announcement. It was an exciting moment for Silverstein, but the response from the punk community was ruthless.

In the early 2000s, Punknews.org was the premier web forum for punk rock, and it embodied all aspects of punk culture, namely strong opinions and snarky commentary about which bands and subgenres were cool and which were not. According to Punknews.org, Silverstein was absolutely not cool; they were seen as trend-hopping poseurs who wanted to ride the coattails of better bands that had come before them. A reviewer for the site gave *When Broken Is Easily Fixed* a rating of half a star out of five—the lowest possible score—and called it "a waste of shelf space," taking issue not only with Silverstein's music but with Victory's shift into signing emo and pop-punk bands. "Absolutely nothing distinguishes this band from any other in their genre," the review read. "Except perhaps for the fact that, if possible, Silverstein is even worse than your average pop-punk calamity." The comment section largely agreed. Silverstein's haters were loud, they were mean, and they were tenacious.

"I learned very early on that I needed to have thick skin," Told says. "It was right away. After that first album came out, I was reading scathing things about our band and myself. I just had to suck it up and learn to laugh at it. It was my defence mechanism."

Besides, it didn't matter what punk scenesters were saying about Silverstein. After all, the success of emo bands like theirs didn't happen in the forums of Punknews.org or the pages of *Maximumrocknroll*. It happened on MySpace.

FURTHER LISTENING

BOYS NIGHT OUT

Hometown: Burlington, Ontario
Years active: 1998, 2001–2016

Boys Night Out played one gig in 1998 before breaking up, but they had more staying power when they reformed in 2001. By the time they released their debut album, *Make Yourself Sick*, in 2003, they had largely sanded down their Grade-indebted hardcore edge in favour of emo-style vocal melodies—though they made sure to punctuate the album's most intense moments with proggy breakdowns and screamed accents. All three of Boys Night Out's albums were released on New Jersey-based label Ferret Records, and the band enjoyed sustained success in Canada and the U.S., including tours with My Chemical Romance and Saves the Day. The band continued to push forward their melodies on their later releases, including 2005 concept album *Trainwreck* and 2007's self-titled album. Later activity included the 2016 EP *Black Dogs* and the archival compilation *Nevermind 2* in 2021.

BEFORE THERE WAS MYSPACE, there was Friendster. Founded by a Canadian computer programmer working in Silicon Valley, Friendster pioneered the social network as we know it: a place where users could browse their friends' profiles, post status updates, send each other messages, and comment on others' posts. Koehler and Boshart were the first of their friends to have a Friendster account after it launched in early 2003.

"Why don't we make a profile for the band?" Boshart asked one day at rehearsal.

"I already did," Koehler replied.

Soon, there were other websites doing the same thing. Just a few months after Friendster went live, a group of employees at the Los Angeles–based internet marketing company eUniverse created their own social networking website that mimicked the features they liked about their own Friendster accounts. They called their website MySpace, and it quickly usurped Friendster as the internet's hottest social network shortly after it launched in the summer of 2003. Again, Koehler was quick to sign up. And again, he made a profile for Silverstein, too.

"Because Paul was one of the first people to sign up, his name was always at the top of every list," says Told. "So Paul became MySpace famous, and in turn, our band kind of became MySpace famous, too, because we were one of the first bands to sign up."

On MySpace, artists could share updates with their fans—as many had begun to do using online fan clubs and email newsletters—and interact with them one on one. What set the platform apart from the other social networking sites that came before and after it, though, was the centrality of music to the MySpace experience. Artists could open an account and post their songs directly onto their profile page, and anyone who stumbled upon their profile would be able to hear their music right there and then.

This made total sense at a time when people had been rapidly discovering the power of the internet as a place for music discovery. In its two short years of existence, Napster had blown the doors open with peer-to-peer file-sharing technology; by the time the company ceased operations in 2001 after losing copyright infringement lawsuits brought by Metallica and Dr. Dre, multiple copycats such as LimeWire, BearShare, and Soulseek had already taken its place. The internet had become a place where you could very easily (and illegally) download thousands of MP3s from the comfort of your personal computer, entirely for free. This was hurting established bands like Metallica, but it was hugely beneficial to new and lesser-known bands like Silverstein.

Within two years, Silverstein amassed more than thirty thousand followers on MySpace, and "Smashed into Pieces" was racking up plays. The band also found fans by uploading songs to MP3.com, a site made specifically for independent artists to share their music. *When Broken Is Easily Fixed* wasn't a chart success—though it did make a brief appearance on Billboard's Heatseekers list—but it ended up selling an impressive one hundred thousand copies by early 2005. That was already far more than Silverstein expected. But the band's total reach couldn't really be determined by traditional quantifiers like album sales. "The craziest part is we have no idea how many albums got downloaded," Told says.

BEGINNING IN THE SUMMER of 2003, Silverstein had begun to gain a reputation for being constantly on tour. Victory sent them out on numerous U.S. tours with other bands on the label's roster, like Spitalfield, Bayside, and Hawthorne Heights, and they joined the Warped Tour in the summer of 2004. The rest of the time, they split their nonstop tour schedule between supporting punk bands like Rise Against, Strike Anywhere, and Hot Water Music, and other emo newcomers, like Senses Fail, Armor for Sleep, From Autumn to Ashes, and Underoath. In their first twenty months on the road, Silverstein played an impressive 315 shows. That meant a couple of things: the band had put in the hours to become an impressively well-tuned, professional live act, and they had played to thousands of kids who were becoming Silverstein fans.

Meanwhile, the emo scene at large was growing rapidly during the two years that Silverstein was touring behind *When Broken Is Easily Fixed.* In that time, emo had become a full-blown cultural phenomenon. It was now normal for an emo album to crack the top 10 on the Billboard 200, like Taking Back Sunday's *Where You Want to Be*, AFI's *Sing the Sorrow*, and the Used's *In Love and Death*, with others appearing farther down the Billboard chart, like Thrice's *The Artist in the Ambulance* and My Chemical Romance's *Three Cheers for Sweet Revenge.*

It wasn't just about the music anymore, either. Emo was a fashion statement, a lifestyle, a state of mind. The subculture especially thrived on MySpace, where hordes of teenagers would show off their jet-black fringe haircuts, dark eyeliner, skinny jeans, and studded belts in their profile pics, set their favourite emo songs to auto-play on their page, and quote the most angst-ridden lyrics in their status updates (along with "</3" to denote a broken heart). Despite all this, emo still hadn't peaked. And Silverstein's second album would be ready just in time for what would go down as emo's biggest year.

* * *

THANKS TO THE SUCCESS of *When Broken Is Easily Fixed*, Silverstein could afford to be more ambitious when it came time to make their second studio effort in early 2005. Two years earlier, the farthest they'd ever been from home was Halifax. Now, they had performed in almost two hundred cities across Canada, the U.S., and the U.K., and they had one hundred thousand album sales to their name. They were ready to get out of Burlington and go somewhere with a bit more glitz and glam. They decided on Los Angeles.

But when Silverstein's first choice of producer for their second album fell through, the band was stuck. They had set aside a six-week period in their busy tour schedule to make a new record. By January, that studio time was only a couple of months away, and they had no producer.

That month, the band was in the U.K. supporting the Florida-based outfit Underoath. Silverstein had made friends with the other opening band, the Hurt Process, a metal group from southeast England that had released their debut album *Drive By Monologue* just a few months after Silverstein had released *When Broken Is Easily Fixed.* The Hurt Process had recorded their album with a newer producer named Cameron Webb at his new studio in Orange County. Since then, Webb had produced heavy music veterans like Motörhead and Social Distortion and worked as an additional engineer on Sum 41's *Chuck*. Silverstein received a personal referral from the Hurt Process drummer Darren Toms—and it helped that Webb had also produced one of Silverstein's favourite albums, Park's

It Won't Snow Where You're Going—but even then, they were hesitant.

"They kind of grilled me," Webb says. "Here's the thing: those kinds of emo bands at that time... I don't want to say this in a mean way, but they were very arrogant. They were kids, and all of a sudden they sold thirty thousand records—or in Silverstein's case, one hundred thousand of their first record. And like, one hundred thousand records on an independent label? That's huge. That's enormous. So Silverstein had this thing where it was like, we're really big right now, we can do whatever we want. That's what happened with those bands on Victory Records."

After their call, Webb won them over. Not that Silverstein had time to be picky, anyway. Only a few weeks after they got home from their U.K. tour, the band hopped on a flight to spend six weeks in California working on their second record. They tracked most of the album at Webb's Maple Sound Studios, but Webb chose to record the drums at Capitol Records' legendary Hollywood studio instead. ("I wanted to impress them," he says.)

When Broken Is Easily Fixed showcased a relatively inexperienced group of musicians with good ideas and a strong vision, but Silverstein's second full-length effort would reveal a road-worn band that had spent several years at the grindstone and was now much sharper for it. Told's voice sounded much stronger, particularly his screaming, which lost its shrieky quality and took on a deeper and more forceful tone. Koehler's drumming was snap-tight and more creative, working in lockstep with Bradford, Boshart, and Hamilton, whose playing was additionally amplified by Webb's punchy production. The band's writing had clearly become more streamlined, which allowed them to introduce more complex instrumentation while still packaging it all into simply structured tunes.

Silverstein wrapped up their recording sessions in early April, and then they immediately headed back out on a three-week tour with Fall Out Boy. They didn't know it yet, but both bands were about to release a scene-defining record that would forever change the trajectory of their careers.

IN MID-APRIL 2005, VICTORY announced that Silverstein's second record, *Discovering the Waterfront*, would be released that summer. By then, emo had reached a whole different level. Fall Out Boy's major-label debut, *From Under the Cork Tree*, spent fourteen weeks in the top 20 of the Billboard 200. "Sugar, We're Goin Down," the album's lead single, was a mainstay on MTV's *Total Request Live* and crossed over into the Billboard pop singles chart, eventually spending five weeks in the top 10. That summer, albums by Motion City Soundtrack, the Academy Is . . ., Funeral for a Friend, Armor for Sleep, and the All-American Rejects also charted on the Billboard 200. All of them were on the Warped Tour, along with dozens of other breakout acts. With a total of 123 artists on the roster, it was the biggest year in the history of the Warped Tour.

"That's when you had Fall Out Boy, My Chemical Romance, and everybody else blowing up all at once," Warped Tour founder and event producer Kevin Lyman said in an interview with the Bay Area newspaper the *Mercury News* in 2019. "You couldn't turn on *TRL* or MTV without seeing them—which almost made the tour too successful, because we started drawing more of a pop crowd."

That year's Warped Tour reflected a major shift in the alternative music scene, as emo, post-hardcore, and metal bands took over a festival that was initially known for good ol' punk rock. There were still members of the old guard of '90s punk—with No Use for a Name, the Offspring, and Strung Out among them—but the tide had clearly shifted in favour of groups like Silverstein, Fall Out Boy, Hawthorne Heights, From First to Last, Senses Fail, Avenged Sevenfold, and Underoath. Skate punk was out, and emo was in.

Silverstein was poised to take advantage of that moment. Their music was a near-perfect synthesis of where pop-punk, emo, hardcore, and metal were coalescing at the midway point of the decade. The material on *Discovering the Waterfront* stuck with Silverstein's tried-and-true formula of melancholy reflections punctuated by bursts of rage, but songs like "Smile in Your Sleep" and "My Heroine" had the kind of uptempo, catchy choruses that were likely to appeal to fans of pop-punk, while the aggressive attacks of guitar riffing in songs like "Your Sword Versus My Dagger" and "Fist Wrapped in Blood" aligned them with the "metalcore" style that was gaining popularity thanks to the success of groups like Killswitch Engage, Bullet for My Valentine, and Atreyu. *Discovering the Waterfront* was an emo record that held huge potential for crossover appeal among both pop-punk kids and metalheads.

That was no accident. Told had started out making upbeat pop-punk tunes in Jerk Circus and Boshart had been headbanging in his metalcore band Maharahj before they and the rest of the band got together over their love of '90s emo and their local hardcore heroes Grade. Between the five of them, they knew how to make a dynamic, efficient song that would incorporate wistful emo verses, anthemic pop-punk choruses, hot-blooded metal riffage, and an ass-kicking hardcore beatdown, all within a three-minute run-time. Within the context of an alternative music scene that was exploding upward and outward in several different directions, Silverstein's music sat perfectly in the centre of all of it.

In mid-July 2005, right at the halfway point of the Warped Tour's two-month run, Silverstein released "Smile in Your Sleep," a catchy and intensely angsty song that instantly became a fan favourite. As the tour continued, Silverstein's crowds became bigger than ever. At a stop in Barrie, Ontario, a city an hour north of Toronto, Victory even booked an airplane to fly over the Warped Tour festival grounds pulling a banner advertising the album's release date.

"That was the year, man. That was when everything exploded," says Told.

"For the first record, we played for ten people a night," Koehler adds. "For our second record, a plane is now promoting it from the sky. At that point, the corporations, the labels, the money, the business, everyone decided to take this scene and blow it up. We didn't realize that's what was happening. But they were just like, yeah, we're gonna throw a bunch of money at this because we clearly know where this band is going."

When *Discovering the Waterfront* arrived on August 16, 2005, it changed Silverstein's trajectory completely. One week after the release, the band was playing the Bottom Lounge in Chicago when their manager emailed them with the sales numbers. They sold twenty-six thousand albums in the first week, enough to make their debut on the Billboard 200, where they peaked at No. 34.

"'How?'" Told remembers asking himself. "That was when it was like, 'Oh fuck.' We're on the Billboard chart, and we're not on the Heatseekers one, we're not just on the rock albums chart—this is the Billboard 200. I have the *Billboard* magazine from that week. It was real. I remember getting that email and thinking, 'How the fuck did we do that?'"

Silverstein's music videos for "Smile in Your Sleep" and "My Heroine" got picked up by MTV, but the band's popularity continued to be driven primarily by teenagers on the internet. By the end of 2005, *Discovering the Waterfront* had sold more than one hundred thousand copies in the U.S., and it was one of the highest-charting emo albums of the year, behind Fall Out Boy and Panic! at the Disco (both of whom were far more pop-oriented compared to Silverstein's harsh screaming and hardcore riffing). Soon enough, Silverstein wasn't just selling T-shirts at their shows, but at Hot Topic stores in shopping malls across the continent. While the band was playing in Vienna with Simple Plan in early 2006, their music even made it to primetime TV back on their home continent when *American Idol* contestant Ryan Hart auditioned with an a cappella version of "Smashed into Pieces" in the first round of the show's fifth season.[52]

"Right place, right time," Webb says. "That's right when that scene was starting to get bigger and bigger, and when we did that record, it sat at the right spot."

Silverstein continued to tour virtually nonstop, including

---

52 "Why on earth are you here?" Simon Cowell responded, which led to a short argument between the judge and contestant. Hart remarked that he was "too hardcore for you," with Cowell sarcastically replying that he was "very frightening." Paula Abdul and Randy Jackson mostly sat there stunned. "I feel like people asked me about that every day for five years," Told says now.

making their first trips through mainland Europe. They racked up a total of 179 shows in 2005, and then kept pressing on to play another two hundred in 2006 while they continued to support *Discovering the Waterfront.* After two years, the album had sold more than two hundred thousand copies.

In the brief periods when they weren't on the road, the five members of Silverstein still lived with their parents in Southern Ontario. But they did use their new income to splurge a little bit, spending some of their pocket money on luxuries like laptops and Diesel jeans. They didn't act like it, but Silverstein had become Canada's first big emo band.

SILVERSTEIN'S THIRD ALBUM, *Arrivals & Departures*, released in the summer of 2007, was what you would probably call a resounding success. It remains their highest- and longest-charting album, spending eight weeks on the Billboard 200 and peaking at No. 25. By those measures, it's their most commercially successful album ever. But to the band, it was their first and only misstep—yet it was one that ultimately helped them become the band that has remained a strong, steady force in the world of emo and hardcore for more than twenty years.

By early 2007, Silverstein had already exceeded their expectations and were still on the ascent. At a time when hip-hop and R&B were pushing out rock as the dominant force in mainstream music, emo was helping to keep rock in the zeitgeist. The previous year, AFI's *Decemberunderground* topped the Billboard 200, with no shortage of scene-mates in the top 10. Their sales numbers were enough to have them hanging around the pop charts with the likes of Rihanna, Nelly Furtado,

Ne-Yo, and Busta Rhymes. It was a bit of a weird time in the world of popular music.

What seemed impossible a few years earlier was now happening regularly. It was not that far-fetched for Silverstein to have a chart-topping album. This was a band that had never expected to be remotely as successful as they already were, and now they could see there was even further they could go. That also meant that, for the first time, they could be disappointed.

For *Arrivals & Departures*, Silverstein turned to producer Mark Trombino, who had become well-known for several major releases in the punk and emo scene, including Blink-182's *Dude Ranch* and three Jimmy Eat World records: *Static Prevails*, *Clarity*, and *Bleed American*. Trombino also came with an air of old-school credibility: he had produced records by the '90s bands Mineral and Knapsack—two of Silverstein's major influences—and was formerly the drummer of the pioneering emo and post-hardcore act Drive Like Jehu. The band spent the winter writing their third record and headed into Trombino's studio in March 2007. But once there, it became clear that it wasn't a good fit.

"I hated the process of making the record. That time in my life was the most depressed I'd ever been. Everything else in my life was going great. I was in a new relationship and the band was doing so well, and then we made this record in L.A. with Mark Trombino, and he was not the right guy for the record," Told says. "He made some of our favourite records. We were excited to work with him. But he wasn't the guy for us. I remember everybody had gone home and I was finishing the vocals in California. My voice was gone, I couldn't sing properly, and I was so depressed. I wasn't sure about the record, and I remember just crying alone in the Oakwood Apartments in L.A."

Still, the band pushed through it and finished the record. By the time they returned home to Burlington and listened back to the final mixes, they thought it turned out pretty well.

When *Arrivals & Departures* hit stores on July 2, 2007, it sold twenty-seven thousand copies in its first week and "If You Could See into My Soul" received regular airplay on MTV. "They were playing it in the morning between, like, Justin Timberlake and Rihanna. It was crazy," Told recalls. The band went on a three-month tour as the direct support for Rise Against, playing the biggest rooms they'd ever played, including the 9,500-seat Red Rocks Amphitheatre in Denver and the 13,500-capacity Long Beach Arena in Los Angeles. In 2008, they went on one of their biggest headlining tours to this day, a two-month excursion that took them across Canada and the U.S. They were bigger than ever, and it showed... but something didn't feel right.

"It really should have been the moment," Told says. "And the reason we didn't capitalize more on that is that the record wasn't very good. It wasn't as compelling. The songs weren't as good. It's my least favourite album I've ever done."

Meanwhile, the emo scene as a whole had abruptly stalled. After two huge years of bands from their scene rocketing up the charts, 2007 was mostly a bust. The biggest breakout that year was Chiodos' *Bone Palace Ballet* landing at No. 5 on the charts. Albums by established acts like Dashboard Confessional, Jimmy Eat World, and Saves the Day sold well enough, but they didn't make nearly the same impression as the records they had released just a few years earlier. More straight-ahead pop-punk bands were still able to churn out some catchy hits, like Paramore's hit single, "Misery Business," and Fall Out Boy's first No. 1 album, *Infinity on High*. But the reality was that emo bands—particularly those like Silverstein that played loud, fast, and hard—weren't the commercial force they had been just a year prior. Meanwhile, MySpace was losing the battle for social network supremacy to Facebook, which meant that one of the largest communities for emo bands and their fans was quickly collapsing.

FURTHER LISTENING

COMEBACK KID

Hometown: Winnipeg, Manitoba
Years active: 2001–present

Originally formed in 2001 as a side project of Winnipeg hardcore band Figure Four, Comeback Kid named themselves after a headline about Mario Lemieux's return to the NHL. Within a couple years, that side project turned into a full-time gig as the band signed to the California-based Facedown Records for their debut album, *Turn It Around*, in 2003, at which point they began touring all over North America and Europe. By 2005, they had joined their Canadian brethren in Silverstein on the Victory Records roster and released four records with the hardcore tastemakers, which earned them multiple chart placements, including their turning-point Victory debut with 2005's *Wake the Dead* and their first appearance on the Billboard 200 with 2007's *Broadcasting* ... Now with seven albums and counting that showcase their fierce vocals, pounding rhythms, and onslaught of guitar riffs, Comeback Kid have been a pillar of hardcore punk on the world stage for more than twenty years.

That trend continued throughout the remainder of the decade as mainstream pop culture shifted away from emo. By the early 2010s, many of the bands that had been part of Silverstein's tours throughout their career had either gone on hiatus, broken up, or just quietly faded away.

But Silverstein kept going. And the disappointment of *Arrivals & Departures* only strengthened their motivation to keep doing what they were doing. "We have the drive," Koehler says. "When you make a record, you're doing the best you possibly can, but when you're done, you just have a little bit more to give."

* * *

FOR THEIR FOURTH ALBUM, Silverstein needed a reset. They returned to Cameron Webb to recapture the working relationship of *Discovering the Waterfront*, but they didn't go down to California. This time, Webb came to Canada—in the dead of winter in late 2008 and early 2009—so the band could stay at home as they worked together out of Metalworks Studios in Mississauga.

"We stripped away the distractions," Koehler says. "We had a guy who we knew could get the best out of us. We brought it back home, steps away from the doors to all the venues we played. Being at home, surrounded by friends and family, that really, really helped us make that record."

A more aggressive record than anything else they'd done but also more dynamic and cinematic in its approach, *A Shipwreck in the Sand* represented not just a return to form but an elevation of their craft. Full of hard-hitting riffs, high-flying choruses, and strong studio performances all around, it was a fourth record they would've liked to have been their third. *A Shipwreck in the Sand* ended up being a commercial success, as well, in spite of emo's falling stock. After the album was released on March 31, 2009, it peaked at No. 33 on the Billboard 200—not as high as *Arrivals & Departures*, but still better than *Discovering the Waterfront.*

"That was a really important turning point, not only for our fans and maybe the critics, but also for me to know that, creatively, we were able to pull that off," Told says. "It was a hard album to make, but it was a really, really important record that, for me, solidified that we're a good band."

"We brought it back to the 905," Koehler adds. "It definitely bought us a future career and allowed us to continue from there, and we've made pretty much everything else locally since."

The band left Victory in 2010 after fulfilling their four-album deal. Since then, they have released seven more albums under the American indie labels Hopeless Records and Rise Records, and then with the Australia-based UNFD.

In all, Silverstein have played more than 2,500 live shows in more than five hundred cities around the world. They played the Warped Tour ten times, and they've sold more than a million records worldwide. By the time the band celebrated the tenth anniversary of their breakthrough album in 2015, *Discovering the Waterfront* had sold more than four hundred thousand copies.

Early in their career, Silverstein rose to a level of stardom that no other emo band from Canada had reached and they will likely never reach again. Thanks to their success in the U.S. market—not an easy feat for Canadian acts, even those in more widely accessible genres—and their tireless work ethic, Silverstein are among the most continuously beloved bands from their scene.

While many of their peers from the mid-2000s flamed out and broke up not long after the genre faded from the mainstream, Silverstein soldiered on. Since their debut, they've only had one lineup change, when Boshart was replaced by guitarist Paul Marc Rousseau shortly before the release of their seventh album, 2013's *This Is How the Wind Shifts.* The band released a new album basically every two years in their first two decades, for a total of eleven studio recordings. Nine of those albums charted on the Billboard 200, and five of them notched in the top 40. Silverstein are undoubtedly the biggest band from their music scene to emerge from Canada.

But they weren't alone. At almost the same time as Silverstein was climbing the Billboard charts, five guys from just down the road in Ontario were about to become one of the most interesting, unique, and unlikely success stories in all of Canadian music.

7

ALEXISONFIRE

At the tail end of August 2006, Alexisonfire have just launched into "Accidents," one of the songs that helped propel the Canadian screamo group to a level of fame they had never expected. Over the past few years, the band has played the song to many hot and sweaty crowds, but never at a venue like this. This time, they're not playing at a club or even on a stage—they're on a passenger boat that's cruising along the River Thames through the heart of London.

As the ferry makes its way through the city, nobody's head turns as they pass by famous landmarks like Big Ben, the London Eye, or Tower Bridge. Everyone's attention is focused on the five men making enough noise to be heard inside Buckingham Palace. The bandmates have dressed up specially for the occasion: guitarist Wade MacNeil is wearing a *marinière*-patterned T-shirt and a white Dixie hat[53] while the rest of the band wears crisp white T-shirts and dark jeans, in contrast with their usual uniform of sweat-soaked black band tees (or vocalist George Pettit's usual outfit of basketball shorts and no shirt).

The performance is a throwback to the spring of 1977, when the Sex Pistols commemorated Queen Elizabeth II's Silver Jubilee by playing their anti-monarchy missive "God Save the Queen" on a similar cruise of the Thames aboard a boat named, fittingly, the *Queen Elizabeth*. The Pistols' set was cut short when police arrived on their own boats to break up the show—leading to a riot on land and multiple arrests—but on this night nearly thirty years later, Alexisonfire's punk-rock excursion carries on without disruption. Nearly six thousand kilometres away from their home in St. Catharines, Ontario, the band rips through an electrifying five-song set for a boatful of fans in celebration of the release of their third album, soon to become the most successful of their career. *Crisis* has been out for only one day, and fans are already singing along enthusiastically as the band finishes "Accidents" and charges into the pounding drums, crushing guitars, ferocious screams, and soaring melodies of "This Could Be Anywhere in the World." The title of the song is fitting. The boat party in London marks the beginning of a massive world tour that will find Alexisonfire bringing their high-energy live show across the U.K., Europe, Australia, the U.S., and Canada multiple times over the course of the next year, playing to bigger crowds than they had ever

---

53 Fittingly dapper, but not authentic, especially for a Canadian in England. Both are naval apparel, but the *marinière* is French and the Dixie hat is American (and later used in Bolivia, the Philippines, and Venezuela).

imagined. During that time, *Crisis* will become their first album to chart internationally and their first to reach the top spot in Canada, where it will be certified platinum in less than a year.

This marks an exceptional achievement for Alexisonfire. In just five years, the Canadian punks have evolved from a local curiosity to nationally beloved oddballs to a global force in an emerging genre known as "post-hardcore" or "screamo." As the boat chugs through London, Alexisonfire has come further than anyone ever expected. Not bad for a bunch of punk kids, mall rats, skaters, and record-store regulars who play a smorgasbord of niche music styles and want nothing more than to make an unbelievable racket everywhere they go.

IN THE LATE '90S, Joel Carriere was working at Sam the Record Man in the Pen Centre, the biggest shopping mall in St. Catharines, Ontario. At its peak, the chain of record shops was Canada's largest music retailer, with 140 locations across the country. It was the perfect job for a teenager who was constantly reading music magazines and looking for new bands to check out. Sure, he had to help customers find CDs of the Backstreet Boys, Britney Spears, and the *Titanic* soundtrack, but he also got to discover lesser-known albums and dive deeper into his love of niche music. After Carriere had been working at Sam's for a while, the manager let him place special orders, and he'd use this newly acquired power to keep the shelves stocked with his favourite punk and hardcore albums from small independent labels, which made the store an unusually bountiful location for local punks to source records they wouldn't be able to find elsewhere.

One of Carriere's regular customers was a high schooler named Dallas Green, who sported glasses, scruffy brown hair, and a healthy pair of sideburns. Green also worked at the Pen Centre throughout high school; he held jobs at the Foot Locker shoe store, the West 49 skate shop, and the Famous Players movie theatre, which he especially enjoyed because he could watch movies for free and help himself to unlimited popcorn. When he was seven, Green had developed an early taste for punk rock, the guitar, and skateboarding thanks to people like his older sister, his cousin, and his best friend's brother. As a teenager working in the mall, Green would visit Sam the Record Man when he was on his break, and Carriere would turn him on to bands like the Guelph indie-rockers Constantines and the Kentucky emo group Elliott.

On one of those workdays in 1998, Green invited Carriere to come see his band, Helicon Blue, at the Mindbomb, one of the last remaining rock bars in St. Catharines. Helicon Blue's dark and moody style of rock reminded Carriere of some of his favourite bands, like Hum, Quicksand, and Mogwai. What really stood out, though, was Green's voice, which even at an early age had the power of a hard-rocker like Alice in Chains' Layne Staley, but also a more soulful flavour that reflected his love of Jeff Buckley and Sade. The music may have sounded like Carriere's favourite '90s rock bands, but none of those bands sounded quite like Green. Carriere wanted in.

"I don't know how to help you, but let's see what I can do," he told Green.

Carriere had been looking for ways to launch a career in the music industry. He had gotten a job at the major label PolyGram Records and worked for the S.C.E.N.E. Music

Festival,[54] an alternative music extravaganza started by a member of a local punk band called Revenge of the Egg People. As Carriere got to know local promoters and booking agents, he and his friend Tricia Ricciuto started helping new bands get noticed. Carriere began boosting Green's band, and over the next few years, Helicon Blue developed a strong local following. On the strength of two EPs, they had become popular enough to fill a room with a couple of hundred people, making them one of St. Catharines' bigger bands, and in September 2001 they landed their biggest gig yet, opening for SoCal post-hardcore band Sense Field in Toronto. But on the day of the show, Green's bandmates were late and missed their set. Instead, Green borrowed an acoustic guitar and fumbled his way through some solo material.

"You saw his heart break on stage," Carriere says.

Green, just shy of his twenty-first birthday, was bummed. If he was going to make something of his music, he needed a band he could count on. As fate would have it, he got a call two days later from a friend, a precocious teenage punk intent on assembling a crew of young music freaks in St. Catharines and stitching them together into a Frankenstein's monster.

ON A TYPICAL SUMMER day in 1998, fourteen-year-old Wade MacNeil would ride his skateboard over to the corner store to meet his friend Chris Steele. MacNeil was a stocky kid who'd often have a wide grin stretched between his big cheeks, on which he grew thick mutton chops as soon as he was able.

---

54 St. Catharines Event for New Music Entertainment.

Steele had bushy brown hair and a mischievous look about him—something in the eyes—that made him seem friendly but potentially unpredictable. The two friends would talk about punk rock while smoking a joint that MacNeil had brought from home, where he had hidden it from his parents in the empty case of a Metallica cassette. Steele went to a different high school in the city's north end, where he hung out with a bunch of jocks who liked hip-hop, hacky sack, and rough housing. Steele was the only one of his group who wore a chain wallet and Doc Martens and listened to punk rock. He and MacNeil had played on the same hockey and baseball teams, but it wasn't until they saw each other at a Misfits concert that they knew they should be friends. Just days after that show, they picked up their guitars and got some friends together to start a skate-punk band called Plan 9.

A natural hustler, MacNeil would book gigs for his band at the nearby Chinese and Jamaican restaurants, having skipped class to beg the owners to host his shows. He and Steele would post flyers up and down St. Catharines' main street and invite classmates from both of their high schools.

If they weren't playing a gig, MacNeil and Steele could be found watching other local bands. Pretty much every weekend they would go see local legends like Sick Boys and Revenge of the Egg People, or take a short drive across the U.S. border to see hardcore bands like Snapcase, Bane, and Majority Rule play basement shows in Buffalo.

By his late teens, MacNeil's musical tastes had grown more intense. He had always loved the classic '70s and '80s punk bands like the Misfits, Necros, and Dead Boys, but by the late '90s that stuff already felt vintage and safe. He was looking for something new, something dangerous, something that would really scare off the parents the same way those older punk bands did back in the day. "What felt akin to that was the screamo stuff that was happening," MacNeil says. "It was wildly abrasive. Bands like Orchid and Pg. 99 felt more punk to me."

While emo had emerged as a softer and more melodic response to the intense physicality of hardcore punk, the advent of screamo in the early '90s saw the pendulum swing back. Starting in San Diego with bands like Heroin and Antioch Arrow, a new version of emo emerged that kept the genre's sense of melody and melodrama, but added chaos, distortion, and screaming—lots and lots of screaming that rendered the lyrics basically unintelligible but ratcheted up the emotional intensity by a thousand percent. By the late '90s, screamo was rapidly spreading to punk scenes across North America.[55]

As MacNeil chased the high of this exciting new era of punk rock, he had a vision for a band of his own that would be equal parts melodic and chaotic, where something hauntingly beautiful could co-exist with something exquisitely ugly. For this band, he wanted to recruit guys from the local scene who were taking their music more seriously than the rest of their groups. His friend Dallas Green fit that description perfectly. With MacNeil and Green both on guitar duty, Steele slid over to bass. They brought along their friend Jesse Ingelevics, who had been drumming in another local punk band called the Banned.

Between the four of them, they had a drummer, a bassist, and two guitarists who could sing. For most new bands, that would be enough. But MacNeil wanted a lead vocalist who

---

55 Like any good subculture, these bands didn't refer to themselves as "screamo," and many of them weren't particularly fond of the term.

would really own the mic, someone who would fire up the crowd, someone whose stage presence was so wildly chaotic that you couldn't take your eyes off him. He knew just the guy.

GEORGE PETTIT GREW UP in Grimsby, Ontario, a small town to the west of St. Catharines. A teenager with dark hair, thick-rimmed glasses, and an excitable personality, Pettit was, in his own words, "the only punk in the village." There were no punk-rock shows in Grimsby, so as soon as he got his driver's licence, he would make the twenty-minute drive to St. Catharines to enjoy the nightlife he couldn't get at home. On the weekends, he would go see bands like Plan 9 and Helicon Blue play at a community arts space or a Chinese restaurant, and he'd go hunting for hard-to-find LPs at independent shops like Tantrum Records. It seemed like wherever he would go, he'd run into Wade MacNeil.

"When you're the only guy in your town with a leather jacket with a Crass patch on it, and then you walk by a guy with a Misfits T-shirt on ... you're both probably socially awkward enough that you won't talk to each other, but you see each other," Pettit says.

Eventually, those knowing looks turned into friendly nods and then into conservations. Pettit learned that if your band wanted to play an all-ages show in St. Catharines, MacNeil was the guy to make it happen. Pettit was playing bass in a metal band called Condemning Salem, so he asked his new friend to book them some shows. Condemning Salem and Plan 9 ended up playing together a lot, and they'd often cross paths with Helicon Blue, too.

"It's a small city, so the weirdos find each other," MacNeil says.

Everyone who saw Condemning Salem would say the same thing: the bassist stole the show. When he'd perform, Pettit would thrash around, jump off the walls—figuratively, but sometimes also literally—and leap into the crowd. "He was just a maniac," says Carriere.

So, when MacNeil went looking for a frontman for the new band he was forming, Pettit seemed like the obvious choice. He just needed to persuade Pettit.

"I don't know how to sing," Pettit said.

MacNeil waved it off. "We just want you to *yell*."

So, they all got together and made some noise. It was the fall of 2001, and the five youngsters were being bombarded by musical influences from all directions, from hardcore to emo to post-rock to mathcore. And they wanted their new band to sound like all of it.

"I don't know if we all really knew the exact vision, because we all had different influences mashed into one," says Steele. "In the beginning, I was a little confused. I couldn't quite see it at first. But once we all got into a room, it clicked."

FURTHER LISTENING

MONEEN

Hometown: Brampton, Ontario
Years active: 1999–2013

Forming just as emo was really starting to take off in the mainstream, Moneen generated enough interest with their noisy, knotty take on the genre to land them a record deal with the California-based tastemakers Vagrant Records in 2003. Beyond their recorded work, Moneen were known for their deafeningly loud and chaotically energetic live shows, where the members of the band would bounce off the walls and fly through the air, which served as a major inspiration to Alexisonfire, who would later sign to Vagrant. (The two bands would also cover each other on a split EP.) After releasing two albums on Vagrant, Moneen moved to Dine Alone for their fourth and final album, *The World I Want to Leave Behind*, in 2009. They haven't released any music since but emerge every few years for anniversary tours and the occasional Alexisonfire support gig.

Around the time of that first jam, Green had watched a documentary on the Discovery Channel that featured a fire-breathing stripper called Alexis Fire, who claimed to be the world's only lactating contortionist. The three-minute segment on the striptease performer-turned-pornographic actress gave him a great idea for a band name.[56] With that, Alexisonfire was born.

NOBODY IN OR AROUND Alexisonfire really knew what they were doing or where they were supposed to go with it. But they had five guys who were dedicated to the idea of the band, and they had a sixth guy who was dedicated to helping them make it a reality. Carriere had graduated from curating the punk section at Sam the Record Man to becoming a full-fledged impresario and tastemaker with his own promotion company, Bedlam Society. At a time when message boards were taking hold in the early days of internet culture, Bedlam Society's website became a popular virtual gathering space for people to talk about new albums, video premieres, and other sorts of local music news. The exact nature of his role with Alexisonfire was undefined—perhaps best described as their unofficial sixth member—but he was always around, and he was the kind of guy it helps to have around. "I didn't know what I was, and I don't think they knew what they were, but we were a group of people trying to do something," Carriere says now.

Alexisonfire played their first show at the Knights of Columbus Hall in Niagara Falls in November 2001 opening

56 "My favourite band of all time is Alice in Chains, so it kind of reminded me of that," Green says.

for Silverstein, at that time an up-and-coming emo band from nearby Burlington. From there, they were gradually subsumed into a punk and hardcore scene that was quickly developing along the western shores of Lake Ontario. No longer just playing shows at makeshift music venues in their hometown, they would regularly drive down the Queen Elizabeth Way to play in other cities along the highway linking the Niagara region to Toronto.

Alexisonfire recorded their first demo at Burning Sound, a small recording studio in a Niagara Falls basement, in early 2002. They tracked three songs that, for the first time, would capture their mishmash of wistful emo chords, ambient post-rock textures, quick-fretted guitar riffs, and Pettit's uncontrolled screaming.[57] They burned the three songs onto CDs, wrapped each disc in a different page of Ingelevics's math homework, and sold them for three dollars at their shows.

Carriere also gave a copy of the *Math Sheets Demo*, as it became known, to Greg Below, a concert promoter and recording engineer he had met at a Deftones show in Toronto back in 1998. Originally from St. Catharines, Below had produced Helicon Blue's two EPs before moving to Toronto, where he cut his teeth engineering hip-hop groups. Below was now working at EMI Music Publishing Canada, which had helped launch Sum 41 and was in the midst of doing the same for Billy Talent. The company's president Michael McCarty had initially brought in Below as an intern before making him the manager and principal engineer of EMI's new in-house

57 Toward the end of the first song on the demo—titled "The Philosophical Significance of Shooting My Sister in the Face: An Essay by James Secord"—you can actually hear Pettit choke on one of his screams.

studio. On the side, Below had become a popular promoter of metal and hardcore shows in the city, bringing bands like Slipknot, System of a Down, and Incubus to Canada for the first time, a couple of years before each rocketed to fame. McCarty recognized that Below had a gift for identifying metal and hard rock bands before they hit it big.

"Here's the deal," McCarty told him. "You start a label. We'll sign these bands to a publishing deal, and that's how they'll get money in their jeans. Then you record them in our studio, and you put them out on your label. You use the gigs to promote the record label, and you use the record label to promote the gigs, and it becomes this circle."

Below emailed his friend Mitch Joel, a music journalist in Montreal who had just been laid off from his day job. Together, they struck up a partnership and called it Distort Entertainment. Below already knew the first band he wanted to sign. He wasted no time and walked into EMI's offices with a CD wrapped in math homework.

"What's this band called? *Alex-is-on-fire*?" McCarty asked.

"No, *Alexis-on-fire*," Below replied as he slipped in the disc and pressed play.

McCarty was far from a headbanger, but he knew a good song when he heard it. Alexisonfire's music was extreme, for sure—with way more screaming than you'd ever hear on the radio—but it was the most melodic and accessible version of this style of hardcore punk that he had ever heard.

McCarty saw potential, and he admired the band's chutzpah for wrapping their demo in Ingelevics's math homework. "You talk about punk—what an incredibly rebellious statement," he says. "'My entire schooling is only good enough to wrap my demo in. My schooling is subservient to my love of music.'"

McCarty and Below drove down to watch Alexisonfire play a Legion hall show in Niagara Falls. There were only about ten people in the crowd, but the band brought the house down anyway. McCarty was sold. "They had an overwhelming amount of energy," he recalls now. "They just had this swirl of energy and melody and noise."

"On stage, they give 120 percent," Below told *Billboard* magazine in 2004. "Each member has the potential of being their own star."

After the show, the guys from EMI took Green, the oldest of the group, out for burgers and beers, as McCarty always did with bands he wanted to sign. "Come with us, and we'll sign you to a publishing deal. We'll help you get a record deal. We'll position you to get the right one," McCarty pitched.

Green was eager, but he was ready to state the band's terms of engagement. Before the meeting, Carriere had told him exactly what to say.

"We want to be as big as possible *on our own terms*," Green recited. "If you help us, but you let us do it our way, I believe that it will work."

McCarty respected that. They had a deal.

"One more thing," Green added. "I have this other side of me that you haven't heard and you're not going to hear for a long time. But you have to promise to support that side of me."

Nobody but Green knew what that was yet, but McCarty knew he had talent. He agreed.

In June 2002, less than a year after forming, Alexisonfire had a publishing deal, a record label, and a studio they could use to write and record their debut album.

* * *

IT'S NOT LIKE THERE was no heavy music in the mainstream before Alexisonfire came along. But whether it was heavy metal traditionalists like Metallica and Iron Maiden, nu-metal titans like Korn, System of a Down, and Linkin Park, or death metal-influenced breakouts Slipknot (who screamed their way to No. 3 on the Billboard 200 with *Iowa* in 2001), those groups had one thing in common: they were all proudly metal bands.

Alexisonfire was something different, something less easily labelled. The bands that they idolized—Saetia, the Appleseed Cast, Snapcase, Bane, Quicksand, Elliott, Mogwai, Converge, and Sunny Day Real Estate among them—existed in a tangled underground ecosystem of rock, punk, and hardcore that neither intuitively fit together nor registered on the radar of the mainstream music industry, with no expectation they ever would.

"This music did not exist in any large space," says MacNeil. "The things that came later for us were unfathomable—completely inconceivable."

Even with the support they got from EMI and Distort, the recording process for Alexisonfire's debut album was a low-budget affair helmed by Below primarily at EMI's in-house studio. Those sessions were free, but it meant using the room at weird intervals over the course of several months—often for short periods in the middle of the night.

When they weren't in the studio, Alexisonfire continued to tour as much as they could, and on those early tours, an inside joke developed. All of the show flyers would list each band's name followed by a short, colourful description in brackets:

marketing-minded slogans like "Whiskey-tinged metalcore from upstate New York," or "punishing D-beat from Syracuse," or "gasoline-soaked Texas hardcore." For Alexisonfire's description on those flyers, they told promoters to write, "Two Catholic schoolgirls in a knife fight."

"I don't know what that sounds like. I don't think anybody does. But you can imagine it," Green said in a promotional video for Dine Alone Records in 2013. "And that's sort of what we sounded like, to be honest—just a bunch of shrieking."

Actually, Alexisonfire's first album sounded like a lot of things. Beginning right away with the opening measures of ".44 Caliber Love Letter," the record's eleven tracks are full of chaotic instrumentation, unconventional structures, intensely melodramatic lyrics, and vocals that run the gamut of singing, shouting, spoken word, and yes, a lot of shrieking. Everything about it is raw, youthful, and full of ideas. And while it's clearly the work of a bunch of young musicians still figuring things out, the album was nonetheless a serious debut that came to define a template for the new wave of post-hardcore. The band's jokey description inspired the lyrics for the fourth track, "A Dagger Through the Heart of St. Angeles," as well as the album's cover artwork, a photograph of two girls wearing traditional Catholic school uniforms—tartan skirts, white dress shirts, and knee-high socks—wielding switchblades.[58]

Simply titled *Alexisonfire*, the band's debut came out in Canada on Halloween 2002. Unlike some of the bigger, major-label deals that McCarty and EMI had been concocting for bands like Sum 41 and Billy Talent, Alexisonfire's record was

---

58 Pettit snapped the photo himself on the baseball diamond at Ferndale Public School.

still a small-scale project. Distort was a new label and there was virtually no marketing budget. So, the band relied on word of mouth and some other creative tactics. Alexisonfire and their team passed out thousands of sampler CDs at the Warped Tour's Ontario stop the following summer. And having smoothed out his ambiguous role as Alexisonfire's booker/promoter/advisor/superfan into the band's official manager ("I didn't really want to say that for a while because you just hear horror stories about managers and pop music," he admits), Carriere helped spread the good word by manufacturing hype on internet message boards with a half-dozen burner accounts.

Another early apostle was MuchMusic VJ George Stroumboulopoulos, who had attended Alexisonfire's first Toronto show and had interviewed the band on his radio show around the release of their debut album. Without a music video to broadcast, the only way Stroumboulopoulos could support the band on MuchMusic at first was to wear their T-shirt on the air. "I was getting letters from kids who said that they were learning about bands from what I was wearing as much as what I was talking about," Stroumboulopoulos says. It helped somewhat, but to truly break through, Alexisonfire needed to make a music video of their own.

As a condition of its licence from the Canadian Radio-television and Telecommunications Commission—the regulatory body governing the country's broadcasting industry—MuchMusic operated a fund called VideoFACT, which used a percentage of the company's gross revenue to provide grants to Canadian recording artists to help them make music videos. That way, up-and-coming artists would be able to make music videos that MuchMusic could play on its channels—and the company, consequently, would be able to meet the CRTC's minimum requirements for Canadian-made content on radio and TV. That's how a two-year-old screamo band managed to score a $20,000 cheque to make their first music video.

"That was like a million dollars at the time," says Pettit, who found out the band had received the grant while he was working a shift at a video store in Grimsby. "It was such a huge amount of money. My initial thought was, 'Can we make the music video for $5,000 and keep the rest?' And they were like, 'No, you can't, you have to use it all on the video.'"

The band hired Marc Ricciardelli, a filmmaker who had been making videos about Toronto's skateboarding scene. Inspired by Refused's video for "New Noise," they rented out a mansion in Toronto and spent an entire night—from sunset to sunrise—shooting a video for "Pulmonary Archery," the last song on the album. They would play the three-minute song as hard as they could—strumming, drumming, stomping, jumping, and windmilling around the room—and then Ricciardelli's team would set up the camera for another angle and the band would do it again and again until morning.[59] "It showed the band pretty perfectly," Pettit says.

The members of Alexisonfire stayed up to see MuchMusic play the video for the first time in the wee hours of a weeknight. It wasn't much at first, but behind the scenes over at MuchMusic headquarters, Stroumboulopoulos was pushing

59 On the night that Alexisonfire were shooting the music video, Steele was booked for a mandatory overnight inventory shift at Blockbuster. "The option was to shoot the music video and no longer work at Blockbuster, or don't shoot the music video and stay employed at Blockbuster with ten free rentals a week," he says. He was subsequently fired.

hard to get Alexisonfire out there. "We just played the shit out of them," he says.

Eventually, enough people had seen and loved "Pulmonary Archery" that they had begun to request it in droves, prompting MuchMusic to play the song not just on Stroumboulopoulos's late-night program, but in primetime rotation. Pretty soon, kids across Canada were coming home from school to see Alexisonfire screaming and thrashing in an abandoned mansion, giving many of these youngsters their first-ever introduction to screamo.

"Up until that point it already felt like the right trajectory, and it was making sense that we could probably do this," says Steele. "And then with a video that's out on the *MuchMusic Countdown* while we're in high school ... that immediately rocketed our career."

From there, Alexisonfire became MuchMusic media darlings. MacNeil and Steele would skip school to appear live on *MuchOnDemand*. "I'm supposed to be in science class and I'm on TV," says MacNeil. "As if no one's gonna find out."

The band ran with the momentum and landed subsequent grants to make two more music videos in the year that followed. "Counterparts and Number Them" showed the band wearing pink polo shirts and all smiles as they played with a big group of kids in a park, and "Waterwings" staged a dance battle to settle the score between five colourfully dressed rival gangs each led by a different band member. As they continued to get aired on MuchMusic, Alexisonfire were not only bringing screamo to primetime, they were changing the genre's image. Their music was intense, but their videos were *fun*. When they appeared on TV, Alexisonfire shocked audiences with their loud, abrasive music and unrestrained performances, but they also showed the folks at home their sense of humour and goofy personalities.[60] It was disarmingly charming, and it stood in stark contrast to the mostly dark imagery of hardcore and metal at the time.

Alexisonfire were quick to see the benefits of their exposure on Canadian TV. They went on their first U.S. tour when MacNeil and Steele had time off school for March break in early 2003, and the three-week excursion was the furthest thing from glamorous: they were playing sparsely attended community art spaces and sleeping in their van, and their album hadn't even been released in America yet. Six months later, they went on a two-week cross-Canada tour with Billy Talent, Spitalfield, and Death from Above,[61] and they watched the crowds get bigger every night. On the second-last day of the tour, they played for 1,500 people at the Croatian Cultural Centre in Vancouver. "It was monumental," says Pettit. "It was the biggest show we'd ever played at that time. People were losing their marbles. They knew the songs and they were very excited about it. So yeah, you could see how MuchMusic had a big effect on us at the time."

But fame in Canada and fame outside of Canada are two completely different things, as the band soon learned. "The other side of that coin is we finished at the Croatian Cultural Centre and we crossed into the States to Olympia, Washington,

60 When they appeared on the late-night talk show *Open Mike with Mike Bullard* on May 21, 2003, Pettit mentioned to the host that he had a big scar on his chest from an incident involving "three pigs, a Twinkie wrapper, and a bucket of congealed milk." After he had baited the audience into cheering for him to show off the scar, he pulled up his shirt to reveal a message written on his chest in black marker: "Buy our CD or we'll starve."

61 Now known as Death from Above 1979.

and played to nine people at a club the next day," Pettit recalls. "We've done this thing in Canada, but you're still in the van eating mayonnaise sandwiches the next day."

At that point, Alexisonfire hadn't had any distribution for their album in the U.S. That changed when they landed a partnership deal with Equal Vision Records, the Albany-based label founded by New York hardcore veteran Ray Cappo that was best known for releasing records by Converge and Bane. Equal Vision released Alexisonfire's debut in September 2003, shipping it to American music stores almost a full year after it had come out in Canada.

Alexisonfire's early success in their home country gave them a well-earned confidence boost, and that spring in their step helped them continue slogging it out on U.S. tours playing to barely double-digit crowds. They were determined to repeat their Canadian success south of the border even if it meant stuffing themselves into a van to play small hardcore shows in community centres and Legion halls. But the world is a big place, and they were about to learn just how far they could really go.

TWO YEARS AFTER ALEXISONFIRE'S debut, a lot had changed. Their sudden and unexpected success in Canada meant they were in a completely different position for their second album than with their first. Now, they had more than a few people in their inner circle who believed in them, they had the full attention of the music industry, and, most importantly, fans across the country in their corner. That also meant they had expectations to fulfill.

People were telling them they should hire a big-time producer for their sophomore record, but Alexisonfire rejected that advice. Green had recently had a bad experience in a writing session for another artist's major-label debut with a big producer, and it had validated many of his fears about the music business. Alexisonfire didn't want someone who would shoot down their ideas and tell them what to do. "We were very hard-headed and very opinionated," Green says.

Instead, Alexisonfire went with a basically unknown producer named Julius "Juice" Butty, who had worked for a few years in post-production audio at Canadian kids' channel YTV before building a recording studio in his Hamilton home. Sure, it was soundproofed, but not terribly well; Butty would schedule the band to record the really loud stuff during the daytime and save vocal sessions for later in the evening. His two children spent some time falling asleep to the soothing tones of Pettit screaming at the top of his lungs.

In a 2016 interview with *VICE*, Pettit described Alexisonfire's debut album as "the musical equivalent of being a little kid and sticking a bunch of ingredients in a bowl and stirring it up and thinking that you're cooking." For their second album, they tightened their focus and streamlined their songwriting. Now that they were crafting their music with more traditional structures and dividing up the vocal duties more thoughtfully among their three singers, the songs became much easier to sing (or scream) along to, and they emphasized this by punching them up with plenty of *whoa-oh* group vocals that would inspire World Cup–calibre crowd chants during their live sets. They also expanded upon the atmospheric sounds they had started to explore with "Pulmonary Archery," taking a lot of inspiration from ambient post-rock bands like Mogwai.

They were a much more experienced band than they had been two years prior, and it showed. With Butty at the helm, the recordings sounded tight and massive. Steele and Ingelevics were a thundering rhythm section, Green's and MacNeil's guitars sounded like they could carve through mountains, and Pettit evolved from a screaming teenager into something more animalistic—he was more disciplined,[62] but that only heightened his ferocity.

"People like to talk about the 'sophomore slump,'" Pettit says. "We knew that we needed to do something interesting, and we needed to level it up from what we had just done."

When Alexisonfire released *Watch Out!* in June 2004, it blew away their expectations. The album's strong first-week sales were enough to debut at No. 6 in Canada. *Watch Out!* also reached the top 25 on Billboard's Independent Albums and Heatseekers charts, their first time charting in the U.S. Three months later, Alexisonfire had their first gold record in Canada.

At home, Alexisonfire had become stars of the Canadian music scene. They produced three more music videos with Ricciardelli that all got heavy airplay on MuchMusic. At the 2005 Juno Awards, they were named New Group of the Year. At the MuchMusic Video Awards, "Accidents" won Best Independent Video, and the band took to the MMVAs' outdoor stage to deliver a blistering performance of "No

---

62 Pettit credits his vocal performances from *Watch Out!* onward to Butty's coaching: "On the first record, I was just yelling at the top of my lungs, like screechy, screaming stuff," he says. "Juice was really, really arduous about recording vocals. We would do the same thing fifty times. I would spend six hours in the studio and do two songs. I remember those being long days. I had to learn to suffer through that. And it made me better. It made me a lot better. I never lost my voice again after that."

Transitory" on the streets of downtown Toronto. In the middle of that song, the band would cut out completely to let Pettit unleash a banshee-like scream lasting precisely 2.36 seconds without any accompaniment, his voice a serrated knife cutting viciously through the night. It was something you needed to see to believe—a high-water mark for heavy music in the Canadian mainstream.

But Alexisonfire was reaching further than that. Their label and publishing team had built a network of imprints to represent the band around the world; while Distort released their record in Canada and Equal Vision handled the U.S. release, they now also had partnership deals in place with independent labels in Germany, the United Kingdom, Japan, and Brazil. In late 2004, Alexisonfire toured Australia and England, and by mid-2005 they had spent months on the road with Rise Against in both North America and Europe. Those journeys went so well that they crossed the Atlantic again that fall, this time for a month-long headlining tour through Italy, Germany, the Netherlands, France, and the U.K.

"The world just kept getting bigger and bigger," MacNeil says. "To have the recognition on a continent so far away... that was just jaw-dropping for me. I couldn't believe we were doing this in our lives. We were like, 'What do you mean people care about us in Australia? What do you mean the tour is sold out?' The more we travelled, the more we realized people cared. We started giving those places consistent attention. We were touring nonstop."

Alexisonfire ended up playing more than three hundred shows in the two years that followed *Watch Out!*, as the album converted them from Canada's weird little crossover success story into a world-conquering musical force. In a few short years, they had gone further than they ever expected a screamo band from St. Catharines could go—or really, just about any screamo band from anywhere. They had a gold record in Canada and fans all over the world. But they weren't done yet.

THE ROAD TO ALEXISONFIRE'S commercial high point started with a personal low point. On a tour of Atlantic Canada with Rise Against in March 2005, Ingelevics left Alexisonfire for "personal reasons," according to the band's official statement. The band was right in the middle of a typically hectic touring schedule booked for the rest of the spring—a five-week tour of Canada and the U.S. and then a month in Europe, with only two-week breaks between each. They had to find a new drummer, and fast.

Alexisonfire's tour manager, Sean McNab, recommended his old bandmate Jordan "Ratbeard" Hastings, who he had played with in a Burlington punk band called Jersey, an offshoot of Grade that had briefly signed to Virgin Music and Universal Records before breaking up.[63] The band wasn't sure at first—Jersey were a straightforward punk rock band in the vein of Rancid and Bad Religion and they weren't sure if Hastings could cut it in a band as technical as Alexisonfire—but after some persuading from McNab, MacNeil gave the drummer a call.

63 When Hastings first joined Jersey, bassist Johnny Lubera started calling Hastings "Ratcliff," which then morphed into "Ratcliff Clavin" after the *Cheers* character. Soon after, Hastings grew out his goatee into a scraggly beard; from then on, he was "Ratbeard."

"We're gonna be home in three days," he told him. "Can you learn these twelve songs in three days and then go on a five-week tour?"

Hastings barely had to think about it. "Yeah, I can do that," he said.

It was just the opportunity Hastings had been looking for. He had joined Jersey as a teenager around the time of their major-label deal, but once their little bit of radio success fizzled out, his older bandmates decided to move on from the band. For close to a year, Hastings had been back living in Burlington full-time and working at the Music Gym rehearsal studio. He was even considering finally finishing high school, having dropped out to tour with Jersey, so he could get back on his mom's health insurance and get his wisdom teeth removed.

But Hastings had been a massive Alexisonfire fan from the first time he saw them perform. Plus, the tooth pain was sporadic—his love of music was constant.[64] His kit was already set up at the Music Gym, so he spent three days learning as many Alexisonfire songs as he could before driving out to MacNeil's mom's house in St. Catharines for rehearsals.

FURTHER LISTENING

JERSEY

Hometown: Burlington, Ontario
Years active: 1996–2005

While Grade was gaining notoriety in the hardcore scene, guitarist Greg Taylor and drummer Kevin Harris formed a ska-punk side project that would quickly be on the rise. Jersey debuted in 1998 with *No Turning Back* and then signed with Fueled by Ramen—the American indie label that would later sign Fall Out Boy—for their second album, *The Battle's Just Begun*, the following year. In 2003, Jersey landed a co-venture deal with Virgin Music and Universal Records and made their major-label debut with 2004's *Generation Genocide*, which featured new drummer Jordan Hastings. The band broke up a year later and went in separate directions: Hastings joined Alexisonfire, later formed Say Yes and Cunter, and spent several years filling in for Billy Talent, while the other members formed groups including Saint Alvia, the Artist Life, and the Creepshow.

---

64 He would finally get his wisdom teeth removed around a decade later, when he was in his thirties.

Less than two weeks after Alexisonfire's East Coast tour had ended, they were back on the road with Rise Against, their new drummer in tow. Hastings was just supposed to be a fill-in until the band could reconvene and make a real plan ahead of their next album, but from his first show of the tour, at the Masquerade in Atlanta, it was clear that he was an excellent fit.

Alexisonfire agreed, and Hastings officially joined the band shortly after. They had finally encountered a classic rite of passage for bands—the dreaded lineup change—and had come out the other side stronger, just in time to head back into the studio to record their biggest album yet.

WHILE ALEXISONFIRE WERE THROWING a boat party in England's capital in August 2006, the band's third record became an immediate chart-topper back home. *Crisis* sold twenty thousand copies in Canada in its first week, more than tripling the first-week sales of *Watch Out!* two years earlier. That was enough for it to debut at No. 1 on the Canadian albums chart, knocking Christina Aguilera out of the top spot. In the U.S., the band released *Crisis* on Vagrant Records, home to emo heavyweights the Get Up Kids, Dashboard Confessional, and Saves the Day, leading to their first appearance on the Billboard 200 in the U.S. Additional chart success in the U.K. and Australia further proved that Alexisonfire had broken out of Canada to arrive on the international stage.

"*Crisis* felt special," says Pettit. "I think we knew we were making a really good record at that point. We had found a little bit of confidence and we knew what we wanted to sound like. It was the most concise record thematically, the artwork—everything came together and coalesced really, really nicely with *Crisis*."

Alexisonfire toured the world for the next ten months, paying multiple visits to the U.K., Europe, and Australia while also criss-crossing Canada and the U.S. several times. And with the success of *Crisis*, the band was taking the stage in front of massive crowds the likes of which they had never seen before: they played the main stages at the Reading and Leeds festivals in the week following the album's release, they hung with crowds of thousands of people on travelling festivals, including the U.K. leg of the Taste of Chaos tour and Australia's Soundwave; and they were a smash on the summer festival circuit in Canada, which included an eighty-thousand-person draw at the Festival d'été de Québec. Back home, the demand was so high that they played six straight nights in Toronto in mid-December 2006 (plus a seventh the day after Christmas). *Crisis* continued to sell so many copies that it would be certified platinum in Canada on May 1, 2007, just eight months after it landed in stores. By the end of 2007, Alexisonfire had amassed enough of an audience in the U.K. that they were able to play a headlining show at the nearly five-thousand-capacity Brixton Academy in London.

Since its release, *Crisis* has stood as Alexisonfire's signature album. The record is a musically, thematically, and visually cohesive work that finds Pettit, Green, and MacNeil splitting vocal duties evenly as they sing about social issues including homelessness, addiction, labour, natural disasters, and generational divide. Songs like "Boiled Frogs," "We Are the Sound," "Rough Hands," and "Drunks, Lovers, Sinners and Saints" would become long-term staples of their live sets, guaranteed to send fans into a frenzy of mosh pits, circle pits, and sing-alongs.

"The songs definitely got better," says Butty. "There was definitely an elevation there from a songwriting standpoint, and in an arrangement standpoint, and lyrics and melody."

The album's biggest standout was "This Could Be Anywhere in the World," which became the band's first charting single thanks to MuchMusic and mainstream radio airplay pushing the song onto Canada's rock and alternative charts. It was an unusually structured turn for Alexisonfire; it was hardly pop by any means, but where the groups' three-vocalist dogpile tended to follow no discernible pattern, here Green's clean vocals made the chorus as accessible as any other rock hit, with enough heaviness from Pettit and MacNeil to satisfy older fans.

The new rhythm section is perhaps the song's secret sauce; Steele brought forward the idea to punctuate the intro with a pair of guitar chords so snappy they sound like slash marks, and tasked Hastings to fill the space. "I was like, 'What the fuck am I going to fill that space with? I gotta figure out something that's hooky, because that's a lot of space in a song,'" says Hastings. "I felt like I would be doing the song an injustice if I just let it be straight and boring." His music teacher had recently taught him about polyrhythms, which led to a series of grooving, Latin-inspired drum fills that became almost as much of the song's calling card as Green's chorus. Emphasis on "almost." Green had always been a strong singer, but on *Crisis*, he was noticeably more confident, with plenty of straight-up belting. He wasn't just a great singer by punk-rock standards, he was a great singer by *any* standard. Green's voice was a game changer, an ace-in-the-hole that single-handedly raised Alexisonfire's ceiling.

"I'm sure that there could have been some feelings around

that time, like, 'It might have been a straight shot to the top of the charts for those guys if they just kicked out the weird screamy kid from the band,'" says Pettit. "The obvious thing to do is to put Dallas at the front of the band, and he's clearly a very, very good singer. And I think there was even a heartbeat where we tried that. The band bought me a guitar and an amp, and there was an idea of like, 'Okay, so during these songs, you're gonna play guitar and that way, you've got something to do on stage while Dallas is singing,' and then we abandoned that very quickly. We found that it wasn't what we were supposed to be doing. I was more than happy to do whatever, but the second we started thinking in that regard, it was no longer Alexisonfire. Then, we doubled down on what already existed, and we knew that we could find a good balance."

After a year and a half of near constant touring, Alexisonfire were one of the biggest heavy music acts in the world, and they had done so on independent labels and by staying true to their unorthodox three-vocalist structure and vast range of musical influences. The band's interpersonal relationships remained intact, with a musical drive so fierce that multiple members chose to use the post-touring downtime to make music elsewhere. MacNeil, joined by Pettit and Hastings, started a folk-punk project called Black Lungs, while Green decided to focus on his singer-songwriter pursuits—a decision that marked the beginning of the end for Alexisonfire.

DALLAS GREEN NEVER FORMALLY "started" his solo project—he had kind of been doing it the whole time. He had sold early solo EPs at Alexisonfire shows to make a quick buck and performed solo acoustic shows during breaks in Alexisonfire's touring schedule to keep his singer-songwriter muscles active. "When I first got into rock music, I was always attracted to the aggressiveness of it, but I was also attracted to the melody in there as well," Green explains. "So, when I started writing, I started writing on an acoustic guitar and singing, and also playing guitar really loud and writing riffs. All that stuff is amazing, and I love doing that. I was just always attracted to a song, you know? It was never a question to me whether or not I would do both. Writing simple acoustic songs was just another way for me to explore that outlet of songwriting." By early 2005, he had started using the moniker City and Colour, a spin on the name Dallas Green.

Alexisonfire fans started sharing Green's solo material on the internet and talking to him about it after shows. To sate this new fan-base offshoot, Green made more solo recordings during Alexisonfire's brief breaks, and in November 2005, City and Colour's debut album, *Sometimes*, was released on Carriere's new label, Dine Alone Records.[65] The project made waves early the next year on the strength of lead single "Save Your Scissors," a deceptively simple acoustic folk number about not changing oneself for others. It laid bare the power of Green's voice and lyrics, which often went obscured in Alexisonfire, just one part of the maelstrom and chaos. As "Save Your Scissors" hit the charts, it was joined by "The Grace," a collaboration between Green and his friend Daniel Victor's project Neverending White

---

65 While City and Colour was Dine Alone's first signed artist, *Sometimes* was not the label's first release—DA001 had been snatched up a few weeks earlier by *Short Controlled Bursts* by the Fullblast, the punk band from Oakville, Ontario, that featured former members of Shane Told's pre-Silverstein band Jerk Circus.

Lights. The two songs brought Green's voice where Alexisonfire could not, establishing him as a singer with crossover appeal who could win over the hardcore kids and the indie crowd in equal measure. *Sometimes* was Green's third album to go gold, after *Alexisonfire* and *Watch Out!*, but his first to go platinum, selling one hundred thousand copies in Canada in just over a year. It also earned Green a Juno Award for Alternative Album of the Year in 2007.

"That was the moment where Canada had to make a decision. I think a lot of people said, 'I like this guy.' And a lot of people said, 'Fuck this guy,'" Green says. "But that was a moment for me where all of those things happening at once created the thing that I don't think any of us saw coming. That many people paying attention changed my life, really."

After putting City and Colour to the side for *Crisis*, he dusted off the moniker for a second album, *Bring Me Your Love*, released in February 2008. The album expanded the project's palette by adding pedal steel, organ, slide guitar, mandolin, percussion, and a collaboration with the legendary Gord Downie of the Tragically Hip. It peaked at No. 3 in Canada, going gold in exactly three months, and platinum six months after that, and went to No. 31 in Australia. Two of the album's singles, "Waiting..." and the Downie-featuring "Sleeping Sickness," charted on the format-agnostic Canadian Hot 100 chart. Green was finally able to bring his rigorous approach to touring to his solo project, going on a sold-out U.K. tour with Ontario punk rockers Attack in Black, a Canadian tour with MacNeil's side project Black Lungs, a U.S. tour supporting the twin indie-pop duo Tegan and Sara, and another U.S. tour as headliner.

On New Year's Eve, days before that headlining tour started, Green married his partner of two years, MuchMusic VJ Leah Miller. Days after that tour ended, Green flew to Vancouver to start recording Alexisonfire's fourth album. Every part of his life was ascending to a higher level—but his body was about to start giving out and his mental health was suffering. "Instead of celebrating both of these things happening at the same time—and it was literally my dream coming true—I was basically not celebrating either of them," Green says. "I really became a miserable person."

On the night that Green found out that *Bring Me Your Love* had been certified platinum in Canada, he was in the middle of a tour with Alexisonfire. Not wanting to risk anybody being upset, he didn't bring it up. The band had dinner, and Green quietly paid the cheque himself—a small, private celebration of a momentous milestone in his solo career.

Alexisonfire rallied for a fourth album, *Old Crows / Young Cardinals*, but from the moment they went into the studio, it was evident that things had taken a turn for the worse. Green was in the deep throes of burnout, Steele was struggling with alcoholism, and MacNeil had started going to

FURTHER LISTENING

ATTACK IN BLACK

Hometown: Welland, Ontario
Years active: 2003–2010

Emerging from the Niagara region punk scene, Attack in Black had already shed a lot of their hardcore influences by the time they signed to Dine Alone and started releasing music, but their 2007 debut album *Marriage* still hits pretty hard, no doubt aided by their time on the road with Alexisonfire. *Marriage* is driven by Daniel Romano's raspy, howling vocals that dig in deep even on the twangier numbers, but especially when their punk inclinations are strongest, like on "Hunger of the Young" or the title track. Attack in Black's last two albums were pretty old-school folk, released around the time that Romano brought similar touches to City and Colour's second album, *Bring Me Your Love*. But while the other band members have stayed pretty folky in their solo works, Romano has been known to return to his punk roots every now and then, like with his bands Ancient Shapes and Spider Bite.

therapy. By the time the album was released in June 2009, the cracks were starting to show. All it took was an almost imperceptible step back to shake the band's foundation. While *Crisis* had debuted at No. 1 in Canada, *Old Crows / Young Cardinals* only debuted at No. 2. It was the first time the band had seen anything other than a constant upward trajectory.

"We see a decline in ticket sales, and then you couple that with the fatigue that comes with touring for ten months out of the year, and I think that that was just enough," says Pettit. "We were trying to keep this plate spinning that was keeping everybody really engaged and really confident in what we were doing, and the second it took a little bump or came down even in the slightest bit, it broke. It made it more apparent the things that were killing us."

By the time they finished touring behind *Old Crows / Young Cardinals* in December 2010, Green told the band he'd be quitting. Throughout touring, he would lie awake at night, crying uncontrollably in the bus. At one point he was hospitalized with pneumonia. "I was pushing my body to the end of its limits," he says now. "I was stubborn and not willing to see how deteriorated I had become." The rest of the band initially wanted to move on without him, and even chatted with rapper P.O.S., Jim Ward of Sparta and At the Drive-In, and Melissa Auf der Maur of Hole and Smashing Pumpkins about filling Green's spot. But then MacNeil himself was presented with a new opportunity he couldn't resist, when the English hardcore punk band Gallows asked him to be their new lead vocalist.

With two members gone, that was it. In Pettit's farewell letter to fans the following August, he wrote, "Was the breakup amicable? Not really. Was it necessary? Probably."

* * *

ALEXISONFIRE'S IMPLOSION WAS ULTIMATELY a blessing in disguise. The band reunited for a proper farewell tour in 2012 and then, over the years, began touring in short stints when their other projects would allow it. Green was able to make City and Colour his main focus, yielding four consecutive No. 1 albums in Canada (of which all cracked the top 10 in Australia), while making room for Alexisonfire, finding the balance he so desperately craved. A few months after the band stopped touring, Steele was pursuing alcoholism treatment; following Alexisonfire's 2019 tour, he convinced MacNeil to get treatment as well.

Alexisonfire eventually released a few new singles, and then made their grand return with their fifth album, *Otherness*, in 2022. It may never be the members' main focus again, but they had learned that their friendships and the band itself are better when it's not the only thing going on in their lives. From the very beginning, Alexisonfire started calling themselves "The Only Band Ever," based on an in-joke between Pettit and his pals in Grimsby,

FURTHER LISTENING

FUCKED UP

Hometown: Toronto, Ontario
Years active: 2001–present

If their name isn't enough of an indication, Fucked Up are one of the most provocative bands in Canadian music. Since their formation in Toronto in 2001—with every member initially using a pseudonym—the band has strayed far from the standards of typical hardcore punk as they've experimented with lengthy instrumental jams and unconventional arrangements coupled with cryptic lyrics full of mysticism, obscure references, and character-driven narratives. While all of that sounds inaccessible to a broad audience, Fucked Up managed to not only win over Toronto's underground, but the larger Canadian music industry and American indie-rock scene. Three of their albums have been nominated for Juno Awards, one won the juried Polaris Music Prize in 2009, and vocalist Damian Abraham hosted *The Wedge* on MuchMusic from 2011 until its cancellation in 2014.

who used "the only ____ ever" as a hyperbolic expression that something was really great.[66] From that fall day in 2001 when five teenagers first picked up their instruments together in a basement in St. Catharines through to the glory days of playing for massive crowds at festivals and concert halls around the world, Alexisonfire was, to them, the only band ever—the only thing that mattered. More than twenty years later, that's no longer the case, and they're better for it. And it seems they may never stop making noise.

"We still have this thing with each other that we started because Wade called me and said, 'Would you like to jam with me and Steele?'" Green says. "That's still there and all of the other stuff that comes with it, whether it's finding what shows we want to play, or choosing artwork for a record, or who we play with . . . all that bullshit is one side of it. But at the core of it, we can also be in a room, make each other laugh, and make a really great racket together."

---

66 It also came in handy because Alexisonfire couldn't use alexisonfire.com as their website URL, since that was already taken by the adult entertainer they'd named the band after, so they went with theonlybandever.com instead.

8

FEFE DOBSON

On a brisk Manhattan evening in November 2003, young people line the sidewalk outside MTV's Times Square headquarters illuminated by the bright neon displays of electronic billboards. Dozens of them are holding their own more rudimentary signs made with markers, construction paper, and glue sticks that proclaim NYC ♥S FEFE and FEFE ROCKS!!! As Fefe Dobson skips her way onto the set of MTV's *Total Request Live*, host Damien Fahey takes her hand and leads her over to the studio's floor-to-ceiling windows overlooking the square so she can see the hordes of fans outside. "This does not happen with a lot of first-timers, so you should be very proud of yourself," Fahey tells the perky eighteen-year-old as she grins widely and waves to the fans below.

The feverish reception comes on the back of Dobson's single "Take Me Away," which, as Fahey makes a point to note, has been in constant rotation on MTV throughout the summer and fall of 2003.

"Does it feel like it's taken a long time to get to this point?" Fahey asks her.

Dobson hesitates for a split second before answering. "It's taken the right amount of time," she says. "I wouldn't have wanted it to have come out any time earlier."

It's a diplomatic answer, a humble and gracious one that Dobson may or may not actually believe. After all, she's still a teenager but already a star. She certainly has the confidence down pat: she riffs with Fahey without missing a beat, making jokes, appealing to the audience, and even flirting openly with the hotshot host. Cool and collected, she's a natural in front of the camera, appearing completely unfazed in her blue jeans and studded belt, tank top, and long jacket that swooshes back and forth as she sways nonchalantly throughout their conversation.

In a few weeks, Dobson's debut album will hit stores and solidify her as one of the brightest young stars in the music industry, with a sound and image that combines the hard-edged rock of idols like Kurt Cobain and Sid Vicious with an unapologetic adoration of pop music. And while this young star is only eighteen years old, it must have felt like it took a lifetime to get here as a young Black girl from a poor neighbourhood in a Toronto suburb who dreamed of being the type of rock star the world wasn't ready for.

FEFE DOBSON'S TASTE IN music is as eclectic as her upbringing. When she was a young girl growing up in Scarborough, at the easternmost edge of Toronto, her vibrant musical life was divided into three very different worlds.

First, there was musical theatre: showtunes and vaudeville that Dobson sang on stages across the city, in productions like *The Wizard of Oz*, and during singing lessons at the New Conservatory of Music. "I was never afraid to sing," she recalls. "I was taught that at a very young age: if someone says 'sing,' you sing." And, even if nobody said "sing," she sang anyway: on the street, on public transport, atop coffee tables, in malls.

Then, there was the pop music that she and her friends devoured. They swapped mixtapes filled with the latest '90s boy bands and girl groups like Take 5 and Dream. Dobson regularly made her way across the city to see Hanson, O-Town, and NSYNC, sometimes even alone, with money she had saved up for months. But ultimately, Dobson craved a companion, someone to share her experiences. Memorably, she once sold a high-priced ticket to see NSYNC—which would have allowed her to be up close to the stage where her crush, Justin Timberlake, could notice her—for two tickets in the nosebleeds so that her older sister Tanya could tag along. Thankfully, Tanya chose to swoon over JC Chasez instead, leaving space for Fefe's dreamed-up love affair with Timberlake. "Good thing she didn't choose Justin, because we would've been fighting," says Dobson.

And finally, when Dobson came home from school, she would listen to her mom's record collection filled with hits from the '80s: Donna Summer, Depeche Mode, Lionel Richie, and Phil Collins, among others.

Though everyone in the family loved music, it was clear that Fefe loved it the most. When she was eleven, her mom used a year's worth of savings from her job delivering *Toronto Star* newspapers to buy her daughter a karaoke machine for Christmas. It was a giant box with a CD player, tape deck, microphone, and several knobs. Dobson would play her favourite songs from CD, and the machine would mute the vocal track and record Dobson's vocals over the instrumental to a cassette tape. Week after week, Dobson would create demo tapes, packing cassettes with her karaoke renditions of classic tracks by Shania Twain, Janet Jackson, and Céline Dion. Highly ambitious even then, she'd send those tapes to any music industry address she could find.

For Dobson, having a successful career in music would give her a more stable future. Her mom was raising four kids on her own, and the family moved around every few years, living in subsidized housing in low-income areas like Kingston-Galloway and Malvern. "These were really not the safest neighbourhoods," says Dobson. "There was a lot of poverty in Scarborough when I was growing up. We were living in some crazy times out there."

As a mixed-race child of a white mother and a Black father, Dobson felt out of step with her classmates. "My school was multicultural, to the point where there were no white kids. So I was very different," she told the *Observer* in 2004. "The other kids were like, 'Why aren't you like us? Why don't you listen to hip-hop?' But that wasn't where my passion was. When they were listening to Puff Daddy and Mase, I was listening to R.E.M.'s 'Losing My Religion.'"

Dobson was an eccentric who stood out from the pack—always obsessing over a boy, always wearing some outlandish outfit cobbled together from her mom's hand-me-downs, always wearing her heart on her sleeve. It made her an easy target for a group of bullies who would make fun of her relentlessly. "I recall one instance where a bunch of kids chased me home. And I remember being really tough on the way home and then the minute my mom walked in the door, I fell to my knees and broke down," says Dobson. "It hurt when kids made fun of me, but at the same time ... I didn't give a fuck."[67]

As Dobson entered her teenage years, she was admitted to the local arts high school, Wexford Collegiate Institute, to study musical theatre. At the same time, her after-school ritual changed to incorporate a fourth style of music that would become a key part of her identity. Once she was done listening to her mom's record collection, she would head upstairs and hover outside Tanya's room, pressing one ear close to the door to overhear the music blaring on the other side, bands like Guns N' Roses and Nirvana. Dobson was transfixed. She had never heard such power and vulnerability before. Musical theatre taught Dobson how to belt, pop music taught Dobson how to connect, and her mom's record collection taught Dobson how to groove. But it was her older sister's rock music that would teach Dobson how to *feel.*

ARTS HIGH SCHOOLS ARE a perpetual game of one-upmanship. If you place a few hundred kids with ambitions of stardom in the same few classrooms, they're naturally predisposed to try to outdo each other in increasingly audacious ways. Dobson was no exception. Even as a Grade 9 student, she was already known

---

67 Decades later, when Dobson bumped into one of her childhood bullies at the airport, the bully claimed that she picked on Dobson because "you were so emotional, you were so *easy.*"

at Wexford for her audacity as much as her talent, particularly for one bold statement that she would make over and over again: "Justin Timberlake is going to know me." At that time, in early 2000, Timberlake was one-fifth of NSYNC, whose album *No Strings Attached* had sold more than 2.4 million CDs in its first week, spawning massive pop radio hits like "Bye Bye Bye" and "It's Gonna Be Me." Dobson, on the other hand, was struggling to sit through her math and science classes. But the path to Timberlake was closer than anyone would suspect.

Bonnie Fedrau, the A&R director at Zomba Music Canada, had received one of Dobson's karaoke tapes and was impressed with what she heard. Fedrau got in touch with the young singer to discuss working together, and the moment that Dobson learned that Zomba was an affiliate of Jive Records—home to NSYNC, Britney Spears, and the Backstreet Boys—she jumped at the opportunity.

Zomba offered Dobson a demo deal and teamed her up with a roster of nearly a dozen songwriters. After school, while her classmates would rehearse for school musicals, Dobson was going to recording studios to write songs with a suite of collaborators including Doc McKinney, Dave Hodge, Bryan Potvin, and Terry Sawchuk (not the famed NHL goaltender). But Dobson found that the music she was working on wasn't the rock, grunge, or punk music that was quickly becoming the soundtrack to her life—it was pop, R&B, and dance music.

"It just didn't feel right," she says now. "I love all genres of music, and I can literally enjoy any song you put on if it's a good melody and it feels good or it's just something really special, but it wasn't right for me."

Dobson did her best to push through the sessions and play

nice, but her frustrations worsened when she learned that some staffers had been calling her "Brandy Spears" because they thought she looked like Brandy Norwood and sounded like Britney Spears—a Black girl with a white voice. "I didn't like being compared to someone right off the bat because I hadn't even figured out who I was," says Dobson. "I respect Britney, and Brandy, too, but that's not who I am. It just felt icky."

At home, Dobson had moved on from listening outside her sister's door to become fully immersed in the world of modern rock music. Like any good Canadian teenager, Dobson constantly watched MuchMusic, which is how she discovered Silverchair. The first thing she loved about the Australian rock trio was lead singer Daniel Johns's flowing blond locks, but she was even more captivated by his heart-baring honesty on the band's third album, *Neon Ballroom*, which had come out in March 1999, the week after Dobson's fourteenth birthday. Across the album's twelve songs, Johns opened up about his struggles with depression and anorexia nervosa. Dobson was hooked. "I was going through my own trauma at school, so I think that album helped me verbalize it in a really dramatic, emo way," she says. "I needed someone I could turn to, musically, and feel like I wasn't alone. And I definitely think Silverchair and Daniel Johns feeling alienated from the world really helped."

Dobson had always wanted to be a singer-songwriter, but now she was starting to learn exactly the type of songwriter she wanted to be.

* * *

DESPITE DOBSON'S FRUSTRATIONS WITH Zomba, her dreams of stardom fuelled her through session after session in the hopes that she would finally cut through the noise and find her voice. One day, as she was trying to get through another uninspiring session at Wellesley Sound Studios in downtown Toronto, there was a knock at the door. Dobson's voice had caught the attention of the two guys in the neighbouring booth, Jay Levine and James Bryan McCollum, who were looking for help with a track they were working on for their cartoon pop duo, Prozzäk.

Dobson was thrilled. She loved Prozzäk—many MuchMusic viewers did. They were a parody of a Europop group, with cheesy put-on accents, flamenco guitars, simple drum machines, and crudely animated music videos that looked overly lo-fi even for the late '90s. Levine and McCollum had started the project as a joke while touring Europe with their pop-rock band the Philosopher Kings, but Prozzäk's tongue-in-cheek dance-pop side project eventually became their main focus.

Levine and McCollum invited Dobson to their studio to record background vocals for a song they were working on, the theme to *Get a Clue*, a Disney Channel made-for-TV movie starring Lindsay Lohan as a high-school detective.[68] Instead of Prozzäk's usual Europop production and subdued vocals, there were chugging guitars and nasal sneers reminiscent of Blink-182's Tom DeLonge. All they needed were some background vocals. Dobson agreed instantly. "I was such a big fan of Prozzäk. I loved their music and I had their album." Dobson

68 The song "Get a Clue"—and all of Prozzäk's releases on Hollywood Records—came out under the name "Simon and Milo," presumably because there was no way Disney was going to release music by a band named after an antidepressant.

sang along, adding some shouts and melodies to the chorus. The song was an upbeat burst of in-your-face punk rock energy, and Dobson came alive in the studio.

"She just exploded on it. It was mind-blowing and perfect for her, the energy and fun really came out," Levine recalls. "It was this 'a-ha' moment of her tearing that track up. I was like, 'Wow, this is a different person when rock guitars are happening.'"

After the session, Levine and McCollum's enthusiasm was through the roof. "You shine on this," Levine told Dobson. "You should make this type of music."

"That's what I've been trying to tell everybody!" she replied. "I want to make punk-pop music and I want to make things that are rebellious, and with guitars!"

Levine put it to her straight: "Look, do you want to make a record? I can't promise you anything, I can't tell you that it'll work, I can't say that people are gonna give a shit, but we'll make the records you love, and you'll walk out of here happy."

Dobson's hour in the studio with Levine and McCollum had excited her more than all her sessions with Zomba's songwriters combined. Plus, it just so happened that the production duo were looking for an artist to develop.

The next time Dobson met with Zomba for lunch, she told them she was walking away, and that was that.[69] Instead, she signed a production deal with Levine and McCollum, who had proven to her that, as well-intentioned as Zomba was, she didn't have to try to fit in. She just needed to be herself.

"People compare you right away to someone else or try to

---

69 "I made sure I ate the free lunch first," she told Refinery29 in 2021.

position you in a certain way. It's like, 'What the hell?! Let me carve out my own fuckin' thing,'" says Dobson.

She had been waiting for someone to give her that opportunity, to meet her where she was instead of where they thought she should be. Levine and McCollum were those people. The next step was to get writing.

THE PHILOSOPHER KINGS AND Prozzäk were both signed to Sony-owned labels, so Levine and McCollum had access to the Sony Music Canada offices in northeast Toronto. With Dobson out of school—she had decided not to return for Grade 11 in the fall of 2001—the trio spent their days writing. Though she didn't have much to her name yet, Dobson was adamantly a singer-songwriter. She wasn't going to let a bunch of adult songwriters pitch songs to her like a typical pop star—she had to write them herself.

Levine and McCollum were firmly on board with this plan. They encouraged Dobson to write music that was honest to her life experiences, and to not hold back. "Jay and James gave me the ability to be free, and to express my childhood," says Dobson. "They saw something in me that needed to be nurtured. I don't think that they were trying to create anything, I think they were trying to just let it come out."

"I thought she might have felt she was being pigeonholed for superficial reasons, like 'a Black girl shouldn't do rock' and 'a Black girl should be Brandy,' who was big at the time," says Levine. "There wasn't a lot of thought that someone of that background would gravitate naturally toward a more rock sound. When we started to do it, there was no issue with that at all. She was meant to sing rock and roll music."

In the Sony studios, they wrote "Revolution Song," where Dobson imagines a world free of oppression; "Unforgiven," an excoriating cut directed at her absent father; and "Julia," about a friend's eating disorder. "I felt safe to go there with them, *and* to write about teenage shit," she says.

"I can remember the lines she came up with," Levine adds. "A lot of people say, 'Oh yeah, I wrote this,' but then they have these grownup people holding their hands really doing all the writing. That is not the case with her. Even when she was a teenager, she has absolutely always been a killer writer, no question about it."

While all of this was happening, another teenage girl from Ontario was already laying out a viable pathway to pop-punk supremacy. One day at Sony, while Dobson and Levine were working on a demo, Dobson glanced at the TV and saw a teenager in a tank top and a necktie rocking out on MuchMusic. "She's so pretty," she said to herself. "And damn, she's *good*."

In 2002, Avril Lavigne was doing just about everything Dobson was trying to do. As the world got its first taste of Avrilmania, Dobson wanted to be the next young Canadian girl to become a global superstar. And she wanted to take it up a notch, to make the kind of hard-rocking, punked-up record that even Lavigne was fighting against music industry forces to make for herself. "Avril's album [*Let Go*] and her singles were masterful and massive hits, but very pop," says Levine. "Don't get me wrong, it's a killer album, and those songs are amazing as pop songs to this day. However, what we were doing was pretty hardcore for a teenage girl-pop album."

There was more than enough room for the thousands of men in bands all over the world, so surely the rock world could handle *two* teenage girls from Ontario—right?

IN 2002, LEVINE AND McCollum set Dobson up with Chris Smith, who managed the Philosopher Kings and Prozzäk. Smith was the guy who had convinced Levine and McCollum to strike out on their own, and the pair had complete faith that Smith would encourage Dobson to reach her full potential. The team decided that the best way to get Dobson signed to a label was by way of her theatrical, larger-than-life personality. So, instead of just shopping around demos, they were going to turn her into a live act.

Picking the right live band for Dobson was going to be tricky. The team needed to find musicians who were talented enough to hack it as the backing band for a major-label-calibre artist, but were still green enough to be affordable, since Dobson didn't actually have that major-label deal yet. They distributed flyers at local rock shows, hoping to attract the attention of young musicians who were on the path to becoming professionals. At an Ozzy Osbourne show at Copps Coliseum in Hamilton in March 2002, a university student named Dan Kanter stumbled upon a trove of flyers after a failed attempt to meet Osbourne's guitarist, Zakk Wylde, at the stage door. The flyers read "International Recording Artist Looking for a Band," and Kanter, a second-year music student at York University in Toronto, was immediately interested. He called the number and was asked to prepare songs by Blink-182 and Linkin Park. "I was a rocker at the time, leaning more grungy than punky, but I definitely borrowed a studded belt and dressed a little for the part," Kanter admits.

On the Sony office soundstage, Kanter leaned into the rock 'n' roll theatrics, doling out scissor kicks and jumping off the riser. After the initial audition to a backing track and a callback with Dobson, he got the gig. "Had I met Zakk Wylde, I probably would not have picked up a flyer off the ground," he says. Everyone in the band could *play*—drummer Colin Robinson and the other guitarist Anesti Karantakis had both studied jazz at Humber College—and they all helped one another build the stage presence to make Dobson a formidable live act.

After months of rehearsals at the Sony office, Dobson's band embarked on a series of concerts at small venues around Ontario and slowly amassed more allies. A show in Burlington in mid-2002 was enough to convince Universal Music Canada president Randy Lennox to call up Lyor Cohen, the CEO of Island Def Jam, who was fresh off the worldwide success of Sum 41. "I need you to come up to Toronto," Lennox told Cohen. "And if I'm wrong, I'll never call you again." Cohen and A&R head Jeff Fenster flew to Toronto a few days later for a morning showcase at Reverb, one of three venues housed in the gigantic, purple-painted monolith known as the Big Bop.

The band launched into "Stupid Little Love Song," one of the new pop-punk tunes Dobson had written with Levine and McCollum. There were only about ten people in the room, but the thrashing guitars, skittering drums, and Dobson's snarling vocals ignited them all into a frenzy. Though Dobson had only been performing with a band for a few months, her live persona was already outrageous, with jumps and spins and leaps off the drum kit.

"The minute the band played, it was like I was let out of a cage," says Dobson. "I could just do crazy shit and not get in trouble for it. That felt really great not to have anyone telling me what I could do. Once I was on that stage, it was *my* show, and as long as I was performing and singing and remembering lyrics and giving my best, I basically could do what I wanted out there. And that was awesome to me."

Kanter puts a finer point on it: "Fefe is by far one of the best frontpeople in all of music," he says. "From the beginning, she was amazing."

By the end of the thirty-minute set, Cohen was in. Within minutes, Dobson's lawyer Chris Taylor was on the phone with Island Def Jam's head of business affairs to negotiate a record deal. "It was always a whirlwind, nothing really made sense," she says. "It was just so fast. When it happened, it happened so quickly."

At just seventeen years old, Fefe Dobson—a girl who grew up in the poor neighbourhoods of Scarborough, where she was relentlessly bullied by her classmates—had landed a major-label record deal. Now, she was off to New York to make her debut album.

DURING THEIR SONGWRITING SESSIONS, Levine and McCollum had given Dobson a crash course in punk rock history centred around New York City, the movement's birthplace. Dobson developed an obsession with the legendary nightclub CBGB and many of the genre's pioneers who frequented the space, like Patti Smith, Blondie, and the Ramones. She also became obsessed with the tragic story of Sid Vicious and Nancy

Spungen, which led her to develop a wicked Sid Vicious impression that never failed to make Levine laugh.

Dobson was having fun, but to her, punk was more than just a good time—it was a lifeline. "I had always felt like I didn't belong anywhere," she says. "That's what I love about punk music: you don't have to belong."

When Island Def Jam came on board, Dobson's team made it clear that if they wanted to do it right, they needed to make the album in New York. On Island Def Jam's dime, Dobson and Levine moved into an apartment hotel on 58th Street in Manhattan.

The major-label budget gave Dobson, Levine, and McCollum free rein to make the biggest-sounding album they possibly could. The label also rented out the Shed, a recording studio located on the penthouse floor of a building in Midtown Manhattan, and held further auditions to assemble Dobson's studio band. Her bandmates from Toronto flew down to New York to audition for the album but were passed over in favour of more seasoned studio players like Jack Daley, who had been playing bass for Lenny Kravitz for a decade, and Nir Z, a drummer who had played with Genesis and John Mayer.

Kanter harbours no hard feelings. "I shouldn't have gotten the gig," he says. "I was not at the level to play at the studio at the time." That said, he and some of his other bandmates were invited to record some overdubs at Metalworks Studios, in the same rooms that birthed countless bestselling albums, including Guns N' Roses' *Use Your Illusion II*, Sum 41's *All Killer No Filler*, and NSYNC's *Celebrity*. Kanter had been told that a newer song called "Take Me Away" was "not rockin'," so he rented a Flying V from the nearest Long & McQuade music store and played it through a Marshall amp at Metalworks. After that, says Kanter, "it definitely was rockin'."

With the album done by the middle of 2003, it was just about time for the world to finally meet Fefe Dobson.

DOBSON'S INTRODUCTION TO AUDIENCES was slow at first, with Island Def Jam testing the waters in the summer of 2003 with a Canada-only single. "Bye Bye Boyfriend," a brash kiss-off that alternates between melodramatic pianos and chugging guitars—like a punked-up version of Evanescence's "Bring Me to Life" without the rapping—was a modest success. It did decently on Canadian rock radio and landed on MuchMusic's annual *Big Shiny Tunes* compilation CD, *Big Shiny Tunes 8*, alongside recent hits by Gob, Sum 41, Simple Plan, Linkin Park, Red Hot Chili Peppers, Nickelback, and Jane's Addiction.

But the moment she made her international debut with "Take Me Away," Dobson was on the fast track to stardom. Inspired by the tragic love stories of Sid and Nancy, and John Lennon and Yoko Ono, "Take Me Away" resonated with its message about forbidden love, not just in Canada but in the U.S. as well. "Going by this potent introduction, her potential is limitless," critic Chuck Taylor wrote in *Billboard* that September. The music video introduced the world to Dobson as a microphone-swinging straight-shooter decked out in a tank top and an abundance of chains, and who punctuated her dance moves with boxing jabs and jump kicks. She was tough and not to be messed with, but also passionate and heartfelt. The video quickly found daily rotation on MTV, leading to her hero's welcome at her first of several appearances on *Total Request Live* that November. It was perfect timing for the album's release a few weeks later, on December 9, 2003.

While Fefe Dobson's self-titled debut album spans a range of styles from light and airy pop-rock to super-charged mosh fuel, it's clear that punk rock is the prevailing attitude. Opening with "Stupid Little Love Song," the lightning-fast thrasher that got her signed, the album has no shortage of buzzsaw guitars, pounding drums, and snarling vocals, like on the snarky pop-punk cut, "Kiss Me Fool," and the body-slamming hardcore riffs of "Unforgiven" and "Give It Up." On the album's cover, Dobson is almost a spitting image of a young Joan Jett in her black tank top, rows of chains, and short dark hair as she stares coolly into the camera, her eyes hooded in steel-blue eyeshadow. And with lyrics about young love, adolescent bullying, mental health struggles, and female self-determination, Dobson turned her own real-world personal issues into songs that could light a fire in any teenage girl.

"The punk influence manifested by just being as honest as I could about my childhood and my upbringing in my home life and my heart and combining that with the production being heavy and dramatic and theatrical," Dobson says. "We wanted things to feel honest and raw. Even the way we cut vocals was raw. We didn't tune anything really on that record at all."

Levine agrees. "She sang a little tougher. We weren't afraid to be a little more edgy."

The album's faster, heavier songs push up against the softer, pop-leaning tracks that fit more snugly into the space occupied by Michelle Branch, Vanessa Carlton, and Hilary Duff, revealing an artist whose seemingly conflicting influences were colliding in all sorts of interesting and unexpected ways. The record is just as prone to mid-tempo, acoustic-guitar ballads like "Revolution Song" and "Julia" as it is to straight-up rockers like "Bye Bye Boyfriend." It's also brimming with theatrical flair on tracks like "Kiss Me Fool" and "We Went for a Ride" that would make her former teachers proud. Because, despite the importance of rock and punk to Dobson's career—her unease with Zomba, her initial collaboration with Levine and McCollum, the decision to record the album in New York—the plan was never to record a pure punk-rock album. It wouldn't have been her. She was someone who never wanted to be one thing at a time.

Fefe Dobson debuted at No. 1 on the Heatseekers Albums chart, and it went on to peak at No. 67 on the Billboard 200. Three months after the album's release, *Fefe Dobson* was certified platinum in Canada after selling more than one hundred thousand copies.

Dobson's dreams kept coming true—in the early weeks of 2004, she opened for Justin Timberlake on his U.K. tour. "It was a very big moment for me because it made me realize that manifestation was real," she says. "I had always told my friends in high school that Justin would know me and NSYNC would know me, and they thought I was absolutely just insane and off my rocker. I'm like, 'I don't care what y'all think, it's gonna happen.' And it did. That experience reminded me that you can do anything."

The accolades kept coming. In 2004, the album's third single, "Everything," charted in the U.K., Scotland, and Romania, along with minor placements in Canada and the U.S. Dobson made her TV debut as Tina Turner on the drama series *American Dreams*; she starred in a Tommy Hilfiger ad soundtracked by a new song of hers, "Don't Go (Girls and Boys)"; and she was nominated for two Juno Awards: New Artist of the Year and Pop Album of the Year. She played music festivals throughout North America, along with a handful of clubs. In addition to the one hundred thousand copies sold in Canada, the album went on to sell more than three hundred thousand copies in the United States. Dobson's manifestations were working.

DOBSON HAD SIMPLE EXPECTATIONS for her second album: "I just wanted to make an authentic rock record, and I wanted to work with those I felt would bring that out with me," she says. "I had a lot on my chest, and I needed to get it out. I guess I was kind of pissed, and I just wanted the music to reflect that."

Dobson moved out to Los Angeles to work with a new lineup of songwriters that Island Def Jam had arranged for her, including Tim Armstrong of Rancid, Nina Gordon of Veruca Salt, John 5 of Marilyn Manson, Pharrell Williams and Chad Hugo of the Neptunes, Joan Jett, Cyndi Lauper, and Courtney Love.[70] While Dobson had started working on her debut album with little more than a pair of songwriting partners, a new manager, and an eclectic list of musical inspirations, she went into her second album with a major-label deal that was already paying off, a massive co sign from her favourite artist, a clear vision of the rock album she wanted to make, and hundreds of thousands of fans.

"It was a great experience. That was really rad," she recalls. "Tim Armstrong, who's such a sweetheart, and John 5 and Nina

---

70 Dobson later wrote a song called "Hole," named after Love's band.

Gordon, you know, they're just amazing humans that I got to work with that cosigned the project."

She named the album *Sunday Love* after her mom's stage name from when she worked as a stripper, which also gave Dobson her own alternate identity for her new music. "I have many sides, that's why I named it *Sunday Love*, it was kind of like my alter ego," says Dobson. "It was like, 'I'm gonna make *Sunday Love* this intense rock girl vibe and I'm gonna put *Fefe* to the side.' It was its own thing." Dobson spent eight months in the studio writing and recording a set of fourteen songs that laid out everything that had been weighing on her chest.

Once the record was finished, it was time to get back on the road. To really dial into an authentic punk flavour, Dobson sought out an existing band this time instead of cobbling together another group of individual musicians. She settled on Unwise, a punk band from Trois-Rivières, Quebec. Unwise had landed big gigs opening for Sum 41 and No Warning, and the band members were hungry for more high-profile performance opportunities. At the audition, Unwise played a few songs with Dobson, and she loved them so much that she hired them on the spot.

For their first gig, a free Canada Day show in 2005 that drew thousands of people to Downsview Park in Toronto, Dobson decided she wanted to cover "Blitzkrieg Bop" by the Ramones. During the set, as the band was about to start playing the cover, she told bassist Jean-Phillippe Bourgeois, "I can't remember the lyrics—you sing it!" Bourgeois says, "I had never sung into a mic in my entire life, and she made me sing it in front of all those people." It was a strong start to the next era of Dobson's career. "She made us feel like we're part of the band," Bourgeois says. "She made us feel like we're not only hired guns."

It wasn't long, though, before the problems started. Dobson's new band of punks struggled to acclimatize to Dobson's slower-tempo rock tracks, often playing them faster than intended. "A song that should have been three minutes became a minute and a half," she recalls. Dobson had also begun a relationship with Bourgeois, the band's youngest and newest member, which caused tension with his bandmates.

"You probably shouldn't date someone in your band. They probably tell you that all the time," says Dobson. "But he was my rock on the road. He really helped me through a lot of things."

One night, a confrontation between Bourgeois and his bandmates led Dobson and her team to overhaul the band. Bourgeois got to keep his role as bassist, and he was joined by Kanter, who returned to the band after finishing his degree at York, along with new additions Matthew Wagner and Todd Lefever from progressive metal band the Hollow, later known as Alpha Galates.

Though the reconfigured band got along better, the turmoil continued behind the scenes. Cohen and Fenster, who had signed Dobson, had both left Island Def Jam, and the new management was unsure about her even more rock-oriented turn.

Sunday Love's lead single, the twangy alt-rock track "Don't Let It Go to Your Head," failed to chart, and Dobson's new look in the music video—stark bangs draped over her eyes, ripped-up pantyhose, an eyebrow piercing—seemed to alarm the record label. "I think I was just too dark—not skin colour, but maybe my eyeliner dripped down my face a little too much. Maybe I was a little bit out of control," she acknowledges with hindsight, but at the time, she didn't think anything of it. She was focused on promoting the record.

Dobson recalls there were additional concerns over the cover artwork for the album. Her initial vision involved wearing a ripped prom dress and dripping eyeliner, kneeling in a recreation of her childhood bedroom—complete with a pink four-poster bed—where she's stalked by a dark-winged male figure behind her. It was replaced by a much less provocative image: a portrait of the singer in a black-and-yellow striped V-neck and jeans, pouting in front of a painted heart.

The album's intended release date that fall was pushed to the following summer. While the live performances continued into 2006, including four Grad Night shows at Disney World in Florida opening for Fall Out Boy and Simple Plan, the label's concerns continued to grow when the album's second single, "This Is My Life," also failed to chart.

Then, seemingly out of nowhere, things took a turn for the worse.

DAYS BEFORE *Sunday Love*'s new release date in June 2006, Dobson got a call from Chris Smith, her manager, who had just spoken with a representative from the label. As Dobson recalls, the label had told Smith that they weren't happy with the album or Dobson's creative direction. Dobson's first album, as punk- and rock-influenced as it was, was marketed as a pop album, and *Sunday Love* wasn't crossing over. The release was cancelled, and Dobson's record deal was over.

Dobson was blindsided. "I thought everything was cool."

Fefe Dobson was a fairly scattershot exploration of pop and rock sounds not dissimilar to Avril Lavigne's *Let Go*. *Sunday Love* was a focused, straight-up rock record, not dissimilar to Lavigne's *Under My Skin*—which sold millions of copies—and for what it's worth, Dobson's look fit the part, too. But the label never got behind it.

"It was an almost impossible record to market at that point because it was 'too rock and roll for pop, and too pop for rock and roll,' and so no one knew where to put me because [the music industry] wasn't set up that way. Radio wasn't set up that way," Dobson says now. "There was no place for me."

Dobson's contemporaries Simple Plan, Fall Out Boy, and Avril Lavigne had become staples of pop radio, but Dobson wasn't looking to cater specifically to that audience. She felt she had already done enough of that on her first record. But the label thought that first record was who Dobson should continue to be.

"I had no clue who I was," says Dobson reflecting now. "I was a teenager trying to figure it out. Every human being tries to figure out who they are at some point, and I just did that in front of people. So I can see how it could be like, when *Sunday Love* happened, 'Who is Fefe now?' And *I* don't know! I'm trying to figure it out, too. This is just another side of me that needs to come out because I'm growing up."

Dobson's touring and performance schedule hadn't followed the natural order of a rock band, either. The singer hadn't gotten much of a chance to showcase the true ferocity of her live act in the proving grounds of the club circuit. She had mostly played outdoor festivals and stadiums instead of spending her formative years driving around the continent in a van to play shows to a few hundred kids in small, sweaty bars night after night. That left her without much of a support base who knew the air-punching, scissor-kicking punk rocker in her heart. On *Sunday Love*, Dobson had a strong vision for her edgier look and harder-rocking sound, but she was hard-pressed to sell it to an audience looking for shiny pop hooks.

"With Fefe, everyone was so focused on her being big rather than her being a live artist who grows fans grassroots, one at a time, not so dissimilar from NOFX or New Found Glory," says Kanter, Dobson's guitarist. "When you look at Simple Plan and Alexisonfire, they're live bands. Simple Plan's still touring and selling out huge venues. I think Avril and Alanis are exceptions where they blew up and then they play these giant shows. Fefe's strength was her live show. She got signed by her live show, but they were trying to turn her into Britney Spears and hoping she gets big arena offers based on her calibre rather than earning it by getting in a van and going venue to venue. *That's* punk rock: it's selling T-shirts and shaking hands and signing them after the show for an hour. To me, they were just going for big looks, not building a fan base one fan at a time by kicking ass."

Dobson agrees. "I was torn because I love pop and I love rock and roll. I would have done both. But where music was at that point, if you did pop, then you were taken off the rock stations. There was no middle ground back then."

George Stroumboulopoulos, who encountered Dobson and her band when they first played MuchMusic, sees another problem with the music industry that led to Dobson's shelved album. "Everybody was looking for another Avril, so I don't think Fefe had the runway that Avril did," he says.

"People always pit people against each other," Dobson adds. "I never understood it, but it always happens, especially in the female world. There's Britney Spears and Christina Aguilera and Jessica Simpson, and then there's us: Avril, me, Ashlee Simpson."

But all of this pontificating came later. Back in 2006, when Dobson was dropped by her label, she couldn't process what had happened. All she could do was go back to her loft in Toronto, depressed and unsure about what came next. Her entire career had been built on the idea of signing to a major label and bringing her rock tunes to the world. Now it felt like that dream had ended before it had truly begun.

"I put a lot of work into that album. I was very vulnerable on that album," she says. "It felt like the end of the world."

IN THE YEAR AND a half after she was dropped by Island Def Jam, Dobson stayed mostly holed up in Toronto, ignoring her emails and drinking wine. In early 2008, she was milling about in her kitchen while the sounds of MuchMusic carried over from the living room, when she heard a familiar tune.

She walked over to the TV and saw the latest music video from Miley Cyrus, the teenage performer who was in the midst of breaking out from under her signature character, Hannah Montana. Cyrus's song "Start All Over" was a sprightly mix of rock guitars and new-wave synths that belied melancholic lyrics about reuniting with an ex-lover—a story that Dobson knew all too well. After all, she had written it.

Dobson wrote "Start All Over" during the *Sunday Love* sessions in Los Angeles with Anne Preven and Scott Cutler from the band Ednaswap, whose song "Torn" became a worldwide hit in 1997 when it was covered by Natalie Imbruglia. Dobson,

Preven, and Cutler recorded "Start All Over," but Dobson decided not to include it on the album. Through the endless back rooms of the music industry, the song ended up with Cyrus and found its home on her debut album, *Meet Miley Cyrus*, with the original instrumental intact, even Dobson's backing vocals.

After more than a year of wondering how her music career could have gone so wrong, Dobson finally had proof that her early success hadn't been a fluke. Sure, she had felt confident from her earliest days with Levine and McCollum in the offices of Sony Music Canada, but getting dropped from your label and having your record shelved days before it was supposed to be released would have made any artist second-guess themselves.

Her suspicions were further confirmed the following year when two songs from *Sunday Love* were covered by two more massive pop acts: Selena Gomez & the Scene—the pop-rock band fronted by the namesake Disney breakout star—covered Dobson's "As a Blonde" on her album *Kiss & Tell* with only minor changes to the original arrangement, and *American Idol* winner Jordin Sparks gave Dobson's ill-fated single, "Don't Let It Go to Your Head," an R&B makeover, swapping the guitars and drums for synths and beats.

"The covers validated that the album wasn't bad, and that, clearly, there was something about it," says Dobson. "I had felt that it was a shitty piece of work for the longest time. I had this love-and-hate relationship with *Sunday Love*, and then *that* happened."

"As a Blonde" in particular speaks to the idea that Dobson was delivering radical truth to an industry unwilling to hear it. On the track, she openly questions whether her life would be easier if she didn't look the way she did. While there is definitely a subversive power in hearing Gomez—who is Latina—fight against Eurocentric beauty standards, it's an even more potent message coming from Dobson, the Black woman who wrote the song.

Slowly, Dobson's music career began to pick back up. She returned to Los Angeles to continue songwriting, began performing and touring again, and re-signed to Island Def Jam after being approached by the label's new management. Her second officially released album, *Joy*, which found Dobson splitting her time between modern pop songs and riot grrrl-style punk rockers, came out on Island in November 2010. The album was certified gold in Canada, with its three singles all charting in the top 20 of the Canadian Hot 100, and its second single, "Stuttering," garnering some radio play in the U.S. Gomez released another song co-written by Dobson, "Round & Round," which peaked at No. 24 on the Billboard Hot 100 and charted in nine other countries, including Canada. Dobson remained ever-present in the music industry, with sporadic singles throughout the 2010s, before returning once again with *Emotion Sickness* in 2023, a half-hour blast of raucous synthpop.

When Dobson first burst onto the scene, the music industry struggled to catch up to her. But because of her confidence and her sheer commitment to authenticity, Dobson brought forward a world that was ready for more artists like her—not just Black women making rock and punk music, but someone who could make pop music one year and rock music the next. "Artists should evolve, and they should be able to try anything," Dobson says. "They should be able to create without people saying, 'You need to be this genre.' We're artists! Let us play, let us be artists."

The music industry that Dobson has always envisioned is, in some ways, more of a reality today. And that could have been enough—an industry where artists are free to make the music they like no matter what they look like or what they've done before. But, coolest of all, Dobson is getting some credit for making it happen.

It took nearly two decades, but in the early 2020s, a few pop stars started to drop massive rock- and punk-influenced singles. And, when it happened, those songs drew comparisons to Dobson's music, like in 2021 when Olivia Rodrigo released her pop-punk chart-topper "Good 4 U" and Willow Smith released her Travis Barker–featuring "Transparent Soul" within weeks of each other, or in 2022 when SZA released "F2F."

"I'm trying to collab with Fefe at this point," Willow Smith said in a 2021 interview with *Spin*. "I know that there are so many of us [Black women] that want to play guitar, scream, growl, but are told that that's not our place," she added. "There are so many Black and Brown kids that are shelved at labels that want to do pop-punk, rock, and metal, but for so long, they've just kind of been shelved because [the labels] didn't know what to do with them."

Dobson, for her part, is grateful to be seen as a role model for a new generation. "It's really sweet," she says. "It means a lot to me. I didn't know what the hell I was doing when I started, I just kind of went with it. It means so much that it's helped someone or made an impact of some sort. I feel very blessed that way."

Though Dobson's initial record deal didn't pan out as intended, and though she repeatedly found herself fighting against expectations of what she should look and sound like, she remains to this day a beacon of authenticity, resilience, and self-preservation, someone willing to fight for who they are and what they believe in—because, as she says, if you're true to yourself, your audience will find you, even if it takes them a while to get there.

9

MARIANAS TRENCH

On a Monday night in November 2011, a bottle of champagne and a handwritten note is waiting for the four members of Marianas Trench as they enter their dressing room. The band is getting ready for the ninth show of a U.S. tour headlined by Simple Plan, who have taken the younger Canadian group under their wing to help them reach an audience outside of their home country. Marianas Trench's third album *Ever After* came out today, and Simple Plan knows that congratulations are in order. It's a milestone, for sure: Marianas Trench have been one of the hottest bands in Canada for the last few years, a fixture of MuchMusic and pop radio, and the new album's lead single, "Haven't Had Enough," is already their biggest hit yet. *Ever After* is shaping up to be the pinnacle of the band's career to date.

But that's back in Canada. Right now, they're sitting in a dressing room in Chicago, where they're the opening band on a four-act bill. Marianas Trench haven't been heard on American radio or MTV, and they've only played a few shows in the U.S. in the five years since their debut. As far as the band's concerned, they might as well be anonymous.

But when the group takes the stage and breaks into "Fallout," a new track from *Ever After* they've never played live before tonight, they realize they have way more fans than they thought. "The whole venue was singing it. It had only been out for ten hours, and everybody in the crowd knew it," singer Josh Ramsay says. "We were nobody. And they all knew that fuckin' song."

When they first emerged from Vancouver in the mid-2000s, Marianas Trench were riding a pop-punk wave that, as it turned out, was about to crash. Within a few years, the glory days of mainstream punk would come to an end. Marianas Trench had arrived too late to reap those rewards. But that's fine with them. Marianas Trench aren't destined to be forgotten in the pop-punk bargain bin. A few years before, they decided to forge their own path through the world of pop, and now it seems they've finally found their fans.

JOSH RAMSAY NEVER CONSIDERED a career in anything other than music. As a child growing up in Vancouver, he was surrounded by it. Both of his parents were choir singers, and they'd each made a career out of their passion for music. In the mid-'60s, Miles Ramsay had started a jingle company with two of his friends, and over the following decades they produced more than four thousand commercial jingles, TV themes, and movie scores. In 1972, the trio built a recording studio called Little Mountain Sound, and by the '80s it was a go-to studio for rock legends like Aerosmith, Bon Jovi, Mötley Crüe, and AC/DC, who made some of their biggest albums right there in Vancouver with producers Bob Rock and Bruce Fairbairn. Josh's mother Corlynn Hanney studied music at the University of British Columbia and had a career as a session singer who appeared in TV commercials, film soundtracks, and recordings by numerous artists including Leonard Cohen and the 5th Dimension. She was also a vocal teacher, often giving private lessons at home to singers who were recording at Little Mountain.

Growing up, Josh Ramsay got to see how musicians worked behind the scenes. He would often come to his dad's studio to watch rock legends make records, and he'd frequently accompany his mom to her own studio sessions. On family road trips, his parents would get him and his sister to sing along with them so that they'd form four-part harmonies, and then they'd explain to the kids what each of those chords was called.

"I thought every adult was a musician when I was a kid," Ramsay says. "I only realized people do jobs other than playing music for a living when I was about eight or nine."

When Ramsay was young, his parents exposed him to music that was notable for its vocal arrangements: a cappella groups like the Hi-Lo's, Take 6, and the Real Group, as well as rock bands like the Beach Boys and Queen. The music that was popular among kids Ramsay's age in the early '90s, on the other hand, was focused on loud, gritty instrumentals. A lot of his mother's students were fans of grunge and post-punk bands like Nirvana, the Pixies, Sonic Youth, Pearl Jam, and Soundgarden, and his father—somewhat of a purist—wasn't having any of it. When one of Hanney's students invited the couple to join him at a concert by a band from San Francisco called Jellyfish, she practically had to drag her husband to the show. But by the time the evening was over, Miles had picked up both of Jellyfish's records—1990's *Bellybutton* and 1993's *Spilt Milk*—and excitedly rushed home to play them for his son.

"You've got to listen to this," he told young Josh.

Jellyfish's eclectic mix of prog-rock, Britpop, post-punk, and jazz laced with the complex multi-part harmonies of an a cappella group unlocked something in the boy. Jellyfish quickly became one of Josh Ramsay's favourite bands. Throughout the '90s, he also came to love other popular rock groups like Green Day and Foo Fighters, but Jellyfish's influence was the most lasting. "That sort of became one of my musical bibles, like, 'This is what you do. This is how it's done,'" Ramsay says now. "I still go back to that stuff today."

By the time he was fourteen, Ramsay had started writing his own songs and recording them with his dad in the family's home studio. He would play all the instruments himself, but when he had enough material to start performing live, he decided he needed a backing band.

The first person he recruited to play in his band was his younger sister, Sara Ramsay; he took the role of the lead vocalist and rhythm guitarist, and she served as keyboardist and backup vocalist. Gradually, he added lead guitarist Steve Marshall, bassist Trev Spilchen, and drummer Erik Scott, a mix of friends from high school and the Vancouver music scene. They called the quintet Ramsay Fiction and started playing shows at coffee shops and other small venues around Vancouver. Ramsay's mom would drive him and his sister to gigs because neither of them was old enough to drive yet. When the band played at local bars, they would be allowed on stage but not out on the floor with the crowd because they weren't of legal drinking age; before and after they performed, they'd have to hang out by the kitchen.

At the same time, Ramsay's classmate Matt Webb—a singer and multi-instrumentalist—was playing his own music at many of the same venues around town. The two musicians became friends and recorded an album of Webb's own songs at Ramsay's house.

Elsewhere in Vancouver, drummer Ian Casselman wasn't having any luck finding a band, so he did "the worst thing possible," in his words, and bought a classified ad in the alt-weekly newspaper the *Georgia Straight.* Casselman was inundated with phone calls, mostly from middle-aged men who didn't have much in common with him, musically or otherwise. But there was one voice mail message that seemed promising: Josh Ramsay was looking to fill a vacant spot in his band. Casselman met Ramsay at a coffee shop and they discovered that they liked a lot of the same bands, including Jellyfish.

After their coffees, the pair went back to Ramsay's house to listen to a four-song demo he had recorded with engineer John Webster.[71] Unlike the demos Ramsay had been making for himself and Webb at home, these sounded polished enough to be on the radio. Casselman loved them right away. But just as importantly, he was drawn to Ramsay himself. "I loved his

---

71 John Webster was the keyboardist for the Canadian rock band Red Rider and he continued to work with the band's leader, Tom Cochrane, on his solo albums. He also played on albums by Aerosmith, Mötley Crüe, Rush, Alice Cooper, and AC/DC, and he worked with dozens of artists as an engineer and producer.

vibe," he says. "You could just tell there was something about him."

Over the ensuing months, Ramsay Fiction underwent a number of personnel changes. Sara Ramsay left, Casselman replaced Scott as the drummer, Morgan Hempsted replaced Spilchen on bass, and Webb joined as second guitarist. With an almost entirely new lineup, the band decided to change their name. After a few tries, they settled on a moniker taken from the deepest point on Earth.[72] From there, Marianas Trench set out to break into the music industry.

AFTER RECORDING RAMSAY'S EARLY demos, John Webster had shown them to an industry pal named Jonathan Simkin, a former criminal defence lawyer who had stumbled into entertainment law. Simkin was intrigued. The songs were ambitious, perhaps a little all over the place, but each had at least one amazing moment. He thought that if Ramsay could just figure out how to repackage those amazing moments into more structured, radio-friendly songs, then he could really have something here. "That much talent was going to lead to something," Simkin says. "I just knew it."

Simkin told him to keep working. Ramsay would go quiet for months at a time as he worked on new material, then he'd come back with more demos. Eventually, Simkin liked what

---

72 The Mariana Trench is located in the western Pacific Ocean, about two thousand kilometres east of the Philippines. Its depth is estimated to be 35,814 feet (or 10,916 metres). The deepest point of the Mariana Trench, the Challenger Deep, is farther away from sea level than the peak of Mount Everest. The trench is named after the nearby Mariana Islands, which are themselves named after Mariana of Austria, who was Queen of Spain for part of the seventeenth century.

he was hearing enough that he was ready to shop the demos around to get them a record deal.

During the summer of 2001, he took Ramsay and his band to Los Angeles so they could showcase for the heads of just about every major label in America. All of them passed.

Ramsay's music was often complex, and the band was still young. They didn't really have the chops yet to accomplish what they were trying to do, and the record labels weren't seeing the vision. "When you showcase for a record label, it's not a show—there's no crowd. It's either in an empty bar that they've rented or it's in a rehearsal space, which is even worse," Ramsay says. "You play your whole set for one person with a clipboard. Oh my god, the dead air between songs is palpable. It's an awkward, awkward thing, and it's a difficult thing for any artist to do that."

"They just couldn't pull it off," Simkin adds. "Some artists are great in those showcases, and some aren't. And they weren't. We came so close to the big deal, and it just didn't happen for them. But I'm a bit of a pit bull, and once I clamp down, it's hard for me to let go."

The band headed back to Vancouver to start working on some new demos they hoped would give them another chance to impress a record label. But as it turned out, they didn't need to. They already had.

SIMKIN HAD NEVER INTENDED to run a record label. Hell, Simkin had never intended to be an entertainment lawyer, either. In the early '90s, he was a criminal defence lawyer in Vancouver, mostly doing legal aid for petty crime and dabbling in refugee law. He was always a little out of place. With his long hair and scruffy beard, Simkin looked more like the musicians who lived in the apartment next door to him. But when he'd go to his neighbours' parties and their other musician friends found out what he did for a living, inevitably one of them would ask him for help with a contract.

"Dude, here's my card," Simkin would say. "If you get busted for drunk driving or pot, I'm your guy. Otherwise, I can't help you."

Still, people kept asking. And the more they asked, the more Simkin got to wondering if he was in the right specialty. He'd always loved music, after all, and by 1996 he had become disillusioned with criminal law. Maybe this was a sign.

When Simkin heard a group from nearby Coquitlam called the Matthew Good Band, he decided to go all in. He believed in the band—and himself—enough to make a bold proposal: if he couldn't get them a record deal in six months, they wouldn't owe him a penny. He won that bet when the Matthew Good Band signed a two-album deal with the American indie label Private Music in 1996. With that, Simkin had his first client in the music business.

As word got out and Simkin's new practice grew, he received a call from the singer of a mostly unknown rock band out in oil country. In 1996, almost nobody outside of the small town of Hanna, Alberta, knew about Nickelback. They had self-released their first EP and they needed a lawyer to vet their first management contract. Simkin handled that deal and then became Nickelback's trusted legal advisor as the band got bigger, signing with Roadrunner Records in 1999 and scoring a couple of top 10 hits on U.S. rock radio.

Between tours, Nickelback frontman Chad Kroeger kept busy by trying to help other bands break into the industry. Whenever he started producing for a new group, he'd get Simkin to draw up a contract, and if that band got a record deal, they'd both get a nice little kickback for helping to make it happen. For the most part, those bands didn't pan out. But then, in Burnaby, British Columbia, at a venue called Studebaker's—what Simkin calls "the shithole of all shitholes"—Kroeger saw the band Default. A hard-rock band with a country twang, Default was made to follow in Nickelback's footsteps. Kroeger and Simkin were able to land them a deal with the American imprint TVT Records, and Default's debut record, *The Fallout*, released in the fall of 2001, ended up going platinum thanks to the lead single, "Wasting My Time."

In their first deal together, Kroeger and Simkin had taken a band from a dingy dive bar to rock stardom. And just as that was happening, Nickelback's "How You Remind Me" topped the Billboard pop charts, turning them into one of the biggest bands in the world. "All of a sudden everybody's looking at Chad and me like we're the godfathers of some neo-grunge movement coming out of Vancouver," Simkin says.

So, when he and Kroeger started shopping around their next project—a hard-rock band from Alberta called Theory of a Deadman, who sounded so similar to Nickelback that critics nicknamed them "Theory of a Nickelback"—they signed them to a multi-album commitment in order to put them in a stronger negotiating position to sell that agreement to a major label. Simkin didn't realize what he was actually doing until he was pitching the band to a slightly confused Tom Storms, one of the A&R reps at Atlantic Records who would later sign Billy Talent.

"Are you shopping Theory of a Deadman or are you shopping your label?" he asked.

As if in slow motion, it clicked. Simkin hung up the phone and called Kroeger.

"I think I just started a bidding war on our label," he said.

Kroeger was just as confused. "What label?"

Soon, Kroeger and Simkin were headed to New York to meet with several big-time record executives. In October 2001, they met with Lyor Cohen, head of Island Def Jam, and Cees Wessels, head of Roadrunner,[73] at the Pierre Hotel overlooking Central Park for what turned out to be a ten-hour negotiation that finally ended in a deal. With that, they had the seed money to launch a new record label. It would be distributed by Island Def Jam globally, except in Canada, where they made a separate deal with Universal. They called the label 604 Records, a nod to the area code for southwestern British Columbia.

By mid-2002, Simkin and Kroeger had launched 604 Records with the help of their deep-pocketed financiers in New York. The first band they signed was Theory of a Deadman. The second was Marianas Trench, who had impressed the label before it even existed. "If nobody else gets what this is, then fuck it, I'm going to sign them," Simkin said.

He could tell it wasn't going to be easy, though. Most people who heard Marianas Trench didn't really understand them. Even his own business partner didn't see the appeal.

---

73 At the time, Island Def Jam had just purchased a fifty percent stake in Roadrunner Records, Nickelback's label.

"I don't know … it sounds like they're confused," Simkin recalls Kroeger telling him. "It kind of sounds like they're the Foo Fighters meets the Beach Boys."

"Uh, yeah, *exactly,*" Simkin said. "That's exactly what they are, and that's exactly why I'm signing them."

If Simkin believed in them, then Kroeger would, too. By the first week of 2003, Marianas Trench had officially signed with 604 Records. But they still had a long way to go.

IN THE MONTHS FOLLOWING the release of Marianas Trench's debut album *Fix Me* in the fall of 2006, the band and their record label experienced a marketing crisis.

It had been three years since Marianas Trench signed to 604 Records, and in that time the landscape of mainstream music had changed dramatically. Many of the hottest new rock bands had abandoned the brawny post-grunge sound that was geared toward adult men in favour of a style of pop-punk that was more sensitive and upbeat, and appealed largely to teenage girls. The post-Nickelback boom that had spurred the creation of 604 Records was still viable—Kroeger and his ilk remained near the top of the charts throughout the decade—but when bands like Good Charlotte, My Chemical Romance, Yellowcard, and the All-American Rejects arrived in their skinny jeans, hair dye, and eyeliner with punky pop songs about pain and heartbreak, it signalled a shift in rock music.

This boded well for Marianas Trench, who had since figured out how to streamline their deeply choral, Jellyfish-worshipping mixture of pitch-perfect pop and gritty rock 'n' roll into a collection of energetic pop-punk songs with irresistible hooks.

In the Vancouver scene, they had become a live act you had to see: an electrifying rock band with five-part harmonies that seemed like a relic of the '70s soft rockers and soul groups. Marianas Trench didn't come from the Vancouver punk scene, but they slotted in perfectly with the new pop-punk movement that was taking hold in the mainstream: they played with amped-up, overdriven guitars and a powerful, mostly upbeat rhythm section, and Ramsay sang in a gritty, pronounced tenor style that was in vogue among the pop-punk bands of the day.

When Fall Out Boy exploded into the public consciousness with "Sugar, We're Goin Down" in the spring of 2005, Marianas Trench saw a pathway to success. The band decided that *Fix Me*'s lead single would be "Say Anything," a mid-tempo rocker that burst out of the speakers with a slab of shiny power chords, a bleeding-heart attitude, and a huge, anthemic chorus. They felt it was sure to win over the pop-punk fans who had fallen in love with Fall Out Boy. "I remember hearing 'Sugar, We're Goin Down" on the radio and thinking, 'Well, if this is getting played, then our song is probably going to get played,'" Ramsay says.

But things didn't work out quite how they expected. In mid-2006, the rock stations said "Say Anything" was too pop, and the pop stations said it was too rock. From the outset, the band was stuck in a mushy middle where nobody wanted them. The Fall Out Boy blueprint wasn't a blueprint at all.

The band and their management team gathered for a series of crisis meetings. They weren't getting any radio airplay, which in many ways was still crucial in the music industry of the mid-2000s, and the "Say Anything" music video wasn't getting nearly enough visibility on MuchMusic. They took a step back and looked at what *was* working in their favour. Touring was proving to be a lucrative enterprise, thanks to their must-see live act—wherever they played, they made fans. They already had thousands of followers on MySpace, and they interacted with them daily; "Say Anything" had been making the rounds on the social network since March.[74] And they were early adopters of YouTube, which had just launched in early 2005 to become one of the fastest-growing sites on the internet.

Ever since they were teenagers, Ramsay and his friends had enjoyed running around Vancouver with a camcorder filming themselves doing stupid things. Inspired by the antics of *The Tom Green Show*, they'd cut open bags of grass clippings in back alleys and kick them so the grass would fly into the air; they'd sneak into construction sites and make a mess; and they'd dare each other to behave like unhinged hooligans in front of strangers for a laugh. The camera caught it all.

"It was the era of doing stupid shit like that, and my friends and I would play a game where we would embarrass each other in public and film it," says Ramsay.

When YouTube started gaining popularity for its user-uploaded video clips, the Marianas Trench team saw an opportunity. "You know, we should be putting stuff on YouTube to market the band," one of them said.

"I've got a bunch of these stupid things already," Ramsay offered.

In one of those videos, Ramsay stomps and dances around a mostly empty Subway sandwich shop while dressed as a ninja, playing a harmonica, and screaming "*HOT CHO-CO-LAAATE!*"

74 "What the band understood was that those were real fans on the other end," Simkin says. "I remember Ian, the drummer, spent hours responding to fans on MySpace."

at the top of his lungs. Marianas Trench took that video, slapped some promotional text on top of it, and posted it to their YouTube channel in the summer of 2007. In the days of "Leave Britney Alone," "Chocolate Rain," "Charlie Bit My Finger," and "Grape Lady," Marianas Trench's "Hot Chocolate" video had its own viral moment. The video got more than one hundred thousand views. The band challenged their fans to shoot their own videos re-enacting "Hot Chocolate"—an early example of what would later be called user-generated content marketing.

"Hot Chocolate" exposed Marianas Trench to an audience of curious teens on the internet and galvanized their growing fan base by reflecting their apparent taste for zany buffoonery. Crucially, it showed the band's personality. At a time when even the famous loveable goofballs of pop-punk like Blink-182, Sum 41, and Green Day had started to grow up—trading pot smoke, toilet humour, and practical jokes for politics, poetry, and philanthropy—the majority of rock music in the post-9/11 era was decidedly self-serious. Whether it was the anti-Bush sloganeering of Rise Against and Anti-Flag, the emo angst of My Chemical Romance and the Used, or even the cool-guy aloofness of Jet and Arctic Monkeys, rock bands weren't really goofing off as much as they'd done in the past. Marianas Trench stood out.

"It was the opposite of the rock band paradigm of trying to look cool," Ramsay says. "It made people look at us in a different light, because there was nothing about what we were doing that was trying to look cool. There was nothing cool about it."

"We were idiots," Webb adds. "There's a bit of mystique around rock stars, and we didn't have that."

While the goofy personalities of the band members helped

young people discover Marianas Trench, the ultra-catchy melodies and bleeding-heart earnestness of their music quickly converted many of them into diehard fans. The pain in Ramsay's lyrics—particularly songs like the power ballads "Alibis" and "Low" and the deceivingly peppy "Decided to Break It"—came from a dark place, reflecting Ramsay's struggles with mental health and drug addiction that he had experienced as a teenager. For young people who were struggling with depression, anxiety, self-loathing, or any other sources of angst, the songs on *Fix Me* cut to the core and made them feel understood. Forums and chat rooms were full of young people claiming without any sense of hyperbole that Marianas Trench's music "saved my life."

RIGHT AFTER "HOT CHOCOLATE" became a YouTube sensation, Marianas Trench played a show in Vancouver and were surprised to find a lineup around the block. "Holy shit, what is happening?" Simkin said to himself. When he walked into the venue, he saw kids holding signs that read, *Hot Chocolate.*

Right there, Simkin saw before his eyes that the internet was a powerful tool. Clearly, there was a link between the dumb stuff that was happening online and a measurable increase in ticket sales. From that point, Marianas Trench doubled down on their internet presence, posting more candid, wacky videos and continuing to chat with fans on MySpace.

Then, fifteen months after "Say Anything" failed to make a dent in the radio market, and nearly a year after *Fix Me* had hit the shelves, Marianas Trench finally landed a hit.

The band and their label had just enough money left to make a low-budget video for "Shake Tramp," a high-dose adrenalin shot of a rock song that sounded like a pop-punkification of the Foo Fighters' "Monkey Wrench." The video was ridiculously wacky. In it, Ramsay dances his way down the set of a bustling street, having exaggerated interactions with passersby and making over-the-top faces to the camera. The music video for "Shake Tramp" made it to No. 1 on the *MuchMusic Countdown* on August 10, 2007, pushing Fergie's "Big Girls Don't Cry" out of the top spot. "We didn't have a hit song, but we had a hit video, and that was at least something," Ramsay says.

Now that Marianas Trench had found a base of supporters on MySpace, YouTube, and cable TV, it became painfully obvious that they had been playing all the wrong shows. For most of their touring schedule promoting *Fix Me*, their management had been packaging them with their labelmates and other bands who were part of the post-grunge scene where Chad Kroeger was king. Marianas Trench weren't that kind of band at all.

"The people that liked Three Days Grace and Theory of a Deadman were not the people who were going to like our music," Ramsay says. "We'd get out in front of a hard rock crowd and we'd go, 'Okay, you guys like five-part harmony?' No, they don't."

Things started to change when Marianas Trench got out of the bar scene and started playing all-ages shows with power-pop groups like Everclear and Faber Drive. When that happened, they started connecting with the people they needed to reach. "There still weren't a ton of people at those shows, but there were more of them there, and they were there to see *us*," Ramsay says. "Those were the people who were watching MuchMusic. And as we gained popularity on that network, we gained popularity in real life. We stopped focusing on playing bars, and we found where our audience was. As soon as we started doing that, things started making more sense."

It took almost a full album cycle—the roughly two years of touring and promotion that followed the release of *Fix Me*—for Marianas Trench to figure out where they fit in. This was a time when a new, post–Fall Out Boy wave of pop-punk was producing a steady stream of hits like Panic! at the Disco's "I Write Sins Not Tragedies," Paramore's "Misery Business," and All Time Low's "Dear Maria, Count Me In," all of which crossed over to the Billboard pop charts between 2006 and 2008. While "Say Anything" didn't become the hit single that Marianas Trench hoped it would be, "Shake Tramp" had set them on an upward trajectory; after it hit No. 1 on the *MuchMusic Countdown*, the song made its way up the Canadian Hot 100 and the band was nominated for a Juno Award for Video of the Year.

Marianas Trench had the look, too: Ramsay wore his dark hair in a spiky, side-swept fringe with shocks of blue, and he took a page out of the Avril Lavigne look-book by wearing an assortment of loose-fitting neckties to go with his wardrobe of black T-shirts. After the visibility of the "Shake Tramp" music video, plenty of young fans were taken by his striking appearance, emo-inspired fashion sense, zany personality, and unabashed showmanship. While many teenagers already had magazine cutouts of heartthrob Pete Wentz pasted to the inside of their locker, a growing number of them were taping up Josh Ramsay's photo.

But even as they were finding success, Marianas Trench understood that the age of pop-punk supremacy would soon be coming to an end. They figured that the genre's zenith had come and gone, and that bands like theirs that were just breaking out would have to adapt to survive. And they were right.

BY THE LATTER HALF of the decade, there was an almost imperceptible shift in the landscape of mainstream punk and emo. In 2007, the pop-punk boom was still going strong: Paramore broke out with their era-defining single "Misery Business," Fall Out Boy landed their first chart-topping record with *Infinity on High*, Avril Lavigne scored her first No. 1 single with "Girlfriend," and Sum 41 had major success with their back-to-basics record *Underclass Hero.* But by 2008, the well had seemingly dried up. The most commercially successful pop-punk album of the year was Fall Out Boy's *Folie à Deux*, and even that was a step back from their previous two records. It was a similar story with the Offspring, Hawthorne Heights, Rise Against, and Senses Fail, whose new albums fared well enough but didn't have the same lasting impact as their earlier efforts. In 2009, only Green Day and Paramore went gold, while albums by scene veterans like New Found Glory, Taking Back Sunday, and AFI remained on the margins. It seemed that mainstream audiences had largely moved on from the punk style that had been a dominant force in pop culture for the better part of a decade.

"While we were touring our first album, it was pretty clear," Ramsay says. "Even Blink-182 stopped doing that. They moved away and started doing artsier stuff. If they're moving away from it, then everybody's going to be moving away from it. There are always styles that are popular at any given time, and you make a choice at some point to either stay in one lane and do this one thing forever, or pivot and let the pendulum move where it's going to move."

With that in mind, the band's focus shifted toward making themselves commercially viable in a different stream of the music industry. "My songwriting style is just too poppy to go on rock radio. I accepted that," Ramsay says. "We either had to push it further in the rock direction, which seemed like it was losing popularity, *or* push it further into a pop direction, which seemed like it was gaining popularity."

In the cutthroat world of '90s and early-2000s punk rock, a band that made that kind of statement would have been crucified by their fans. It was bad enough for a punk band to sign to a major label, or to write a song that had even a faint whiff of pop aspirations. For a band to say outright that they were choosing to play a style of music that would make them more popular? Unimaginable.

But Marianas Trench hadn't claimed to be a punk band. They had grown up in a Vancouver music scene completely different from the ones that had produced Gob and D.O.A. Sure, Ramsay would occasionally cite Green Day as an influence, but at that time Green Day was so ubiquitous that it was like a kid saying their favourite food is pizza. Ramsay's influences were all over the place, and Marianas Trench were a pop-punk band almost by accident. Theirs was a sound that fit in perfectly with groups like Fall Out Boy, All Time Low, and Paramore, but that didn't trace its origins back to California's formative '90s punk icons in the same way that other Canadian bands like Sum 41 and Simple Plan did.

"I'm not sure if there was a better way to describe us," Webb says. "We were popular at the same time as the rest of that stuff was popular, and maybe that's why we did well."

Marianas Trench never felt like they actually belonged to the punk scene—they were signed to Chad Kroeger's label, after all—so they had no problem leaving it behind. They didn't want to be lumped into a phase of pop culture that was dying out. They wanted to chart their own path. So, when it came time to record their second album, Marianas Trench set out to detach themselves from the pop-punk scene entirely. "We made a choice: we're not a rock band anymore, we are a pop band," Ramsay says. "We're going to do pop songs, we are a pop band, period."

MARIANAS TRENCH'S SWITCH TO pop music wasn't as much of a hard cut as it was a gradual transition, but the difference was certainly noticeable on their second album, *Masterpiece Theatre.* Ramsay and Webb dialled back the distortion on their guitar amps and started adding more keyboards and string sections. Casselman took it easier on the crash cymbals and started to play more on the hi-hats and ride. Everything sounded tighter and cleaner, and the songs were far more diverse in their sonic palettes, textures, and arrangements. The recording sessions involved more than a dozen guest musicians, including six additional vocalists and a string section. *Masterpiece Theatre* was arguably just as full of catchy hooks and emo-pop earnestness as a Fall Out Boy or All-American Rejects record, but it was also the most theatrical pop-punk album this side of Panic! at the Disco. Several of the songs seemed like they were written specifically for the silver screen, including a three-part suite that threaded a miniature rock opera into an album full of pop-punk bops.

"It wasn't trying to be a rock record anymore," says Ramsay. "We were just trying to write good songs and let them be however they were going to be."

While Marianas Trench had spent the years before and after the release of *Fix Me* trying to connect with a fan base, the response to *Masterpiece Theatre* in Canada was immediate. MuchMusic put a preview of the new record on its website before its release on February 24, 2009, and the album debuted at No. 4 on the Canadian albums chart. By the end of the year, Marianas Trench had their first gold record in Canada. The singles "Cross My Heart" and "All to Myself" became fixtures of MuchMusic and Canadian pop radio, each of them peaking in the top 15 of the Canadian Hot 100. Both of those songs went double platinum in Canada within a year, and the other three of the five singles from *Masterpiece Theatre*—"Beside You," "Celebrity Status," and "Good to You"—were certified at least gold by the end of the album cycle in mid-2011.

Still, Marianas Trench's success was mostly limited to within Canada's borders. Like many of the country's artists, they had yet to figure out how to break out internationally. But that would happen soon, just as a new wave of decidedly un-punk music was taking over.

BY THE EARLY 2010S, the changing landscape of mainstream music had validated Ramsay's theory that pop-punk and emo were losing steam. Sure, established groups like Green Day, Sum 41, Fall Out Boy, and My Chemical Romance were able to squeeze out albums that landed in the top 10 of the Billboard charts during the twilight years of the 2000s punk boom, but they were the too-big-to-fail exceptions in a scene where most of their peers had either disbanded or been discarded. Punk rock and its many offshoots had largely gone back underground, where you had to go looking in blogs, forums, social media, and local punk shows—all of those not-so-secret corners of the media-consuming public sphere—to find your new favourite band.

In the new decade, there was a particular cultural phenomenon that boded well for a band like Marianas Trench: the return of the boy band. In the wake of the Jonas Brothers becoming a chart-topping sensation, One Direction, Big Time Rush, and 5 Seconds of Summer subsequently sang and danced their way into the hearts of Gen Z kids in practically the same way that the Backstreet Boys and NSYNC had defined the childhoods of so many millennials. Marianas Trench met this audience at a moment when they had an appetite for exactly the type of big-league pop that Ramsay and the group had spent years perfecting. And they weren't the only band that had followed that path: the All-American Rejects and Panic! at the Disco had made similar pivots (and Fall Out Boy were a couple of years out from doing the same). And then there was Simple Plan, the veteran Canadian pop-punk hitmakers who were themselves venturing further into the pop world than ever. And with Simple Plan's help, Marianas Trench would finally realize their potential as an international act.

While Marianas Trench's first five years of touring were almost entirely restricted to Canada, they had finally gotten a real crack at the U.S. market in early 2011 when they were brought along for part of the Glamour Kills Tour, an annual tour package—headlined that year by the electro-pop artist the

Ready Set—that was put together by the namesake clothing company that was visibly prominent in the emo and pop-punk scene. Marianas Trench were only around for a handful of dates in the Midwest and upper East Coast, but it was a quality run: they played with bands that fit with their fan base—the Ready Set and Allstar Weekend were playing the sort of neon electro-pop that was gaining popularity among both Warped Tour attendees and Disney kids, while We Are the In Crowd was an easy sell among Paramore fans—and it was a high-profile, sponsored tour that had a cultural stronghold in exactly the kind of young and eager fan base that their band was looking to access.

Meanwhile, Marianas Trench were now big enough to justify a full-blown arena tour back home in Canada, but they still didn't feel ready for the pressure of being the headliner. So, they made a deal with Simple Plan to take them out as their supporting act as they promoted their fourth album *Get Your Heart On!* In many ways, Simple Plan became mentors who would show them how to take their live shows to the next level as they played to bigger crowds. It also meant that Marianas Trench were getting their first proper look at American audiences after years of touring almost solely in Canada. They were floored by what they saw.

"We really didn't know if people were going to come out," Ramsay says. "But somehow there were people coming out. They had found us through the internet. When we move outside of Canada, it's always in countries where we've never been officially promoted. We're still so indie. So when we do come to places, I think they're a little more excited because they have found us organically. They haven't had it rammed down their throats. And maybe they've been waiting for years for us to come. So all of a sudden we had gotten this great reaction in the United States that we didn't expect. People knew the fuckin' songs. We were like, *what*? On the Simple Plan tour, we were always asking people, 'How did you even find our band?' We didn't even understand how people knew of the band. Everybody knew the songs."

With 2011's *Ever After*, an elaborate concept album that completed their transformation into a narratively driven and extravagantly theatrical pop act, Marianas Trench fully rounded into form as mainstage entertainers wholly realizing their stadium-size ambitions. Four of the album's five singles have been certified three-times platinum in Canada, and "Haven't Had Enough" gave them their first top-10 hit. It was also their first album to chart in America, reaching No. 5 on the U.S. Heatseekers chart and No. 48 among independent albums. *Ever After* completed the band's transition to a pop band and solidified Marianas Trench as a group that could not only stay afloat in the changing tide of mainstream music but thrive as a globe-trotting act that was now headlining tours not just in Canada but in the U.S., Australia, and other parts of the world. Ramsay's pop gambit paid off further when he produced and co-wrote a smash hit for his 604 Records labelmate and fellow Vancouverite Carly Rae Jepsen, "Call Me Maybe," which rocketed to No. 1 in eighteen countries and became the biggest song of 2012.

In 2015, Marianas Trench's fourth album, *Astoria*, was released in Canada by 604 Records and internationally by Cherrytree Records, the Interscope imprint that had helped to develop and break Lady Gaga and LMFAO. That record peaked at No. 2 in Canada, making it their highest-charting album at home. It was also their first to appear on the Billboard 200 in the United States and their first to chart in Australia. Throughout the 2010s and beyond, the band went on to become a perennial headliner on numerous major tours of Canada, the U.S., Australia, the U.K., and Europe.

"Quietly, Marianas Trench have built a hell of a fan base internationally," Simkin says. "We never had that moment where it's like, 'Oh my god, you have the No. 1 hit all over the world.' We never had a 'Call Me Maybe' moment. But we had quite a few moments. And I mean, this is a band that can tour Asia, Europe, Australia—sold out, like, sold out."

Marianas Trench didn't need a No. 1 hit to earn their place in the zeitgeist. All they ever needed was a willingness to survive and adapt. Though they arrived too late for pop-punk's golden age, they were around long enough to get the ball rolling before pivoting toward a new sound that would highlight their songwriting strengths. Besides, change is inevitable, and Marianas Trench embraced that from day one.

"I think most artists that have long careers generally reinvent constantly," says Ramsay. "Except for AC/DC, because they got it right the first time and they should never change. But other than AC/DC, artists that have a super long career generally have a lot of different stages of their sound."

It's an attitude that all of Canada's punk-rock exports of the 2000s embraced at one point or another: a willingness to flip their middle fingers at tradition and do what they wanted to do when they wanted to do it. It was true when Gob decided to deviate from Vancouver's hardcore punk scene in the early '90s, and it was true over a decade later when Marianas Trench decided, in the very same city, to leave punk behind entirely. It was all done with the same goal in mind: to share their message with as many people as possible, no matter who they pissed off along the way. What could be more punk than that?

EPILOGUE

A massive crowd of more than eighty thousand people has packed the Las Vegas Festival Grounds. It's nothing but clear blue skies on a sunny Sunday afternoon in October 2022, the first day of the feverishly hyped-up When We Were Young festival. Over the course of twelve hours, what seems like a logistically impossible lineup of sixty-five artists is playing across five stages, with a virtually endless stream of iconic pop-punk and emo acts, including Avril Lavigne, Paramore, My Chemical Romance, Jimmy Eat World, Silverstein, Taking Back Sunday, Hawthorne Heights, and Dashboard Confessional. It's a considerable feat of event production and an endurance test for the tens of thousands of fans in attendance, who are likely all so overwhelmed by the non-stop excitement—not to mention wave after wave of joyous nostalgia—that they don't notice their feet aching in their Vans Old Skools on the artificial turf.

Meanwhile, similar festivals have cropped up across the continent, some of them drawing particular attention to Canada's outsize role in pop-punk's heyday. Subsequent When We Were Young festivals in 2023 and 2024 featured Sum 41 and Simple Plan, along with Blink-182, Green Day, the Offspring, New Found Glory, Rise Against, Fall Out Boy, and the Used. An Ontario equivalent, All Your Friends Fest, emerged in 2024 north of Toronto, headlined by Fall Out Boy and Billy Talent, and also featuring national heroes Silverstein, Gob, and Fefe Dobson. In 2022, Alexisonfire launched their own festival called Born & Raised, a two-day event in St. Catharines headlined by themselves (and City and Colour), and supported by a mix of fellow Canadians, including Billy Talent, Metric, Sloan, Broken Social Scene, PUP, Counterparts, and Sam Roberts Band.

When the Warped Tour ended its twenty-five-year run in 2019, something was bound to fill the void. The pop-punk and emo bands that had swept into the mainstream in the 2000s had too profound an impact on the youth of that era to fade quietly into obscurity. Now, two decades later, thousands of grown-ups are eagerly dropping hundreds of dollars to fly to Las Vegas and relive their teenage years by watching Avril Lavigne sing "Sk8er Boi," Sum 41 bounce around to "Fat Lip," or Simple Plan belt out "I'm Just a Kid."

But it's not just people in their thirties and forties coming out to see these bands. The entire scene has seen a resurgence among a younger generation. The pop-cultural influence of punk rock may have faded in time, but it never went away.

As the kids used to say—it's not a phase.

* * *

LIKE MANY ERAS OF pop culture, the wave of punk rock that swept into the mainstream at the turn of the twenty-first century had a beginning and an end. You can argue about the specifics, but it was roughly an eight-year span between 1999 and 2007. Today, if you hear an aging millennial waxing nostalgic about the "pop-punk era" or you go to an emo-themed dance party at a local nightclub, you'll be hearing songs almost entirely from those eight years that essentially defined the adolescence of a generation.

But while the sun eventually set on the genre's cultural ubiquity, and mainstream audiences moved on to other things—hip-hop, indie rock, EDM, Eurodance, K-pop—many of the artists themselves have continued to sell out major music venues around the world and put up respectable sales numbers for new albums as they've sustained thriving careers for more than twenty years. Much like the enduring influence of punk at large, the effects of Canada's early-aughts superstars can still be felt in the later waves of the genre and across all of contemporary pop music, even before pop-punk returned to prominence in the early 2020s.

More specifically, the artists featured in this book have—with very few exceptions—remained active and enduringly popular since their beginnings while also influencing a new generation of artists. Sum 41's impact has been cited by bands like Welsh pop-punk group Neck Deep, American indie-rock acts Foxing and Bully, and Australian pop-rockers 5 Seconds of Summer. Simple Plan have collaborated with younger pop-punk artists like Chad Tepper and Jax, while Marianas Trench's influence can perhaps best be felt in the aftershock of "Call Me Maybe" and the wave of feel-good pop music that surged in its wake. Billy Talent, Silverstein, and Alexisonfire have been cited by numerous hardcore and metal acts in Canada as having kicked open the door for heavy music in the country, and the bands themselves have been particularly vocal advocates for up-and-coming artists, having influenced and platformed punk groups like PUP, the Dirty Nil, the OBGMs, Seaway, Like Pacific, and NOBRO. Fefe Dobson has served as an inspiration to several of the biggest female pop stars of the 2020s, including Olivia Rodrigo, SZA, and Willow Smith. At one point, Gob would have been every Canadian punk band's favourite Canadian punk band. And Avril Lavigne's influence is almost too far-reaching to summarize: she's been name-checked by pop stars like Rodrigo, Billie Eilish, Charli XCX, and Ed Sheeran; indie rockers such as Snail Mail, Soccer Mommy, and Phoebe Bridgers; and hip-hop artists like Lil Uzi Vert, Rico Nasty, Noname, and Princess Nokia.

"I think a lot of young people are discovering old music thanks to pop-punk finding its way back into the mainstream," Avril Lavigne told a reporter for *Vulture* after her performance at the When We Were Young festival in 2022. "It's really cool and exciting to see, and I'm happy to be a part of it."

"Since the beginning, the audiences at our shows have always looked the same to me. As far as I can see, they just look the same age they always did: mid-teens, early twenties," Sum 41's Deryck Whibley told *Exclaim!* that same year. "It's just gotta be this kind of music. It's youthful, it's exciting, it's fun, and I think it just keeps a younger audience. It seems like every time we put out a record, it appeals to the fifteen-year-olds getting into punk rock."

The pop-punk music of the 2020s is very different from what roared into prominence twenty years ago. It's way more diverse both in terms of race and gender: artists of colour like KennyHoopla, Meet Me @ the Altar, and Beabadoobee have risen to prominence in a scene that sadly wouldn't have been nearly as welcoming even a decade before. The institutional limitations that stifled Fefe Dobson's creative voice or practically forced Avril Lavigne to take a punk-music quiz in every interview appear to be less pervasive, due in no small part to the impact that the two made in the 2000s. Despite the name "emo rap," the mid-2010s microgenre was certainly influenced by pop-punk; scene trailblazer Juice Wrld chatted with Lavigne for *Interview* magazine in 2019, while Sum 41's initial goal of bringing punk and hip-hop together returned with their 2021 collaboration with Nothing, Nowhere.

Amid the constantly shifting tides of contemporary culture, the enduring influence of the artists in this book on both underground scenes and major-label pop music speaks to how powerful they have remained. And it makes the unlikely rise of these suburban Canadian teenagers all the more remarkable—that they were able to break out of unassuming communities that had been neglected and ignored by the larger music industry to become not just a passing fad but a seemingly unstoppable force.

It's almost impossible to predict how Canada will shape popular music in the future. Here in the present, the world domination of Drake, the Weeknd, and Justin Bieber since 2010 has given the country more pop-cultural pedigree than ever before, and the emergence of other homegrown pop stars like Shawn Mendes, Alessia Cara, and Tate McRae has only bolstered Canada's international reputation. Even still, every Canadian story is an underdog story—that's just the Canadian way. And you can only wonder who's going to be next.

ACKNOWLEDGEMENTS

Huge thanks to our editor, Doug Richmond, for turning the overeager thoughts of two scrappy music critics into something cohesive, and to the rest of the House of Anansi team for welcoming us with open arms and forgiving us when we had to push back the deadline for the photo section yet again.

We're forever grateful to everyone who took the time to speak to us for this book, including many of our childhood heroes, who, it turns out, are even cooler than we imagined. We also couldn't have done this without the support of Adam Bentley, Cameron Drew, Kevin Drew, Lenny Levine, Sarah Lycanlang, Tania Natscheff, Danny Reiner, and Menno Versteeg.

Thanks to Michael Barclay, Jonny Dovercourt, James Keast, Anna Maxymiw, and Josh O'Kane, who took us along the path from writers to authors; to Ian Danzig and Atsuko Kobasigawa of *Exclaim!* for building and sustaining a vital pillar of the Canadian music community for over 30 years; and to our editors at *Exclaim!* and beyond for the opportunities that gave us the confidence to write this thing.

Matt would like to thank:

My partner, Madeline, for her boundless love, enthusiasm, and patience. My parents, Celia and Stephen, respectively my first editor and the first person I ever edited. My brother, Ryan, for always encouraging me to believe in myself. My friends and family, for forgiving me when I would emerge in their lives spontaneously, after weeks without contact, only able to discuss the intricacies of the major label system or Canadian copyright law. The ER doctor at Toronto Western Hospital who took the earplug out of my ear hours before Adam and I interviewed George Pettit. And Adam, a more exceptional writing partner, co-conspirator, and friend than I ever could have imagined, whose even-keeled demeanour kept the project moving steadily in spite of my more chaotic impulses.

Adam would like to thank:

My partner, Kaitlyn, for her love, support, and generosity, and for believing in me so unreservedly and enthusiastically. My parents, Carrie and Robert, for raising me with an appreciation for music, books, and art. My Oma, for keeping all of my clippings when I was a young reporter in Ottawa. My siblings, Jordan and Michaela, for their curiosity and ego-checks. My found family, Kristyn, Mary Ann, and Dave, for taking such pride in their son-in-law's work. My close friends and one-time bandmates, for all of those nights playing rock 'n' roll in basements and dive bars, learning (the hard way) about teamwork, patience, anger management, and going broke for your art. All of my good friends and family members who have been my biggest cheerleaders during this project. Henry, who sat on my lap as a puppy, keeping me company during those late nights spent writing and editing. And Matt, a deeply thoughtful, savvy, and resourceful collaborator whose great idea turned into a successful project and, more importantly, a wonderful friendship and creative partnership comprising two people who, through our perfectly overlapping strengths and weaknesses, make up something resembling one normal, fully functioning human.

Listen on Apple Music

PLAYLIST

Sum 41—"Fat Lip"
Gob—"Soda"
Sum 41—"Makes No Difference"
Gob—"I Hear You Calling"
Avril Lavigne—"Sk8er Boi"
Simple Plan—"I'd Do Anything"
Sum 41—"The Hell Song"
Fefe Dobson—"Stupid Little Love Song"
Avril Lavigne—"He Wasn't"
Billy Talent—"Try Honesty"
Silverstein—"Smashed into Pieces"
Alexisonfire—"Pulmonary Archery"
Sum 41—"We're All to Blame"
Alexisonfire—"Accidents"
Silverstein—"Smile in Your Sleep"
Billy Talent—"Red Flag"
Alexisonfire—"This Could Be Anywhere in the World"
Marianas Trench—"Say Anything"
Fefe Dobson—"As a Blonde"
Marianas Trench—"Shake Tramp"
Gob—"Give Up the Grudge"
Simple Plan—"I'm Just a Kid"
Avril Lavigne—"Complicated"
Sum 41—"In Too Deep"

SOURCES

The majority of the content of this book comes from the authors' own original interviews with the artists: Tom Thacker of Gob; Steve Jocz and Jason "Cone" McCaslin of Sum 41; Pierre Bouvier and Chuck Comeau of Simple Plan; Ian D'Sa, Jonathan Gallant, Ben Kowalewicz, and Aaron Solowoniuk of Billy Talent; Paul Koehler and Shane Told of Silverstein; Dallas Green, Jordan Hastings, Wade MacNeil, George Pettit, and Chris Steele of Alexisonfire; Fefe Dobson; and Ian Casselman, Josh Ramsay, and Matt Webb of Marianas Trench.

Additional material was gleaned from original interviews with the artists' friends and colleagues, including Ric Arboit, Bill Baker, Jean-Philippe Bourgeois, Trevor Bowman, Gavin Brown, Julius Butty, Joel Carriere, Marc Costanzo, Miska Csepreghi, Nick Farkas, Bonnie Fedrau, Cristina Fernandes, Terry Flood,

Jen Hirst, Philippe Jolicoeur, Mark Jowett, Dan Kanter, Ole Kirchhoff, Justin Koop, Ken Krongard, Patrick Langlois, Eric Lawrence, Grant Lawrence, Larry LeBlanc, Jay Levine, Terry McBride, Michael McCarty, Terry David Mulligan, Tim Park, Mike Renaud, David Rogers, Chris Schembri, Bernie Schick, Joanne Setterington, Jonathan Simkin, Tom Storms, George Stroumboulopoulos, Chris Taylor, Ray Tombran, Livia Tortella, Cameron Webb, Paget Williams, and Kevin Williamson.

In addition to these first-hand accounts, the authors consulted hundreds of external sources, including news articles, magazine features, videos, and podcasts. All of this supporting material helped the authors to tell these stories as thoroughly and accurately as possible.

ARTICLES

"All About Avril Lavigne." *NBC News*, January 10, 2003. nbcnews.com/id/wbna3080073.

Bilcik, Tori. "Interview with Tom Thacker of Gob." *Daily Slice*, October 1, 2014. dailyslicemag.wordpress.com/2014/10/01/interview-with-tom-thacker-of-gob.

Bliss, Karen. "Billy Talent." *Access*, 2003.

———. "Billy Talent Debuts in Top 10." *Jam! Music*, September 25, 2003. web.archive.org/web/20041107044942/http://www.canoe.com/JamMusicArtistsB/billytalent.html.

———. "Chad Kroeger's 604 Signs B.C. Band." *Jam! Music*, January 8, 2003. web.archive.org/web/20160611093328/http://jam.canoe.com/Music/Lowdown/2004/11/22/pf-726063.html.

———. "Everyone Who Knows Screamo Knows . . . Alexisonfire." *Canadian Musician*, September/October 2004.

Caramanica, Jon. "*No Helmets No Pads... Just Balls*: Simple Plan: Review." *Rolling Stone*, February 25, 2003. web.archive.org/web/20070825094213/http://www.rollingstone.com/reviews/album/153426/review/5944233/no_helmets_no_pads_just_balls.

"Cover Story: Sum 41." Pollstar, November 2, 2001. news.pollstar.com/2001/11/02/sum-41.

Davis, Erin. "Back with New Music but the Same Unapologetic Attitude: Fefe Dobson." View the Vibe, July 6, 2023. viewthevibe.com/back-with-new-music-but-the-same-unapologetic-attitude/.

DeCaro, Alessandro. "The Untold Story of Shane Told of Silverstein's First Band Jerk Circus." *Alternative Press*, March 23, 2023. altpress.com/shane-told-silverstein-first-band-jerk-circus.

Deziel, Shanda. "Avril's Edge." *Maclean's*, July 13, 2003.

Ebner, Dave. "Pop Goes the Punk." *Globe and Mail*, September 29, 2001. theglobeandmail.com/arts/pop-goes-the-punk/article18418590.

Edwards, Gavin. "People of the Year 2001: Sum 41." *Rolling Stone*, December 17, 2001. web.archive.org/web/20090211183220/http://www.rollingstone.com/artists/sum41/articles/story/5918959/people_of_the_year_2001_sum_41.

———. "Sum 41: Teenage Rock & Roll Machine." *Rolling Stone*, September 24, 2001. rollingstone.com/music/music-news/sum-41-teenage-rock-roll-machine-181266.

Eliscu, Jenny. "Avril Lavigne: Little Miss Can't Be Wrong." *Rolling Stone*, March 20, 2003. rollingstone.com/music/music-news/avril-lavigne-little-miss-cant-be-wrong-180369.

Ewens, Hannah. "The VICE Interview: Deryck Whibley." *VICE*, September 6, 2016. vice.com/sv/article/the-vice-interview-deryck-whibley.

"Flash-forward: Fefe Dobson." *Observer Music Monthly*, February 22, 2004. theguardian.com/observer/omm/story/0,,1150751,00.html.

Friend, David. "Life as a Rock Mom: Deryck Whibley's Mother on What It's Like Raising a Rock Star." *CTV News*, May 12, 2017. ctvnews.ca/entertainment/life-as-a-rock-mom-deryck-whibley-s-mother-on-what-it-s-like-raising-a-rock-star-1.3410609.

Goh, Yang-Yi. "Sum 41's Deryck Whibley Has Been on One Hell of a Ride." *GQ*, December 7, 2023. gq.com/story/sum-41-deryck-whibley-profile.

Gormely, Ian. "Inside the Career of Alexisonfire, Canada's Greatest, Least Likely Success Story." *Exclaim!*, April 21, 2019. exclaim.ca/music/article/inside_the_career_of_alexisonfire_canadas_greatest_least_likely_success_story.

———. "Sum 41 Survive Teen Stardom, Substance Abuse and Changing Tastes to Rise Again on *Out for Blood*." *Exclaim!*, July 11, 2019. exclaim.ca/music/article/sum_41_survive_teen_stardom_substance_abuse_and_changing_tastes_to_rise_again_on_out_for_blood.

———. "The Complicated Life and Times of Avril Lavigne." *Exclaim!*, February 26, 2019. exclaim.ca/music/article/the_complicated_life_and_times_of_avril_lavigne.

"Hometown Proud: When Avril Lavigne Was the Toast of Napanee, Ont." *CBC Archives*, March 13, 2020. cbc.ca/archives/hometownproud-when-avril-lavigne-was-the-toast-of-napanee-ont-1.5480305.

Horner, Al. "10 Albums That Wouldn't Exist Without Green Day's *Dookie*." *NME*, October 31, 2019. nme.com/blogs/nme-blogs/10-albums-that-wouldnt-exist-without-green-days-dookie-768209.

Hudson, Alex. "Call Him Maybe: Jonathan Simkin Celebrates 20 Years of 604 Records and Becoming 'Godfathers of a Neo-Grunge Movement.'" *Exclaim!*, July 12, 2023. exclaim.ca/music/article/604_records_20th_anniversary_jonathan_simkin_interview.

Jago, Kyle. "Odd Job for Gob." *Sun Media*, December 3, 1999. web.archive.org/web/20000903183108/http://www.canoe.com/JamMusicArtistsG/gob.html.

Lau, Melody. "Fefe Dobson Revisits Her Debut Album 20 Years Later: 'I'm Very Proud of the Younger Version of Myself.'" *CBC Music*, November 28, 2023. cbc.ca/music/fefe-dobson-2003-debut-album-20th-anniversary-interview-1.7039598.

Lindsay, Cam. "Rank Your Records: George Pettit Scrupulously Rates Alexisonfire's Six Records." *VICE*, September 15, 2016. vice.com/en/article/rank-your-records-george-pettit-scrupulously-rates-alexisonfires-six-records/.

———. "Tom Thacker of Gob and Sum 41 Speaks on Rocking Out Gracefully." *VICE*, August 25, 2014. vice.com/en/article/tom-thacker-of-gob-and-sum-41-interview.

Linstrum, Cory Michael. "Some Kinda Fun: The Live Fast Story of Teenage Head." *Punk Globe*, September 1, 2012. punkglobe.com/teenageheadarticle0912.php.

MacDonald, Gayle. "Napanee Girl Becomes Pop Phenomenon." *Globe and Mail*, February 21, 2003. theglobeandmail.com/arts/napanee-girl-becomes-pop-phenomenon/article1157939.

McNeil, Mark. "Remembering the Infamous Teenage Head Riot at Ontario Place." *Hamilton Spectator*, May 31, 2021. thespec.com/news/hamilton-region/flashbacks-hamilton/remembering-the-infamous-teenage-head-riot-at-ontario-place/article_98a2a874-1af6-5171-b15d-683670bfce0.html.

McQueen, Ann Marie. "Avril's Wild Ride to Stardom." *Jam! Music*, February 9, 2003. archive.ph/20121206033901/http://jam.canoe.ca/Music/Artists/L/Lavigne_Avril/2003/02/09/746834.html#selection-1077.1-1084.0.

Menapace, Brendan. "Still Killer: Deryck Whibley on Sum 41's 'Fat Lip' 20 Years Later." *Stereogum*, April 22, 2021. stereogum.com/2144152/sum-41-fat-lip-all-killer-no-filler/interviews/qa.

Modern Drummer. "Chuck Comeau of Simple Plan." May 12, 2004. moderndrummer.com/2004/05/chuck-comeau/.

"Napanee Rocks to Lavigne's Success." *Globe and Mail*, February 23, 2003. theglobeandmail.com/arts/napanee-rocks-to-lavignessuccess/article24452664.

Newman-Bremang, Kathleen. "Fefe Dobson Is Ready to Let It All Out Again." *Refinery29*, June 24, 2021. refinery29.com/en-ca/2021/06/10481736/fefe-dobson-interview-new-album.

Nixon, Geoff. "How 'Force of Nature' Sum 41 Made Their Way to the Top." *CBC News*, May 28, 2014. cbc.ca/news/canada/toronto/how-force-of-nature-sum-41-made-their-way-to-the-top-1.2651210.

Nolfi, Joey. "Fefe Dobson Revisits the Raw Heartbreak of her Sunday Love Cancellation, 15 Years Later." *Entertainment Weekly*, June 9, 2021. ew.com/music/fefe-dobson-sunday-love-interview-new-album.

Nott, Glen. "Tales of the Head: The Up-and-Down Story of a Truly Hamilton Band." *Hamilton Spectator*, October 16, 2008. thespec.com/entertainment/tales-of-the-head-the-up-and-down-story-of-a-truly-hamilton-band/article_e77c116b-f170-5b70-8a13-eac3758d6f23.html.

Pak, SuChin. "Avril Lavigne: The Real Deal." *MTV News*, July 12, 2002. web.archive.org/web/20081226022208/http://www.mtv.com/bands/l/lavigne_avril/news_feature_071202/index.jhtml.

Payne, Chris. "'The Crowd Was Very Emo': On the Ground at the Nostalgia-Fueled Pop-Punk When We Were Young Festival." *Vulture*, October 27, 2022. vulture.com/2022/10/when-we-were-young-festival-photos.html.

Peden, Lauren David. "A Night Out with Avril Lavigne: Punk Rocker, Pop Queen and Tomboy All in One." *New York Times*, November 10, 2002. nytimes.com/2002/11/10/style/a-night-out-with-avril-lavigne-punk-rocker-pop-queen-and-tomboy-all-in-one.html.

Plummer, Sean. "Fefe Dobson, Canada's Latest Teen Musical It Girl, Takes On the World." *Access*, February, 2004. web.archive.org/

web/20090117015640/http://www.accessmag.com/Archives/68-Fefe.html.

Rockingham, Graham. "40 years of Teenage Head." *Hamilton Spectator*, October 17, 2015. thespec.com/entertainment/music/40-years-of-teenage-head/article_4aabb752-bf5c-5dbe-aaf8-10855f11a55.html.

Scaggs, Austin. "Q&A: Avril Lavigne." *Rolling Stone*, June 24, 2004. rollingstone.com/music/music-news/qa-avril-lavigne-171370.

Segal, David. "Avril Lavigne, Unvarnished." *Washington Post*, January 13, 2003. washingtonpost.com/archive/lifestyle/2003/01/14/avril-lavigne-unvarnished/ee05983b-a783-4054-b742-0b1cc6f48aa4.

Shemesh, Yasmine. "Sum 41's Deryck Whibley on *All Killer No Filler* at 20: 'For the Longest Time, I Thought It Wasn't Very Good.'" *Billboard*, April 7, 2021. billboard.com/music/rock/sum-41-interview-all-killer-no-filler-9552792.

Shinn, Travis. "Sum 41 Says Farewell: Deryck Whibley Shares His Favorite Memories with the Pop-Punk Icons." *Grammy.com*, April 1, 2024. grammy.com/news/sum-41-deryck-whibley-interview-final-album-tour.

"Simple Plan Tell the Real Story Behind *No Pads, No Helmets … Just Balls*." *Alternative Press*, May 18, 2017. altpress.com/simple_plan_oral_history_no_pads_no_helmets_just_balls.

Stern, Bradley. "Fefe Dobson Is Starting Over, but Still 'Kicking Doors Down.'" *Billboard*, February 25, 2022. billboard.com/music/pop/fefe-dobson-interview-new-music-feature-1235036367/.

"Things Happen Quickly for Fefe Dobson." *Canadian Music*, September 4–10, 2003.

uDiscover Canada Team. "Teenage Head – Tornado Turns 40." uDiscoverMusic, May 3, 2023. udiscovermusic.ca/news/teenage-head-tornado-turns-40/.

Weingarten, Christopher R., et al. "The 50 Greatest Pop-Punk Albums." *Rolling Stone*, November 15, 2017. rollingstone.com/music/music-lists/50-greatest-pop-punk-albums-122677/.

"'Where Do We Put Her?': How the Music Industry Struggled with Black Pop Artists Like Fefe Dobson." *CBC Music*, February 18, 2021. cbc.ca/music/where-do-we-put-her-how-the-music-industry-struggledwith-black-pop-artists-like-fefe-dobson-1.5918326.

Willman, Chris. "Avril Lavigne: The Anti-Britney." *Entertainment Weekly*, November 1, 2002. ew.com/article/2002/11/01/avril-lavigne-anti-britney.

Winters, Rebecca. "Q&A with Avril Lavigne." *TIME*, May 31, 2004. content.time.com/time/subscriber/article/0,33009,994294,00.html.

Wonsiewicz, Steve. "Alternative Heeding Gob's Call." *Radio & Records*, March 29, 2002.

BOOKS

Barclay, Michael. *Hearts on Fire: Six Years that Changed Canadian Music 2000–2005*. ECW Press, 2022.

Fontana, Kaitlin. *Fresh at Twenty: The Oral History of Mint Records*. ECW Press, 2011.

Lavoie, Kathleen. *Simple Plan: The Official Story*. Éditions La Presse, 2012.

Whibley, Deryck. *Walking Disaster: My Life Through Heaven and Hell*. Gallery Books, 2024.

FILM, TV, VIDEOS, AND PODCASTS

Alternative Press. "Sum 41: The Complete History from *Half Hour of Power* to *Order in Decline*." July 11, 2019. YouTube, 18 min., 4 sec. youtube.com/watch?v=t496oJrHoL8.

Gordon, Dennie, dir. *New York Minute*. Warner Bros., 2004.

Loudwire. "*Sum 41—Wikipedia: Fact or Fiction?*" November 2, 2016. YouTube, 10 min. 15 sec. youtube.com/watch?v=BAolcNY6wt8.

Mayek, Chris. "*Singer/Songwriter Clif Magness Interview.*" July 11, 2022. YouTube, 1 hr., 31 min. youtube.com/watch?v=W54H_eRB_Uk.

MTV. *Total Request Live.* November 17, 2003.

MuchMusic. *Born to Be... Marianas Trench.* May 25, 2012.

Starlight Media. "Avril Lavigne—Sk8er Boi (Live at the 45th Grammy Awards, 2003)." July 11, 2021. YouTube, 3 min., 56 sec. youtube.com/watch?v=jnHogEWO74k.

Winters, Tyler, host. "On the Record with... Thriller Records/ex-Fearless Records President Bob Becker." *All Punked Up*, February 26, 2023. allpunkedup.com/on-the-recorded-with-thriller-records-ex-fearless-records-president-bob-becker.

PUBLICATIONS

Additional details for this book were gleaned from online sources, including *519 Magazine*, *Access*, AllMusic, *Alternative Press*, *American Songwriter*, *Billboard*, the *Boston Globe*, *Canadian Musician*, the Canadian Press, CBC News, *Celebrity Access*, the *Chicago Tribune*, *CTV News*, the Daily Slice, Discogs, *DIY Magazine*, Drowned in Sound, the *East Bay Express*, *Entertainment Weekly*, *Exclaim!*, ESPN, Far Out, the *Georgia Straight*, *Glamour*, the *Globe and Mail*, GQ, Grammy.com, *The Guardian*, Hit Quarters, HuffPost, IMDb, the *Independent*, *Interview Magazine*, Jam! Music, *Kerrang!*, Lambgoat, the *Los Angeles Times*, Loudwire, *Maclean's*, the *Mercury News*, Mixonline, *Modern Drummer*, the *Montreal Gazette*, MTV *News*, MuchMusic, the Music, Music Canada, Music Radar, the *New York Times*, *Niagara This Week*, *NME*, *Nylon*, *People*, Pollstar, Postmedia, Punknews.org, Refinery29, *Revolver*, RIAA, *Rolling Stone*, *SOCAN Magazine*, *Sound on Sound*, *SPIN*, Stereogum, Sun Media, *TIME*, the *Toronto Star*, uDiscover Music, Ultimate Guitar, the *Vancouver Sun*, *Variety*, *VICE*, View the Vibe, *Vulture*, and the *Washington Post*.

[illegible] "Sam [illegible]" [illegible] November 14, 2019. [illegible] NME [illegible]

[illegible] *Vogue* [illegible] [illegible] *Complex* [illegible]

[illegible] *New Musical Express* [illegible]

[illegible] *Mojo* [illegible]

[illegible] *Media* [illegible] [illegible]

[illegible] *Billboard*, February 26, 2014. [illegible]

[illegible]

Additional details for this book were gleaned from many sources [illegible] *Rolling Stone* [illegible] the *Boston Globe* [illegible] the *Chicago Tribune* [illegible] the *Daily Mail* [illegible] *Drowned in Sound* [illegible] the *Evening Standard* [illegible] the *Financial Times* [illegible] *GQ* [illegible] the *Independent* [illegible] *MTV* [illegible] the *New York Times* [illegible] *NME* [illegible] *Pitchfork* [illegible] *Stereogum* [illegible] the *Telegraph* [illegible] the *Village Voice* and the *Washington Post*.

INDEX

Page numbers with fl represent Further Listening side bar, i represents photo insert pages, and n represents note.

Chelsea Williams, @visualsbychelsea

MATT BOBKIN and ADAM FEIBEL are Toronto-based music journalists whose work has appeared in *Exclaim!*, Bandcamp, *VICE*, the *National Post*, and the *Toronto Star*. *In Too Deep* is their first book.